C-318   **CAREER EXAMINATION SERIES**

This is your
PASSBOOK for...

Principal Civil Engineer

Test Preparation Study Guide
Questions & Answers

COPYRIGHT NOTICE

This book is SOLELY intended for, is sold ONLY to, and its use is RESTRICTED to individual, bona fide applicants or candidates who qualify by virtue of having seriously filed applications for appropriate license, certificate, professional and/or promotional advancement, higher school matriculation, scholarship, or other legitimate requirements of education and/or governmental authorities.

This book is NOT intended for use, class instruction, tutoring, training, duplication, copying, reprinting, excerption, or adaptation, etc., by:

1) Other publishers
2) Proprietors and/or Instructors of "Coaching" and/or Preparatory Courses
3) Personnel and/or Training Divisions of commercial, industrial, and governmental organizations
4) Schools, colleges, or universities and/or their departments and staffs, including teachers and other personnel
5) Testing Agencies or Bureaus
6) Study groups which seek by the purchase of a single volume to copy and/or duplicate and/or adapt this material for use by the group as a whole without having purchased individual volumes for each of the members of the group
7) Et al.

Such persons would be in violation of appropriate Federal and State statutes.

PROVISION OF LICENSING AGREEMENTS – Recognized educational, commercial, industrial, and governmental institutions and organizations, and others legitimately engaged in educational pursuits, including training, testing, and measurement activities, may address request for a licensing agreement to the copyright owners, who will determine whether, and under what conditions, including fees and charges, the materials in this book may be used them. In other words, a licensing facility exists for the legitimate use of the material in this book on other than an individual basis. However, it is asseverated and affirmed here that the material in this book CANNOT be used without the receipt of the express permission of such a licensing agreement from the Publishers. Inquiries re licensing should be addressed to the company, attention rights and permissions department.

All rights reserved, including the right of reproduction in whole or in part, in any form or by any means, electronic or mechanical, including photocopying, recording, or by any information storage and retrieval system, without permission in writing from the Publisher.

Copyright © 2025 by
National Learning Corporation

212 Michael Drive, Syosset, NY 11791
(516) 921-8888 • www.passbooks.com
E-mail: info@passbooks.com

PASSBOOK® SERIES

THE *PASSBOOK® SERIES* has been created to prepare applicants and candidates for the ultimate academic battlefield – the examination room.

At some time in our lives, each and every one of us may be required to take an examination – for validation, matriculation, admission, qualification, registration, certification, or licensure.

Based on the assumption that every applicant or candidate has met the basic formal educational standards, has taken the required number of courses, and read the necessary texts, the *PASSBOOK® SERIES* furnishes the one special preparation which may assure passing with confidence, instead of failing with insecurity. Examination questions – together with answers – are furnished as the basic vehicle for study so that the mysteries of the examination and its compounding difficulties may be eliminated or diminished by a sure method.

This book is meant to help you pass your examination provided that you qualify and are serious in your objective.

The entire field is reviewed through the huge store of content information which is succinctly presented through a provocative and challenging approach – the question-and-answer method.

A climate of success is established by furnishing the correct answers at the end of each test.

You soon learn to recognize types of questions, forms of questions, and patterns of questioning. You may even begin to anticipate expected outcomes.

You perceive that many questions are repeated or adapted so that you can gain acute insights, which may enable you to score many sure points.

You learn how to confront new questions, or types of questions, and to attack them confidently and work out the correct answers.

You note objectives and emphases, and recognize pitfalls and dangers, so that you may make positive educational adjustments.

Moreover, you are kept fully informed in relation to new concepts, methods, practices, and directions in the field.

You discover that you are actually taking the examination all the time: you are preparing for the examination by "taking" an examination, not by reading extraneous and/or supererogatory textbooks.

In short, this PASSBOOK®, used directedly, should be an important factor in helping you to pass your test.

PRINCIPAL CIVIL ENGINEER

DUTIES
Performs professional civil engineering work in administrating a major operating division of a public works department such as highway design division, bridge design division, waterways division, or material and soils testing laboratory. Directs and coordinates the activities of subordinate professional, technical, and clerical assistants. Does related work as required.

SCOPE OF THE WRITTEN TEST
The written test will cover knowledge, skills, and/or abilities in such areas as:
1. Principles and practices of civil engineering;
2. Engineering specifications and estimates;
3. Methods and materials of construction;
4. Construction and maintenance of highways, bridges, drainage, and related structures;
5. Contracts and contract administration;
6. Preparation of written material; and
7. Supervision.

HOW TO TAKE A TEST

I. YOU MUST PASS AN EXAMINATION

A. WHAT EVERY CANDIDATE SHOULD KNOW

Examination applicants often ask us for help in preparing for the written test. What can I study in advance? What kinds of questions will be asked? How will the test be given? How will the papers be graded?

As an applicant for a civil service examination, you may be wondering about some of these things. Our purpose here is to suggest effective methods of advance study and to describe civil service examinations.

Your chances for success on this examination can be increased if you know how to prepare. Those "pre-examination jitters" can be reduced if you know what to expect. You can even experience an adventure in good citizenship if you know why civil service exams are given.

B. WHY ARE CIVIL SERVICE EXAMINATIONS GIVEN?

Civil service examinations are important to you in two ways. As a citizen, you want public jobs filled by employees who know how to do their work. As a job seeker, you want a fair chance to compete for that job on an equal footing with other candidates. The best-known means of accomplishing this two-fold goal is the competitive examination.

Exams are widely publicized throughout the nation. They may be administered for jobs in federal, state, city, municipal, town or village governments or agencies.

Any citizen may apply, with some limitations, such as the age or residence of applicants. Your experience and education may be reviewed to see whether you meet the requirements for the particular examination. When these requirements exist, they are reasonable and applied consistently to all applicants. Thus, a competitive examination may cause you some uneasiness now, but it is your privilege and safeguard.

C. HOW ARE CIVIL SERVICE EXAMS DEVELOPED?

Examinations are carefully written by trained technicians who are specialists in the field known as "psychological measurement," in consultation with recognized authorities in the field of work that the test will cover. These experts recommend the subject matter areas or skills to be tested; only those knowledges or skills important to your success on the job are included. The most reliable books and source materials available are used as references. Together, the experts and technicians judge the difficulty level of the questions.

Test technicians know how to phrase questions so that the problem is clearly stated. Their ethics do not permit "trick" or "catch" questions. Questions may have been tried out on sample groups, or subjected to statistical analysis, to determine their usefulness.

Written tests are often used in combination with performance tests, ratings of training and experience, and oral interviews. All of these measures combine to form the best-known means of finding the right person for the right job.

II. HOW TO PASS THE WRITTEN TEST

A. NATURE OF THE EXAMINATION

To prepare intelligently for civil service examinations, you should know how they differ from school examinations you have taken. In school you were assigned certain definite pages to read or subjects to cover. The examination questions were quite detailed and usually emphasized memory. Civil service exams, on the other hand, try to discover your present ability to perform the duties of a position, plus your potentiality to learn these duties. In other words, a civil service exam attempts to predict how successful you will be. Questions cover such a broad area that they cannot be as minute and detailed as school exam questions.

In the public service similar kinds of work, or positions, are grouped together in one "class." This process is known as *position-classification*. All the positions in a class are paid according to the salary range for that class. One class title covers all of these positions, and they are all tested by the same examination.

B. FOUR BASIC STEPS

1) Study the announcement

How, then, can you know what subjects to study? Our best answer is: "Learn as much as possible about the class of positions for which you've applied." The exam will test the knowledge, skills and abilities needed to do the work.

Your most valuable source of information about the position you want is the official exam announcement. This announcement lists the training and experience qualifications. Check these standards and apply only if you come reasonably close to meeting them.

The brief description of the position in the examination announcement offers some clues to the subjects which will be tested. Think about the job itself. Review the duties in your mind. Can you perform them, or are there some in which you are rusty? Fill in the blank spots in your preparation.

Many jurisdictions preview the written test in the exam announcement by including a section called "Knowledge and Abilities Required," "Scope of the Examination," or some similar heading. Here you will find out specifically what fields will be tested.

2) Review your own background

Once you learn in general what the position is all about, and what you need to know to do the work, ask yourself which subjects you already know fairly well and which need improvement. You may wonder whether to concentrate on improving your strong areas or on building some background in your fields of weakness. When the announcement has specified "some knowledge" or "considerable knowledge," or has used adjectives like "beginning principles of…" or "advanced … methods," you can get a clue as to the number and difficulty of questions to be asked in any given field. More questions, and hence broader coverage, would be included for those subjects which are more important in the work. Now weigh your strengths and weaknesses against the job requirements and prepare accordingly.

3) Determine the level of the position

Another way to tell how intensively you should prepare is to understand the level of the job for which you are applying. Is it the entering level? In other words, is this the position in which beginners in a field of work are hired? Or is it an intermediate or advanced level? Sometimes this is indicated by such words as "Junior" or "Senior" in the class title. Other jurisdictions use Roman numerals to designate the level – Clerk I, Clerk II, for example. The word "Supervisor" sometimes appears in the title. If the level is not indicated by the title, check the description of duties. Will you be working under very close supervision, or will you have responsibility for independent decisions in this work?

4) Choose appropriate study materials

Now that you know the subjects to be examined and the relative amount of each subject to be covered, you can choose suitable study materials. For beginning level jobs, or even advanced ones, if you have a pronounced weakness in some aspect of your training, read a modern, standard textbook in that field. Be sure it is up to date and has general coverage. Such books are normally available at your library, and the librarian will be glad to help you locate one. For entry-level positions, questions of appropriate difficulty are chosen – neither highly advanced questions, nor those too simple. Such questions require careful thought but not advanced training.

If the position for which you are applying is technical or advanced, you will read more advanced, specialized material. If you are already familiar with the basic principles of your field, elementary textbooks would waste your time. Concentrate on advanced textbooks and technical periodicals. Think through the concepts and review difficult problems in your field.

These are all general sources. You can get more ideas on your own initiative, following these leads. For example, training manuals and publications of the government agency which employs workers in your field can be useful, particularly for technical and professional positions. A letter or visit to the government department involved may result in more specific study suggestions, and certainly will provide you with a more definite idea of the exact nature of the position you are seeking.

III. KINDS OF TESTS

Tests are used for purposes other than measuring knowledge and ability to perform specified duties. For some positions, it is equally important to test ability to make adjustments to new situations or to profit from training. In others, basic mental abilities not dependent on information are essential. Questions which test these things may not appear as pertinent to the duties of the position as those which test for knowledge and information. Yet they are often highly important parts of a fair examination. For very general questions, it is almost impossible to help you direct your study efforts. What we can do is to point out some of the more common of these general abilities needed in public service positions and describe some typical questions.

1) General information

Broad, general information has been found useful for predicting job success in some kinds of work. This is tested in a variety of ways, from vocabulary lists to questions about current events. Basic background in some field of work, such as sociology or economics, may be sampled in a group of questions. Often these are principles which have become familiar to most persons through exposure rather than through formal training. It is difficult to advise you how to study for these questions; being alert to the world around you is our best suggestion.

2) Verbal ability

An example of an ability needed in many positions is verbal or language ability. Verbal ability is, in brief, the ability to use and understand words. Vocabulary and grammar tests are typical measures of this ability. Reading comprehension or paragraph interpretation questions are common in many kinds of civil service tests. You are given a paragraph of written material and asked to find its central meaning.

3) Numerical ability

Number skills can be tested by the familiar arithmetic problem, by checking paired lists of numbers to see which are alike and which are different, or by interpreting charts and graphs. In the latter test, a graph may be printed in the test booklet which you are asked to use as the basis for answering questions.

4) Observation

A popular test for law-enforcement positions is the observation test. A picture is shown to you for several minutes, then taken away. Questions about the picture test your ability to observe both details and larger elements.

5) Following directions

In many positions in the public service, the employee must be able to carry out written instructions dependably and accurately. You may be given a chart with several columns, each column listing a variety of information. The questions require you to carry out directions involving the information given in the chart.

6) Skills and aptitudes

Performance tests effectively measure some manual skills and aptitudes. When the skill is one in which you are trained, such as typing or shorthand, you can practice. These tests are often very much like those given in business school or high school courses. For many of the other skills and aptitudes, however, no short-time preparation can be made. Skills and abilities natural to you or that you have developed throughout your lifetime are being tested.

Many of the general questions just described provide all the data needed to answer the questions and ask you to use your reasoning ability to find the answers. Your best preparation for these tests, as well as for tests of facts and ideas, is to be at your physical and mental best. You, no doubt, have your own methods of getting into an exam-taking mood and keeping "in shape." The next section lists some ideas on this subject.

IV. KINDS OF QUESTIONS

Only rarely is the "essay" question, which you answer in narrative form, used in civil service tests. Civil service tests are usually of the short-answer type. Full instructions for answering these questions will be given to you at the examination. But in case this is your first experience with short-answer questions and separate answer sheets, here is what you need to know:

1) Multiple-choice Questions

Most popular of the short-answer questions is the "multiple choice" or "best answer" question. It can be used, for example, to test for factual knowledge, ability to solve problems or judgment in meeting situations found at work.

A multiple-choice question is normally one of three types—
- It can begin with an incomplete statement followed by several possible endings. You are to find the one ending which *best* completes the statement, although some of the others may not be entirely wrong.
- It can also be a complete statement in the form of a question which is answered by choosing one of the statements listed.

- It can be in the form of a problem – again you select the best answer.

Here is an example of a multiple-choice question with a discussion which should give you some clues as to the method for choosing the right answer:

When an employee has a complaint about his assignment, the action which will *best* help him overcome his difficulty is to
- A. discuss his difficulty with his coworkers
- B. take the problem to the head of the organization
- C. take the problem to the person who gave him the assignment
- D. say nothing to anyone about his complaint

In answering this question, you should study each of the choices to find which is best. Consider choice "A" – Certainly an employee may discuss his complaint with fellow employees, but no change or improvement can result, and the complaint remains unresolved. Choice "B" is a poor choice since the head of the organization probably does not know what assignment you have been given, and taking your problem to him is known as "going over the head" of the supervisor. The supervisor, or person who made the assignment, is the person who can clarify it or correct any injustice. Choice "C" is, therefore, correct. To say nothing, as in choice "D," is unwise. Supervisors have and interest in knowing the problems employees are facing, and the employee is seeking a solution to his problem.

2) True/False Questions

The "true/false" or "right/wrong" form of question is sometimes used. Here a complete statement is given. Your job is to decide whether the statement is right or wrong.

SAMPLE: A roaming cell-phone call to a nearby city costs less than a non-roaming call to a distant city.

This statement is wrong, or false, since roaming calls are more expensive.

This is not a complete list of all possible question forms, although most of the others are variations of these common types. You will always get complete directions for answering questions. Be sure you understand *how* to mark your answers – ask questions until you do.

V. RECORDING YOUR ANSWERS

Computer terminals are used more and more today for many different kinds of exams.
For an examination with very few applicants, you may be told to record your answers in the test booklet itself. Separate answer sheets are much more common. If this separate answer sheet is to be scored by machine – and this is often the case – it is highly important that you mark your answers correctly in order to get credit.
An electronic scoring machine is often used in civil service offices because of the speed with which papers can be scored. Machine-scored answer sheets must be marked with a pencil, which will be given to you. This pencil has a high graphite content which responds to the electronic scoring machine. As a matter of fact, stray dots may register as answers, so do not let your pencil rest on the answer sheet while you are pondering the correct answer. Also, if your pencil lead breaks or is otherwise defective, ask for another.

Since the answer sheet will be dropped in a slot in the scoring machine, be careful not to bend the corners or get the paper crumpled.

The answer sheet normally has five vertical columns of numbers, with 30 numbers to a column. These numbers correspond to the question numbers in your test booklet. After each number, going across the page are four or five pairs of dotted lines. These short dotted lines have small letters or numbers above them. The first two pairs may also have a "T" or "F" above the letters. This indicates that the first two pairs only are to be used if the questions are of the true-false type. If the questions are multiple choice, disregard the "T" and "F" and pay attention only to the small letters or numbers.

Answer your questions in the manner of the sample that follows:

32. The largest city in the United States is
    A. Washington, D.C.
    B. New York City
    C. Chicago
    D. Detroit
    E. San Francisco

1) Choose the answer you think is best. (New York City is the largest, so "B" is correct.)
2) Find the row of dotted lines numbered the same as the question you are answering. (Find row number 32)
3) Find the pair of dotted lines corresponding to the answer. (Find the pair of lines under the mark "B.")
4) Make a solid black mark between the dotted lines.

VI. BEFORE THE TEST

Common sense will help you find procedures to follow to get ready for an examination. Too many of us, however, overlook these sensible measures. Indeed, nervousness and fatigue have been found to be the most serious reasons why applicants fail to do their best on civil service tests. Here is a list of reminders:

- Begin your preparation early – Don't wait until the last minute to go scurrying around for books and materials or to find out what the position is all about.
- Prepare continuously – An hour a night for a week is better than an all-night cram session. This has been definitely established. What is more, a night a week for a month will return better dividends than crowding your study into a shorter period of time.
- Locate the place of the exam – You have been sent a notice telling you when and where to report for the examination. If the location is in a different town or otherwise unfamiliar to you, it would be well to inquire the best route and learn something about the building.
- Relax the night before the test – Allow your mind to rest. Do not study at all that night. Plan some mild recreation or diversion; then go to bed early and get a good night's sleep.
- Get up early enough to make a leisurely trip to the place for the test – This way unforeseen events, traffic snarls, unfamiliar buildings, etc. will not upset you.
- Dress comfortably – A written test is not a fashion show. You will be known by number and not by name, so wear something comfortable.

- Leave excess paraphernalia at home – Shopping bags and odd bundles will get in your way. You need bring only the items mentioned in the official notice you received; usually everything you need is provided. Do not bring reference books to the exam. They will only confuse those last minutes and be taken away from you when in the test room.
- Arrive somewhat ahead of time – If because of transportation schedules you must get there very early, bring a newspaper or magazine to take your mind off yourself while waiting.
- Locate the examination room – When you have found the proper room, you will be directed to the seat or part of the room where you will sit. Sometimes you are given a sheet of instructions to read while you are waiting. Do not fill out any forms until you are told to do so; just read them and be prepared.
- Relax and prepare to listen to the instructions
- If you have any physical problem that may keep you from doing your best, be sure to tell the test administrator. If you are sick or in poor health, you really cannot do your best on the exam. You can come back and take the test some other time.

VII. AT THE TEST

The day of the test is here and you have the test booklet in your hand. The temptation to get going is very strong. Caution! There is more to success than knowing the right answers. You must know how to identify your papers and understand variations in the type of short-answer question used in this particular examination. Follow these suggestions for maximum results from your efforts:

1) Cooperate with the monitor
The test administrator has a duty to create a situation in which you can be as much at ease as possible. He will give instructions, tell you when to begin, check to see that you are marking your answer sheet correctly, and so on. He is not there to guard you, although he will see that your competitors do not take unfair advantage. He wants to help you do your best.

2) Listen to all instructions
Don't jump the gun! Wait until you understand all directions. In most civil service tests you get more time than you need to answer the questions. So don't be in a hurry. Read each word of instructions until you clearly understand the meaning. Study the examples, listen to all announcements and follow directions. Ask questions if you do not understand what to do.

3) Identify your papers
Civil service exams are usually identified by number only. You will be assigned a number; you must not put your name on your test papers. Be sure to copy your number correctly. Since more than one exam may be given, copy your exact examination title.

4) Plan your time
Unless you are told that a test is a "speed" or "rate of work" test, speed itself is usually not important. Time enough to answer all the questions will be provided, but this does not mean that you have all day. An overall time limit has been set. Divide the total time (in minutes) by the number of questions to determine the approximate time you have for each question.

5) Do not linger over difficult questions

If you come across a difficult question, mark it with a paper clip (useful to have along) and come back to it when you have been through the booklet. One caution if you do this – be sure to skip a number on your answer sheet as well. Check often to be sure that you have not lost your place and that you are marking in the row numbered the same as the question you are answering.

6) Read the questions

Be sure you know what the question asks! Many capable people are unsuccessful because they failed to *read* the questions correctly.

7) Answer all questions

Unless you have been instructed that a penalty will be deducted for incorrect answers, it is better to guess than to omit a question.

8) Speed tests

It is often better NOT to guess on speed tests. It has been found that on timed tests people are tempted to spend the last few seconds before time is called in marking answers at random – without even reading them – in the hope of picking up a few extra points. To discourage this practice, the instructions may warn you that your score will be "corrected" for guessing. That is, a penalty will be applied. The incorrect answers will be deducted from the correct ones, or some other penalty formula will be used.

9) Review your answers

If you finish before time is called, go back to the questions you guessed or omitted to give them further thought. Review other answers if you have time.

10) Return your test materials

If you are ready to leave before others have finished or time is called, take ALL your materials to the monitor and leave quietly. Never take any test material with you. The monitor can discover whose papers are not complete, and taking a test booklet may be grounds for disqualification.

VIII. EXAMINATION TECHNIQUES

1) Read the general instructions carefully. These are usually printed on the first page of the exam booklet. As a rule, these instructions refer to the timing of the examination; the fact that you should not start work until the signal and must stop work at a signal, etc. If there are any *special* instructions, such as a choice of questions to be answered, make sure that you note this instruction carefully.

2) When you are ready to start work on the examination, that is as soon as the signal has been given, read the instructions to each question booklet, underline any key words or phrases, such as *least, best, outline, describe* and the like. In this way you will tend to answer as requested rather than discover on reviewing your paper that you *listed without describing*, that you selected the *worst* choice rather than the *best* choice, etc.

3) If the examination is of the objective or multiple-choice type – that is, each question will also give a series of possible answers: A, B, C or D, and you are called upon to select the best answer and write the letter next to that answer on your answer paper – it is advisable to start answering each question in turn. There may be anywhere from 50 to 100 such questions in the three or four hours allotted and you can see how much time would be taken if you read through all the questions before beginning to answer any. Furthermore, if you come across a question or group of questions which you know would be difficult to answer, it would undoubtedly affect your handling of all the other questions.

4) If the examination is of the essay type and contains but a few questions, it is a moot point as to whether you should read all the questions before starting to answer any one. Of course, if you are given a choice – say five out of seven and the like – then it is essential to read all the questions so you can eliminate the two that are most difficult. If, however, you are asked to answer all the questions, there may be danger in trying to answer the easiest one first because you may find that you will spend too much time on it. The best technique is to answer the first question, then proceed to the second, etc.

5) Time your answers. Before the exam begins, write down the time it started, then add the time allowed for the examination and write down the time it must be completed, then divide the time available somewhat as follows:
   - If 3-1/2 hours are allowed, that would be 210 minutes. If you have 80 objective-type questions, that would be an average of 2-1/2 minutes per question. Allow yourself no more than 2 minutes per question, or a total of 160 minutes, which will permit about 50 minutes to review.
   - If for the time allotment of 210 minutes there are 7 essay questions to answer, that would average about 30 minutes a question. Give yourself only 25 minutes per question so that you have about 35 minutes to review.

6) The most important instruction is to *read each question* and make sure you know what is wanted. The second most important instruction is to *time yourself properly* so that you answer every question. The third most important instruction is to *answer every question*. Guess if you have to but include something for each question. Remember that you will receive no credit for a blank and will probably receive some credit if you write something in answer to an essay question. If you guess a letter – say "B" for a multiple-choice question – you may have guessed right. If you leave a blank as an answer to a multiple-choice question, the examiners may respect your feelings but it will not add a point to your score. Some exams may penalize you for wrong answers, so in such cases *only*, you may not want to guess unless you have some basis for your answer.

7) Suggestions
   a. Objective-type questions
      1. Examine the question booklet for proper sequence of pages and questions
      2. Read all instructions carefully
      3. Skip any question which seems too difficult; return to it after all other questions have been answered
      4. Apportion your time properly; do not spend too much time on any single question or group of questions

5. Note and underline key words – *all, most, fewest, least, best, worst, same, opposite,* etc.
6. Pay particular attention to negatives
7. Note unusual option, e.g., unduly long, short, complex, different or similar in content to the body of the question
8. Observe the use of "hedging" words – *probably, may, most likely,* etc.
9. Make sure that your answer is put next to the same number as the question
10. Do not second-guess unless you have good reason to believe the second answer is definitely more correct
11. Cross out original answer if you decide another answer is more accurate; do not erase until you are ready to hand your paper in
12. Answer all questions; guess unless instructed otherwise
13. Leave time for review

  b. Essay questions
1. Read each question carefully
2. Determine exactly what is wanted. Underline key words or phrases.
3. Decide on outline or paragraph answer
4. Include many different points and elements unless asked to develop any one or two points or elements
5. Show impartiality by giving pros and cons unless directed to select one side only
6. Make and write down any assumptions you find necessary to answer the questions
7. Watch your English, grammar, punctuation and choice of words
8. Time your answers; don't crowd material

8) Answering the essay question

Most essay questions can be answered by framing the specific response around several key words or ideas. Here are a few such key words or ideas:

M's: manpower, materials, methods, money, management
P's: purpose, program, policy, plan, procedure, practice, problems, pitfalls, personnel, public relations

  a. Six basic steps in handling problems:
1. Preliminary plan and background development
2. Collect information, data and facts
3. Analyze and interpret information, data and facts
4. Analyze and develop solutions as well as make recommendations
5. Prepare report and sell recommendations
6. Install recommendations and follow up effectiveness

  b. Pitfalls to avoid
1. *Taking things for granted* – A statement of the situation does not necessarily imply that each of the elements is necessarily true; for example, a complaint may be invalid and biased so that all that can be taken for granted is that a complaint has been registered

2. *Considering only one side of a situation* – Wherever possible, indicate several alternatives and then point out the reasons you selected the best one
3. *Failing to indicate follow up* – Whenever your answer indicates action on your part, make certain that you will take proper follow-up action to see how successful your recommendations, procedures or actions turn out to be
4. *Taking too long in answering any single question* – Remember to time your answers properly

IX. AFTER THE TEST

Scoring procedures differ in detail among civil service jurisdictions although the general principles are the same. Whether the papers are hand-scored or graded by machine we have described, they are nearly always graded by number. That is, the person who marks the paper knows only the number – never the name – of the applicant. Not until all the papers have been graded will they be matched with names. If other tests, such as training and experience or oral interview ratings have been given, scores will be combined. Different parts of the examination usually have different weights. For example, the written test might count 60 percent of the final grade, and a rating of training and experience 40 percent. In many jurisdictions, veterans will have a certain number of points added to their grades.

After the final grade has been determined, the names are placed in grade order and an eligible list is established. There are various methods for resolving ties between those who get the same final grade – probably the most common is to place first the name of the person whose application was received first. Job offers are made from the eligible list in the order the names appear on it. You will be notified of your grade and your rank as soon as all these computations have been made. This will be done as rapidly as possible.

People who are found to meet the requirements in the announcement are called "eligibles." Their names are put on a list of eligible candidates. An eligible's chances of getting a job depend on how high he stands on this list and how fast agencies are filling jobs from the list.

When a job is to be filled from a list of eligibles, the agency asks for the names of people on the list of eligibles for that job. When the civil service commission receives this request, it sends to the agency the names of the three people highest on this list. Or, if the job to be filled has specialized requirements, the office sends the agency the names of the top three persons who meet these requirements from the general list.

The appointing officer makes a choice from among the three people whose names were sent to him. If the selected person accepts the appointment, the names of the others are put back on the list to be considered for future openings.

That is the rule in hiring from all kinds of eligible lists, whether they are for typist, carpenter, chemist, or something else. For every vacancy, the appointing officer has his choice of any one of the top three eligibles on the list. This explains why the person whose name is on top of the list sometimes does not get an appointment when some of the persons lower on the list do. If the appointing officer chooses the second or third eligible, the No. 1 eligible does not get a job at once, but stays on the list until he is appointed or the list is terminated.

X. HOW TO PASS THE INTERVIEW TEST

The examination for which you applied requires an oral interview test. You have already taken the written test and you are now being called for the interview test – the final part of the formal examination.

You may think that it is not possible to prepare for an interview test and that there are no procedures to follow during an interview. Our purpose is to point out some things you can do in advance that will help you and some good rules to follow and pitfalls to avoid while you are being interviewed.

What is an interview supposed to test?

The written examination is designed to test the technical knowledge and competence of the candidate; the oral is designed to evaluate intangible qualities, not readily measured otherwise, and to establish a list showing the relative fitness of each candidate – as measured against his competitors – for the position sought. Scoring is not on the basis of "right" and "wrong," but on a sliding scale of values ranging from "not passable" to "outstanding." As a matter of fact, it is possible to achieve a relatively low score without a single "incorrect" answer because of evident weakness in the qualities being measured.

Occasionally, an examination may consist entirely of an oral test – either an individual or a group oral. In such cases, information is sought concerning the technical knowledges and abilities of the candidate, since there has been no written examination for this purpose. More commonly, however, an oral test is used to supplement a written examination.

Who conducts interviews?

The composition of oral boards varies among different jurisdictions. In nearly all, a representative of the personnel department serves as chairman. One of the members of the board may be a representative of the department in which the candidate would work. In some cases, "outside experts" are used, and, frequently, a businessman or some other representative of the general public is asked to serve. Labor and management or other special groups may be represented. The aim is to secure the services of experts in the appropriate field.

However the board is composed, it is a good idea (and not at all improper or unethical) to ascertain in advance of the interview who the members are and what groups they represent. When you are introduced to them, you will have some idea of their backgrounds and interests, and at least you will not stutter and stammer over their names.

What should be done before the interview?

While knowledge about the board members is useful and takes some of the surprise element out of the interview, there is other preparation which is more substantive. It *is* possible to prepare for an oral interview – in several ways:

1) Keep a copy of your application and review it carefully before the interview

This may be the only document before the oral board, and the starting point of the interview. Know what education and experience you have listed there, and the sequence and dates of all of it. Sometimes the board will ask you to review the highlights of your experience for them; you should not have to hem and haw doing it.

2) Study the class specification and the examination announcement

Usually, the oral board has one or both of these to guide them. The qualities, characteristics or knowledges required by the position sought are stated in these documents. They offer valuable clues as to the nature of the oral interview. For example, if the job involves supervisory responsibilities, the announcement will usually indicate that knowledge of modern supervisory methods and the qualifications of the candidate as a supervisor will be tested. If so, you can expect such questions, frequently in the form of a hypothetical situation which you are expected to solve. NEVER go into an oral without knowledge of the duties and responsibilities of the job you seek.

3) Think through each qualification required

Try to visualize the kind of questions you would ask if you were a board member. How well could you answer them? Try especially to appraise your own knowledge and background in each area, *measured against the job sought*, and identify any areas in which you are weak. Be critical and realistic – do not flatter yourself.

4) Do some general reading in areas in which you feel you may be weak

For example, if the job involves supervision and your past experience has NOT, some general reading in supervisory methods and practices, particularly in the field of human relations, might be useful. Do NOT study agency procedures or detailed manuals. The oral board will be testing your understanding and capacity, not your memory.

5) Get a good night's sleep and watch your general health and mental attitude

You will want a clear head at the interview. Take care of a cold or any other minor ailment, and of course, no hangovers.

What should be done on the day of the interview?

Now comes the day of the interview itself. Give yourself plenty of time to get there. Plan to arrive somewhat ahead of the scheduled time, particularly if your appointment is in the fore part of the day. If a previous candidate fails to appear, the board might be ready for you a bit early. By early afternoon an oral board is almost invariably behind schedule if there are many candidates, and you may have to wait. Take along a book or magazine to read, or your application to review, but leave any extraneous material in the waiting room when you go in for your interview. In any event, relax and compose yourself.

The matter of dress is important. The board is forming impressions about you – from your experience, your manners, your attitude, and your appearance. Give your personal appearance careful attention. Dress your best, but not your flashiest. Choose conservative, appropriate clothing, and be sure it is immaculate. This is a business interview, and your appearance should indicate that you regard it as such. Besides, being well groomed and properly dressed will help boost your confidence.

Sooner or later, someone will call your name and escort you into the interview room. *This is it.* From here on you are on your own. It is too late for any more preparation. But remember, you asked for this opportunity to prove your fitness, and you are here because your request was granted.

What happens when you go in?

The usual sequence of events will be as follows: The clerk (who is often the board stenographer) will introduce you to the chairman of the oral board, who will introduce you to the other members of the board. Acknowledge the introductions before you sit down. Do not be surprised if you find a microphone facing you or a stenotypist sitting by. Oral interviews are usually recorded in the event of an appeal or other review.

Usually the chairman of the board will open the interview by reviewing the highlights of your education and work experience from your application – primarily for the benefit of the other members of the board, as well as to get the material into the record. Do not interrupt or comment unless there is an error or significant misinterpretation; if that is the case, do not hesitate. But do not quibble about insignificant matters. Also, he will usually ask you some question about your education, experience or your present job – partly to get you to start talking and to establish the interviewing "rapport." He may start the actual questioning, or turn it over to one of the other members. Frequently, each member undertakes the questioning on a particular area, one in which he is perhaps most competent, so you can expect each member to participate in the examination. Because time is limited, you may also expect some rather abrupt switches in the direction the questioning takes, so do not be upset by it. Normally, a board member will not pursue a single line of questioning unless he discovers a particular strength or weakness.

After each member has participated, the chairman will usually ask whether any member has any further questions, then will ask you if you have anything you wish to add. Unless you are expecting this question, it may floor you. Worse, it may start you off on an extended, extemporaneous speech. The board is not usually seeking more information. The question is principally to offer you a last opportunity to present further qualifications or to indicate that you have nothing to add. So, if you feel that a significant qualification or characteristic has been overlooked, it is proper to point it out in a sentence or so. Do not compliment the board on the thoroughness of their examination – they have been sketchy, and you know it. If you wish, merely say, "No thank you, I have nothing further to add." This is a point where you can "talk yourself out" of a good impression or fail to present an important bit of information. Remember, *you close the interview yourself.*

The chairman will then say, "That is all, Mr. _____, thank you." Do not be startled; the interview is over, and quicker than you think. Thank him, gather your belongings and take your leave. Save your sigh of relief for the other side of the door.

How to put your best foot forward

Throughout this entire process, you may feel that the board individually and collectively is trying to pierce your defenses, seek out your hidden weaknesses and embarrass and confuse you. Actually, this is not true. They are obliged to make an appraisal of your qualifications for the job you are seeking, and they want to see you in your best light. Remember, they must interview all candidates and a non-cooperative candidate may become a failure in spite of their best efforts to bring out his qualifications. Here are 15 suggestions that will help you:

1) Be natural – Keep your attitude confident, not cocky

If you are not confident that you can do the job, do not expect the board to be. Do not apologize for your weaknesses, try to bring out your strong points. The board is interested in a positive, not negative, presentation. Cockiness will antagonize any board member and make him wonder if you are covering up a weakness by a false show of strength.

2) Get comfortable, but don't lounge or sprawl

Sit erectly but not stiffly. A careless posture may lead the board to conclude that you are careless in other things, or at least that you are not impressed by the importance of the occasion. Either conclusion is natural, even if incorrect. Do not fuss with your clothing, a pencil or an ashtray. Your hands may occasionally be useful to emphasize a point; do not let them become a point of distraction.

3) Do not wisecrack or make small talk

This is a serious situation, and your attitude should show that you consider it as such. Further, the time of the board is limited – they do not want to waste it, and neither should you.

4) Do not exaggerate your experience or abilities
In the first place, from information in the application or other interviews and sources, the board may know more about you than you think. Secondly, you probably will not get away with it. An experienced board is rather adept at spotting such a situation, so do not take the chance.

5) If you know a board member, do not make a point of it, yet do not hide it
Certainly you are not fooling him, and probably not the other members of the board. Do not try to take advantage of your acquaintanceship – it will probably do you little good.

6) Do not dominate the interview
Let the board do that. They will give you the clues – do not assume that you have to do all the talking. Realize that the board has a number of questions to ask you, and do not try to take up all the interview time by showing off your extensive knowledge of the answer to the first one.

7) Be attentive
You only have 20 minutes or so, and you should keep your attention at its sharpest throughout. When a member is addressing a problem or question to you, give him your undivided attention. Address your reply principally to him, but do not exclude the other board members.

8) Do not interrupt
A board member may be stating a problem for you to analyze. He will ask you a question when the time comes. Let him state the problem, and wait for the question.

9) Make sure you understand the question
Do not try to answer until you are sure what the question is. If it is not clear, restate it in your own words or ask the board member to clarify it for you. However, do not haggle about minor elements.

10) Reply promptly but not hastily
A common entry on oral board rating sheets is "candidate responded readily," or "candidate hesitated in replies." Respond as promptly and quickly as you can, but do not jump to a hasty, ill-considered answer.

11) Do not be peremptory in your answers
A brief answer is proper – but do not fire your answer back. That is a losing game from your point of view. The board member can probably ask questions much faster than you can answer them.

12) Do not try to create the answer you think the board member wants
He is interested in what kind of mind you have and how it works – not in playing games. Furthermore, he can usually spot this practice and will actually grade you down on it.

13) Do not switch sides in your reply merely to agree with a board member
Frequently, a member will take a contrary position merely to draw you out and to see if you are willing and able to defend your point of view. Do not start a debate, yet do not surrender a good position. If a position is worth taking, it is worth defending.

14) Do not be afraid to admit an error in judgment if you are shown to be wrong

The board knows that you are forced to reply without any opportunity for careful consideration. Your answer may be demonstrably wrong. If so, admit it and get on with the interview.

15) Do not dwell at length on your present job

The opening question may relate to your present assignment. Answer the question but do not go into an extended discussion. You are being examined for a *new* job, not your present one. As a matter of fact, try to phrase ALL your answers in terms of the job for which you are being examined.

Basis of Rating

Probably you will forget most of these "do's" and "don'ts" when you walk into the oral interview room. Even remembering them all will not ensure you a passing grade. Perhaps you did not have the qualifications in the first place. But remembering them will help you to put your best foot forward, without treading on the toes of the board members.

Rumor and popular opinion to the contrary notwithstanding, an oral board wants you to make the best appearance possible. They know you are under pressure – but they also want to see how you respond to it as a guide to what your reaction would be under the pressures of the job you seek. They will be influenced by the degree of poise you display, the personal traits you show and the manner in which you respond.

ABOUT THIS BOOK

This book contains tests divided into Examination Sections. Go through each test, answering every question in the margin. We have also attached a sample answer sheet at the back of the book that can be removed and used. At the end of each test look at the answer key and check your answers. On the ones you got wrong, look at the right answer choice and learn. Do not fill in the answers first. Do not memorize the questions and answers, but understand the answer and principles involved. On your test, the questions will likely be different from the samples. Questions are changed and new ones added. If you understand these past questions you should have success with any changes that arise. Tests may consist of several types of questions. We have additional books on each subject should more study be advisable or necessary for you. Finally, the more you study, the better prepared you will be. This book is intended to be the last thing you study before you walk into the examination room. Prior study of relevant texts is also recommended. NLC publishes some of these in our Fundamental Series. Knowledge and good sense are important factors in passing your exam. Good luck also helps. So now study this Passbook, absorb the material contained within and take that knowledge into the examination. Then do your best to pass that exam.

EXAMINATION SECTION

EXAMINATION SECTION
TEST 1

DIRECTIONS: Each question or incomplete statement is followed by several suggested answers or completions. Select the one that BEST answers the question or completes the statement. *PRINT THE LETTER OF THE CORRECT ANSWER IN THE SPACE AT THE RIGHT.*

1. Reinforcing steel is coated with epoxy primarily to _____ of the steel.   1._____

   A. prevent corrosion
   B. improve the electric conductivity
   C. increase the tensile strength
   D. increase the compressive strength

2. Specifications for concrete require that concrete shall reach or exceed the design strength at the end of days.   2._____

   A. 14   B. 21   C. 28   D. 35

3. A #G reinforcing bar has a cross-section area of square inches.   3._____

   A. .44   B. .48   C. .52   D. .56

4. Mixing time for concrete which is measured from the time all ingredients are in the drum should be at least 1.5 minutes for a one cubic yard mixer plus 0.5 minutes for each cubic yard of capacity over one cubic yard.
   The MINIMUM time to mix 7 cubic yards of concrete is, in minutes,   4._____

   A. 3.0   B. 3.5   C. 4.0   D. 4.5

5. It is recommended that a maximum limit be set on mixing time for machine-mixed concrete because overmixing may remove entrained air and   5._____

   A. increase the water/cement ratio of the mixture
   B. increase the amount of fine aggregates in the concrete mixture
   C. the concrete mix may set prematurely
   D. cause excess water to rise in the placed concrete causing alligator cracks in the surface

6.   6._____

   Of the following curves, the shape of the roadway section shown above is

   A. circular   B. elliptical   C. parabolic   D. hyperbolic

1

7.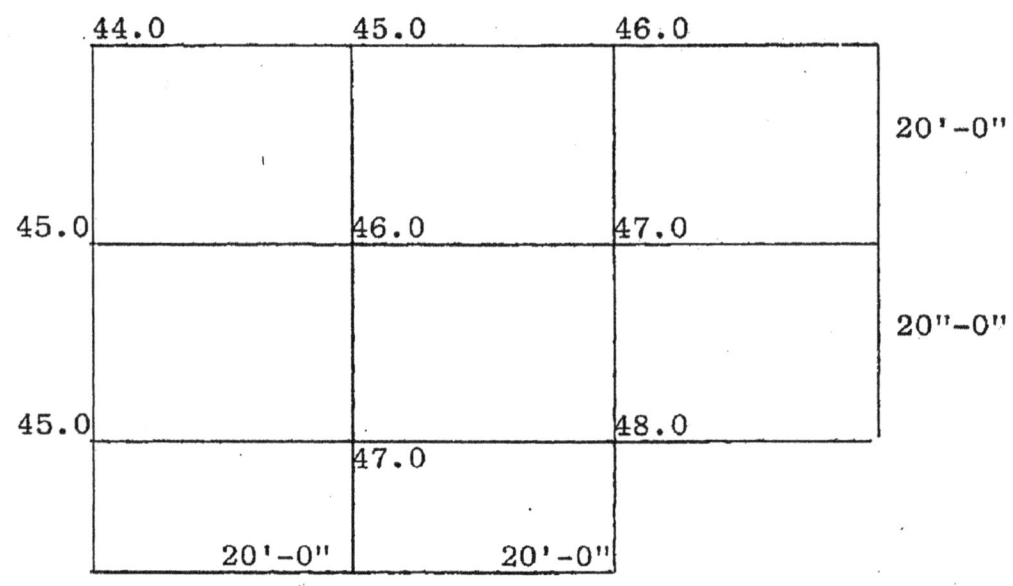

Shown above are the elevations of a borrow pit. The final elevation of the borrow pit after removing the soil is 40.0. Neglecting earth removal outside the borrow pit area, the volume of earth removed is, in cubic yards, MOST NEARLY
A. 347   B. 352   C. 357   D. 362

8. The shaded area is, in square inches, MOST NEARLY
   A. 18.3
   B. 19.1
   C. 20.0
   D. 20.9

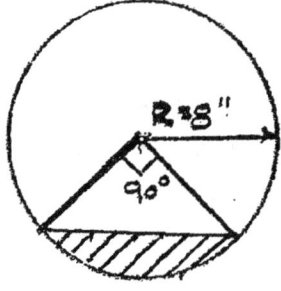

9. Of the following properties of polymer concrete that make it attractive for maintenance of Portland cement concrete roadways, the one that is MOST important is

   A. light weight
   B. immunity to corrosion
   C. resistance to abrasion
   D. rapid hardening qualities

10. A gallon of water weighs MOST NEARLY _____ pounds.

    A. 7.53   B. 8.33   C. 9.13   D. 9.53

11. Air-entrained concrete is used in concrete roadways primarily to

    A. reduce the weight of the concrete
    B. prevent corrosion of the steel reinforcement in the concrete
    C. make the concrete less porous to the intrusion of water in the concrete
    D. resist damage to the roadway due to freezing and thawing

12. The slump test in concrete is used to test its

    A. air content
    B. workability
    C. porosity
    D. uniformity

13. The criterion for water that is to be used for mixing concrete is that it should be potable. This means that the water should

    A. have high turbidity
    B. should be hard
    C. contain no sulfates
    D. be fit for human consumption

14. A test that can be used on an asphalt roadway to measure changes in hardness due to age hardening is a _____ test.

    A. ductility
    B. viscosity
    C. ring and ball softening point
    D. penetration

15. A densely graded bituminous mixture is called a large stone mix if the nominal size of aggregates is equal to or greater than a minimum of

    A. 1 inch
    B. 1 1/4 inches
    C. 1 1/2 inches
    D. 1 3/4 inches

16. The specifications state that the surface on which the bituminous material is applied must have a temperature of 20°C or higher.
    20°C is, in degrees Fahrenheit,

    A. 62°
    B. 64°
    C. 66°
    D. 68°

17. The largest size aggregate in sheet asphalt is usually

    A. 1/8 inch
    B. 1/4 inch
    C. 3/8 inch
    D. 1/2 inch

18. Sheet asphalt is used mainly in

    A. rural areas
    B. major highways
    C. overpasses
    D. city streets

19. Of the following, a slurry seal is NOT used on a bituminous pavement to

    A. fill potholes
    B. fill cracks
    C. repair raveling asphalt pavement
    D. provide a skid-resistant surface

20. Pozzolan is a *siliceous* material. Another example of a siliceous material is

    A. clay
    B. limestone
    C. granite
    D. sand

21. The primary purpose of a tack coat that precedes the application of a bitumimous mix on an existing surface is to

    A. remove dust from the existing surface
    B. fill in cracks in the existing surface
    C. allow the new mixture to adhere to the existing surface
    D. prevent the asphalt in the bituminous paving material from seeping into the existing pavement

    21.____

22. The lowest temperature at which asphalt pavements should be laid is

    A. 30°F   B. 40°F   C. 50°F   D. 60°F?

    22.____

23. Steam will rise from an asphalt mix when it is dumped into the hopper of a paver if

    A. there is too little asphalt in the mix
    B. excess moisture is present in the mix
    C. the mix is too hot
    D. there is an excess of asphalt in the mix

    23.____

24. The number of millimeters in an inch is MOST NEARLY

    A. 20   B. 25   C. 30   D. 35

    24.____

25. The number of inches in a meter is MOST NEARLY

    A. 39.37   B. 39.57   C. 39.77   D. 39.97

    25.____

KEY (CORRECT ANSWERS)

1. A	11. D
2. C	12. B
3. A	13. D
4. D	14. D
5. B	15. A
6. C	16. D
7. B	17. B
8. A	18. D
9. D	19. A
10. B	20. D

21. C
22. B
23. B
24. B
25. A

TEST 2

DIRECTIONS: Each question or incomplete statement is followed by several suggested answers or completions. Select the one that BEST answers the question or completes the statement. *PRINT THE LETTER OF THE CORRECT ANSWER IN THE SPACE AT THE RIGHT.*

1. Overheated asphalt can often be identified from the _____ in the truck.　　　　1._____
    A. rich black appearance and the tendency to slump
    B. slump and leveling out
    C. blue smoke rising from the mix
    D. lean, granular appearance of the mix

2. Of the following, the traffic sign shown at the right indicates a　　　　2._____
    A. school crossing
    B. no passing zone
    C. railroad crossing
    D. deer crossing

3. 90 kilometers per hour is MOST NEARLY _____ miles per hour.　　　　3._____
    A. 40　　　B. 45　　　C. 50　　　D. 55

4. One kilometer is equal to _____ miles.　　　　4._____
    A. 0.5　　　B. 0.6　　　C. 0.7　　　D. 0.8

5. Steel weighs 490 pounds per cubic foot. A one inch square bar of steel one foot long weighs MOST NEARLY _____ pounds.　　　　5._____
    A. 3.0　　　B. 3.4　　　C. 3.8　　　D. 4.2

6. The size of the fillet weld is dimension　　　　6._____
    A. A
    B. B
    C. C
    D. D

7. In mowing planted and natural grass adjacent to a roadway, the preferable period is　　　　7._____
    A. winter　　　B. spring　　　C. summer　　　D. fall

8. Pumping of a roadway surface occurs on

   A. bituminous pavements only
   B. bituminous and concrete pavements
   C. concrete pavements only
   D. concrete pavements only if they are not air-entrained

9. Pumping of a roadway surface is associated with soils in the subgrade that are

   A. gravelly
   B. fine grained
   C. coarse grained
   D. distributed in size from fine grained soils to coarse grained soils

10. The buckling or blowup of old concrete pavements is due primarily to the

    A. failure of longitudinal and transverse joints to function properly
    B. pounding by trucks that the pavement was not designed to carry
    C. failure of the subgrade to transfer the loads upon it
    D. subsurface water that is not drained from beneath the pavement

11. The MOST common type of construction equipment used for clearing and grubbing activities is a bulldozer. Bulldozer size is determined by

    A. tread area
    B. blade size
    C. drawbar pull
    D. flywheel horsepower

12. Sheepsfoot rollers are BEST used to compact

    A. clay soils
    B. sandy soils
    C. gravelly soils
    D. graded sand and gravel mix

13. A smooth-wheeled steel roller that is typically water ballasted are most effective on

    A. granular material such as sand and gravel
    B. clayed material
    C. mixtures of silt, sand and clay
    D. mixtures of sand and clay

14. Of the following machines, the one that would be MOST suitable for grading and shaping surfaces, ditching and bank sloping would be a

    A. bulldozer
    B. motor grader
    C. front end loader
    D. backhoe

15. Supercompactors which are useful for all types of soils weigh from _____ tons.

    A. 10 to 40   B. 20 to 50   C. 30 to 60   D. 40 to 70

16. A basic objective of the Critical Path Method used on a highway construction project would be to

    A. achieve economies in the use of material
    B. achieve economies in the use of equipment
    C. improve the quality of construction
    D. prevent the creation of bottlenecks

17. In the Critical Path Method, free float is the amount of time

    A. an activity requires to be completed
    B. an activity can be delayed without causing a delay in the succeeding activity
    C. an activity takes to make up for the time lag in the following activity
    D. needed to make up for lost time in a preceding activity

18. Another name for the bar chart used in construction planning and scheduling is the _____ chart.

    A. Fischer   B. Schiff   C. Banff   D. Gantt

19. Of the following, the machine that would LEAST likely be used to excavate large volumes of earth is a

    A. scraper   B. front end loader
    C. shovel   D. clamshell

20. Roadside maintenance generally includes the area between the

    A. traveled surface and the limits of the right of way
    B. distance between the outer edges of the shoulders on opposite sides of the highway
    C. median strip of the highway
    D. distance between the right of way on opposite sides of the highway

21. The sewer that usually has the greatest depth below grade is usually a(n) _____ sewer.

    A. sanitary   B. combined
    C. intercepting   D. relieving

22. A combined sewer is a sewer that

    A. carries storm water and salty water
    B. is made of steel and lined on the inside with concrete
    C. sometimes flow less than full and sometimes is under pressure
    D. carries sewage and storm water

23. If the grade of a sewer is 0.5%, the change in the elevation of the invert of the sewer in 350 feet is, in feet and inches,

    A. 1'-9"   B. 1'-10"   C. 1'-11"   D. 2'-0"

24. The National Joint Committee has adopted a color code for traffic control devices. The color brown is used for

    A. direction guidance
    B. general warning
    C. motorist service guidance
    D. public recreation and scenic guidance

25. Of the following, the isosceles traffic sign shown at the right indicates a
    A. traffic separation
    B. no U turn
    C. narrow median-urban
    D. no passing zone

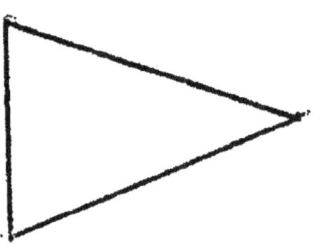

25.____

KEY (CORRECT ANSWERS)

1. C
2. A
3. D
4. B
5. B

6. A
7. D
8. C
9. B
10. A

11. D
12. A
13. A
14. B
15. B

16. D
17. B
18. D
19. D
20. A

21. C
22. D
23. A
24. D
25. D

EXAMINATION SECTION
TEST 1

DIRECTIONS: Each question or incomplete statement is followed by several suggested answers or completions. Select the one that BEST answers the question or completes the statement. *PRINT THE LETTER OF THE CORRECT ANSWER IN THE SPACE AT THE RIGHT.*

Questions 1-2.

DIRECTIONS: Questions 1 and 2 refer to the formula below.

The formula for stopping sight distance SSD13

$$SSD = 1.47tV + \frac{V^2}{30(f+G)}$$

1. The number 1.47 is a(n)

   A. empirically derived constant
   B. conversion factor
   C. factor based on perception reaction time
   D. factor of safety

2. The term t is usually assumed to be _____ seconds.

   A. 1.5   B. 2.0   C. 2.5   D. 3.0

3. An automobile weighing W is rounding a curve of radius R with a velocity V. Neglecting the friction between the tires and the roadway, if the forces acting on the car are in equilibrium, then

   A. $\sin \theta = \dfrac{V^2}{gR}$

   B. $\cos \theta = \dfrac{V^2}{gR}$

   C. $\tan \theta = \dfrac{V^2}{gR}$

   D. $\cot \theta = \dfrac{V^2}{gR}$

Questions 4-5.

DIRECTIONS: Questions 4 and 5 refer to the horizontal curve below.

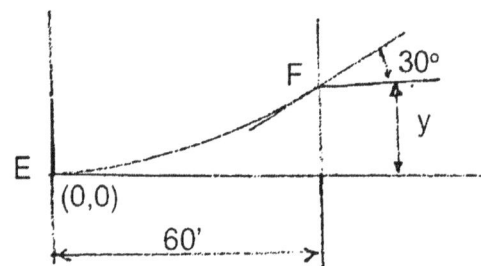

The equation of the curve is $y = kx^3$. The slope of the curve at F is 30°.

4. The value of k is

   A. .000023   B. .000033   C. .000043   D. .000053

5. The value of y is

   A. 5.0   B. 7.1   C. 9.3   D. 11.5

6. A 4° horizontal curve has a radius of _____ feet.

   A. 1232.4   B. 1332.4   C. 1432.4   D. 1532.4

Questions 7-10.

DIRECTIONS: Questions 7 through 10, inclusive, refer to the diagram of a horizontal circular highway curve.

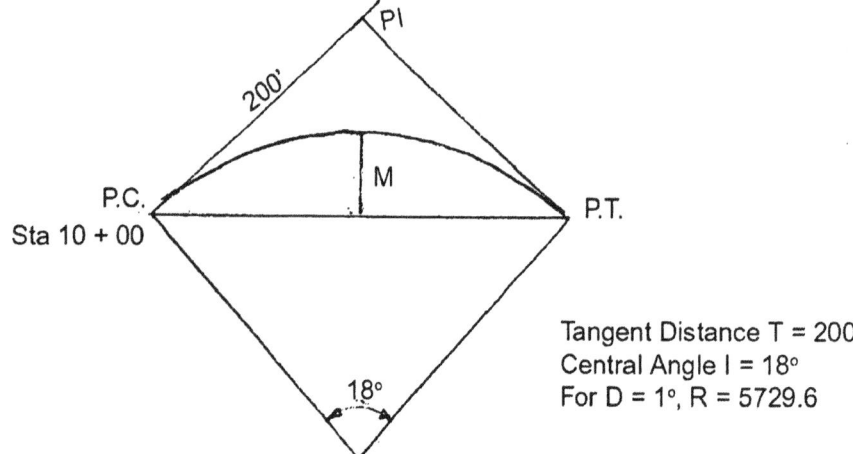

Tangent Distance T = 200'
Central Angle I = 18°
For D = 1°, R = 5729.6

7. The radius of the curve is _____ feet.

   A. 1212.7   B. 1232.7   C. 1262.7   D. 1292.7

8. The length of the arc of the circular curve is MOST NEARLY _____ feet.

   A. 396.7   B. 397.0   C. 397.7   D. 398.0

9. The long chord P.C. to P.T. is MOST NEARLY _____ feet.

   A. 392.06   B. 393.06   C. 394.06   D. 395.06

10. The middle ordinate M is most nearly _____ feet.

    A. 14.95   B. 15.15   C. 15.35   D. 15.55

11.

The sight distance EF is MOST NEARLY _____ feet.

A. 324   B. 364   C. 404   D. 444

12. For crest vertical curves, the length of the curve depends on the change in grade and H_e and H_o where He is the driver's eye height and H_o is the object height. Their relation is usually

    A. $H_e < H_o$
    B. $H_e = H_o$
    C. $H_e > H_o$
    D. H_e is either greater, equal or less than H_o, depending on the judgment of chief of design

13. The length of a transition curve which connects a tangent to a circular curve should be sufficient to

    A. keep the rate of change of direction small
    B. achieve the superelevation of the road section
    C. prevent disruption of the drainage system
    D. prevent an abrupt change of direction when the circular curve is reached

14. It is desirable to have a minimum road grade of at least 0.3% in order to

    A. follow the land contours
    B. facilitate keeping the shoulders clear of debris
    C. secure adequate drainage for the roadway
    D. prevent drivers becoming drowsy on long stretches of level roadway

Questions 15-16.

DIRECTIONS: Questions 15 and 16 refer to the horizontal highway curve below.

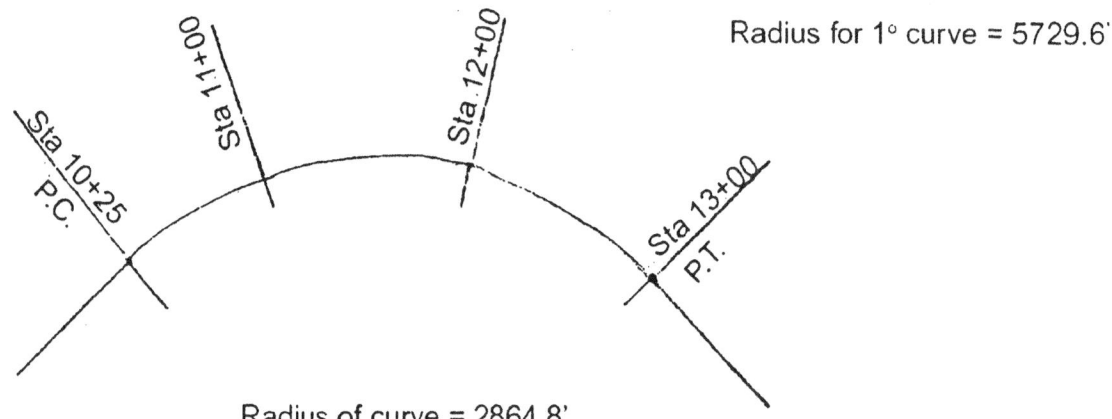

Radius for 1° curve = 5729.6'

Radius of curve = 2864.8'

15. The deflection angle from the P.C. to Sta 11+00 is

   A. 0°45' B. 1°00' C. 1°15' D. 1°30'

16. The deflection angle to Sta 13+00 is

   A. 2°00' B. 2°45' C. 3°45' D. 5°30'

17. Air entrained cement is used in air entrained concrete. The acceptable amount of air is generally between _____ percent of the total volume.

   A. 1 and 5 B. 2 and 6 C. 3 and 7 D. 4 and 8

18. Pumping of joints in a concrete roadway slab will occur during frequent occurrence of heavy wheel loads, the presence in the subgrade soil that is susceptible to pumping and

   A. inadequate thickness of the concrete slab
   B. air entrained cement is used in the roadway
   C. surplus water in the subgrade
   D. coarse and fine sand subgrades

19. Distributed steel reinforcing is primarily used to control cracking of a concrete roadway pavement and to maintain the integrity of the slab between transverse joints. Wire fabric or bar mats are used.
    In a concrete roadway section, the steel is usually placed at _____ of the slab.

   A. or near the center
   B. the bottom
   C. the top
   D. the bottom and at the top

20. In slipform paving for a concrete roadway, the slump in the concrete being poured should be _____ inch(es).

   A. 1/2 to 1 B. 1 to 1 1/2 C. 1 1/2 to 2 D. 2 to 2 1/2

21. The collapse of a section of the New England Thruway at Mianus was due primarily to faulty   21._____

    A. steel
    B. design
    C. construction
    D. periodic inspections

22. The coefficient of expansion of concrete due to temperature change is considered   22._____

    A. the same as that for steel
    B. less than that for steel
    C. more than that for steel
    D. more or less than that for steel, depending on the type of steel being used

23. Design hourly volume is a future hourly volume used for design. It is usually taken as the _____ hourly volume of the year.   23._____

    A. 10th B. 15th C. 20th D. 30th

24. Let E be an experiment and S a sample space associated with the experiment. A function X assigned to every element SES a real number X(S) is called a   24._____

    A. relative frequency
    B. likely outcome
    C. random variable
    D. conditional probability

25. The color code brown on a traffic device denotes   25._____

    A. public recreation and scenic guidance
    B. construction and maintenance warning
    C. general warning
    D. motorist service guidance

KEY (CORRECT ANSWERS)

1. B	11. D
2. C	12. C
3. C	13. B
4. D	14. C
5. D	15. A
6. C	16. B
7. C	17. D
8. A	18. C
9. D	19. A
10. D	20. B

21. D
22. A
23. D
24. C
25. A

TEST 2

DIRECTIONS: Each question or incomplete statement is followed by several suggested answers or completions. Select the one that BEST answers the question or completes the statement. *PRINT THE LETTER OF THE CORRECT ANSWER IN THE SPACE AT THE RIGHT.*

1. The minimum headroom clearance for a sign over a roadway, according to the Federal Highway Administration, should be _____ feet.

   A. 15   B. 16   C. 17   D. 18

   1.____

2. In traffic flow, time mean speed _____ space mean speed.

   A. equals
   B. is less than
   C. is greater than
   D. may be greater or less than

   2.____

3. Overall speed and running speed are speeds over a relatively long section of street or highway between an origin and a destination. Test vehicles are driven over the test section of the roadway. The driver attempts to float in the traffic stream.
   This means

   A. driving as fast as he can under the speed limit
   B. driving in the middle lane of a three lane road
   C. passing as many vehicles as pass the test vehicle
   D. trying to keep his speed the same as the average speed of the vehicles on the road

   3.____

4. The difference between overall speed and running speed on a test run between origin and destination is overall speed is the

   A. average of the maximum and minimum speed while running speed is the distance covered divided by the time elapsed
   B. distance traveled divided by the time required while running speed is the distance traveled divided by the time required reduced by time for stop delays
   C. distance traveled divided by the total time required while running speed is the minimum time needed to cover the distance
   D. distance traveled divided by the total time required while running speed is the effort by the driver to stay in the flow of traffic

   4.____

5. The ductility test on asphalt is considered a measure of the _____ of the asphalt.

   A. impact resistance   B. elasticity
   C. durability   D. cementing power

   5.____

6. In asphalt paving work, there are three different types of specific gravity: bulk, apparent, and effective. Of the following statements relating to specific gravity, the one that is CORRECT is:

   A. Water absorption is normally not used in determining the quantity of permeable voids in the volume of aggregates
   B. The apparent specific gravity is less than the bulk specific gravity

   6.____

C. The effective specific gravity is less than the bulk specific gravity
D. The effective specific gravity falls between the bulk specific gravity and the apparent specific gravity

7. The temperature range of asphalt prior to entering the mixer in a batch or continuous plant is usually

   A. 150 to 250° F   B. 175 to 275° F
   C. 200 to 300° F   D. 225 to 325° F

8. The most likely cause of the various distress types in asphalt concrete pavements is

   A. structural failure   B. temperature changes
   C. moisture changes   D. faulty construction

9. Bleeding in asphalt concrete pavements is MOST likely caused by

   A. faulty mix composition   B. structural failure
   C. temperature changes   D. moisture changes

10. Depressions in asphalt concrete pavements is MOST likely caused by

    A. faulty construction   B. faulty mix composition
    C. temperature changes   D. moisture changes

11. The gradation curve of particle sizes is represented graphically with the ordinate defining the percent by weight passing a given size and the abscissa representing the particle size.
    The ordinate is plotted on a(n) _____ scale and the abscissa is plotted on a(n) _____ scale.

    A. arithmetic; arithmetic
    B. logarithmic; arithmetic
    C. arithmetic; logarithmic
    D. logarithmic; logarithmic

12. The viscosity of a liquid is a measure of its

    A. resistance to flow
    B. volatility
    C. solubility in carbon tetrachloride
    D. elasticity

13. Failures that occur in soil masses as a result of the action of highway loads are primarily _____ failures.

    A. tensile   B. torsion   C. shear   D. buckling

14. Bitumens composed primarily of high molecular weight hydrocarbons are soluble in

    A. toluene   B. carbon sulfate
    C. carbon disulfide   D. ammonium chloride

15. One pascal-second equals _____ poise(s).

    A. 1   B. 5   C. 10   D. 20

16. RS emulsions are best used

    A. where deep penetration is desired
    B. with coarse aggregates
    C. in warm weather
    D. in spraying applications

17. The specific gravity of bituminous material is generally determined

    A. with a pyenometer
    B. with a hygrometer
    C. by displacement
    D. with a hydrometer

18. The principal reason for determining the specific gravity of a bituminous material is

    A. converting from volume to weight measurements and vice versa
    B. identifying the type of bituminous material used in a mix
    C. for checking the uniformity of a mix where large quantities are involved
    D. insure that the properties of the mix continue to meet specifications

19. The specific gravity of asphaltic products derived from petroleum vary from

    A. .80 to .84
    B. .92 to 1.06
    C. 1.04 to 1.18
    D. 1.16 to 1.30

20. The flash point is an indirect measurement of the quality and kind of volatiles present in the asphalt being tested.
    Rapid cure cutback asphalts have a flashpoint of _____ or less.

    A. 100° F
    B. 130° F
    C. 150° F
    D. 180° F

21. Traffic density is defined as the

    A. number of vehicles passing a given point in a given period of time
    B. average number of vehicles occupying a given length of roadway at a given instant
    C. average center to center distance of vehicles on a given stretch of roadway at a given instant
    D. minimum distance center to center of vehicles on a given stretch of roadway at a given instant

22. Of the following, the best distribution that describes the vehicle distribution on a given stretch of highway at a given instant is the _____ distribution.

    A. Poisson
    B. Pascal
    C. normal
    D. hypergeometric

23. In slipform paving for a concrete roadway, the slump in the concrete being poured should be _____ inch(es).

    A. 1/2 to 1
    B. 1 to 1 1/2
    C. 1 1/2 to 2
    D. 2 to 2 1/2

24. A water-cement ratio of 6 gallons per sack of cement is equal to a water-cement ratio of _____ by weight.

    A. .50
    B. .53
    C. .56
    D. .59

25. One micron is equal to _____ centimeters. 25._____

   A. 10^{-2} B. 10^{-3} C. 10^{-4} D. 10^{-5}

KEY (CORRECT ANSWERS)

1.	C	11.	C
2.	C	12.	A
3.	C	13.	C
4.	B	14.	C
5.	D	15.	C
6.	D	16.	D
7.	D	17.	A
8.	D	18.	A
9.	A	19.	B
10.	A	20.	A

21. B
22. A
23. B
24. B
25. C

EXAMINATION SECTION
TEST 1

DIRECTIONS: Each question or incomplete statement is followed by several suggested answers or completions. Select the one that BEST answers the question or completes the statement. *PRINT THE LETTER OF THE CORRECT ANSWER IN THE SPACE AT THE RIGHT.*

1. Of the following statements relating to new bell and spigot pipe being laid in a trench, the one that is CORRECT is that 1.____

    A. the enlarged end of the pipe faces downstream
    B. bell and spigot pipe is usually elliptical in shape
    C. when building a new line using bell and spigot pipe, you start from the downstream end
    D. vitrified pipe is usually thicker than concrete pipe of the same diameter

2. Vitrified pipe is made of 2.____

    A. clay
    B. vermiculite
    C. gypsum
    D. Portland cement

3. The invert of a sewer pipe is its 3.____

    A. outer top
    B. inner bottom
    C. inner top
    D. outer bottom

4. A cradle is usually placed under a sewer pipe when the 4.____

    A. trench is narrow
    B. trench is wide
    C. soil is poor
    D. pipe is near the surface

5. A monolithic sewer is a 5.____

    A. vitrified pipe sewer
    B. sewer carrying only storm water
    C. cast-iron sewer containing bell and spigot joints
    D. reinforced concrete cast-in-place sewer

6. Of the following, the BEST reason for placing manholes on sewers is to 6.____

    A. provide access for inspection and maintenance
    B. allow for overflow during a heavy storm
    C. pinpoint the location of the sewer
    D. give access to the sewer for the purpose of snow removal

7. The sheeting in a trench for a sheeted sewer is ordered left in place after the sewer has been built and backfilled. The BEST reason for ordering the sheeting left in place is that 7.____

    A. the sheeting is too expensive to remove
    B. the removal of the sheeting would disturb the sewer
    C. this minimizes the settlement outside the sheeted area
    D. the sheeting is too difficult to remove

8. The two MOST frequently used types of sheeting for normal soil conditions and average depths are

   A. soldier beams with horizontal sheeting and vertical wood sheeting with bracing
   B. steel sheet piling and vertical wood sheeting
   C. precast concrete planks with soldier beams and steel sheet piling
   D. slurry walls and vertical wood sheeting

9. A specification for a new sewer requires that the pavement NOT be restored for a period of at least six months after the backfill is in place.
   The BEST reason for this requirement is to

   A. be sure that the sewer will work before restoring the pavement
   B. minimize the settlement of the pavement
   C. defer final payment to the contractor
   D. allow the use of a lighter pavement

10. In reinforced concrete sewers, the reinforcing steel must have a minimum cover of concrete.
    Of the following, the BEST reason for this requirement is to

    A. make the sewer watertight
    B. protect the reinforcing steel against corrosion
    C. allow the use of smaller sized stone in the concrete
    D. eliminate the need for vibrating concrete

11. As used in relation to sewers, infiltration refers to the

    A. leakage of sewage from the sewer to the surrounding soil
    B. connection of sanitary sewer lines into storm water sewers
    C. inflow of ground water into the sewer
    D. loss of mortar at the joints of prefabricated sewers

12. A BAD effect of infiltration in a sanitary sewer is that it

    A. tends to overload the sewage treatment plant
    B. corrodes the sewer
    C. causes cavitation in the sewer
    D. increases the carrying capacity of the sewer

13. A storm sewer GENERALLY differs from a sanitary sewer in that a storm sewer

    A. is generally larger in size than a sanitary sewer and carries little dry-weather flow
    B. is generally made of concrete whereas a sanitary sewer is generally made of cast iron
    C. generally requires fewer manholes than a sanitary sewer
    D. generally has a large slope whereas a sanitary sewer generally has a small slope

14. Manhole frames and covers are USUALLY made of

    A. aluminum   B. malleable iron
    C. cast iron   D. steel

15. The spacing of rungs used for steps in a manhole is MOST NEARLY _____ inches. 15._____

    A. 4   B. 12   C. 20   D. 26

16. Steel is galvanized by coating it with 16._____

    A. tin   B. lead   C. copper   D. zinc

17. The reinforcing steel in a cast-in-place concrete sewer section would MOST likely be placed as shown in 17._____

18. Well points would MOST likely be used in the construction of a sewer when the 18._____

    A. sewer is very deep
    B. sewer is in rock
    C. soil is clayey
    D. water table is above the sewer

19. The purpose of jetting the well points in sewer construc-tion is to 19._____

    A. clean out the screen
    B. set the well point in place
    C. clean out the area outside the screen
    D. remove water from the surrounding area

20. The type of soil in which well points operate MOST efficiently is 20._____

    A. sand   B. clay   C. rock   D. silt

21. The water-cement ratio of a concrete mix is USUALLY expressed in terms of 21._____

    A. barrels of cement per gallon of water
    B. bags of cement per gallon of water
    C. gallons of water per bag of cement
    D. gallons of water per barrel of cement

22. The effective diameter of a number 4 reinforcing bar is MOST NEARLY _____ inch.

    A. 1/4   B. 1/2   C. 3/4   D. 1

23. The PRIMARY purpose of curing freshly poured concrete is to

    A. keep the surface smooth
    B. prevent honeycombing of the surface
    C. improve the appearance of the surface
    D. prevent evaporation of water from the surface

24. A bag of cement weighs MOST NEARLY _____ pounds.

    A. 94   B. 104   C. 114   D. 124

25. Of the following, the material that may be used as the coarse aggregate in ordinary Portland cement concrete is

    A. well graded sand   B. sand of uniform size
    C. crushed rock   D. micaschist

26. In a 1:2:4 concrete mix, the 2 stands for the quantity of

    A. water   B. fine aggregate
    C. coarse aggregate   D. cement

27. The height of a slump cone used in concrete testing is _____ inches.

    A. 6   B. 8   C. 10   D. 12

28. As commonly used, 3000-pound concrete refers to 3000 pounds per

    A. inch   B. square inch
    C. cubic inch   D. foot

29. The factor that has the GREATEST effect on the strength of concrete is the

    A. size of coarse aggregate
    B. uniformity of the aggregate
    C. water-cement ratio
    D. quality of the fine aggregate

30. The number of bags of cement needed to produce a cubic yard of concrete is called the _____ factor.

    A. cement   B. yield   C. bulk   D. output

31. The MAIN purpose of vibrating newly poured concrete when it is in the forms is to

    A. remove high points on the surface
    B. eliminate air pockets on the surface
    C. remove excess water
    D. distribute the aggregate evenly in the concrete

32. A cubic foot of ordinary Portland cement concrete weighs MOST NEARLY _____ pounds.

    A. 145   B. 165   C. 195   D. 220

33. The MAIN purpose of adding an air entraining agent to a concrete mix used for sidewalks is to

    A. improve the resistance of the concrete to freezing and thawing conditions
    B. decrease the weight of the concrete to lighten the dead load of the concrete
    C. increase the compressive strength of the concrete
    D. decrease the resistance of the concrete to bleeding

34. Of the following operations on a fresh concrete surface, the one that should be performed FIRST is

    A. screeding   B. floating
    C. trowelling   D. brooming

35. When concrete is referred to as *3000-pound concrete,* the *3000* refers to its strength at the end of _____ days.

    A. 7   B. 14   C. 21   D. 28

KEY (CORRECT ANSWERS)

1. C		16. D
2. A		17. A
3. B		18. D
4. C		19. B
5. D		20. A
6. A		21. C
7. C		22. B
8. A		23. D
9. B		24. A
10. B		25. C
11. C		26. B
12. A		27. D
13. A		28. B
14. C		29. C
15. B		30. A

31. B
32. A
33. A
34. A
35. D

TEST 2

DIRECTIONS: Each question or incomplete statement is followed by several suggested answers or completions. Select the one that BEST answers the question or completes the statement. *PRINT THE LETTER OF THE CORRECT ANSWER IN THE SPACE AT THE RIGHT.*

1. If a batch of concrete is very stiff, its MAIN characteristic is that it

    A. has a low slump
    B. has a high slump
    C. is undersanded
    D. is oversanded

    1.____

2. Reinforcing steel should have the GREATEST cover of concrete when the concrete surface is

    A. in contact with the ground
    B. in contact with outside air
    C. an interior wall
    D. an interior ceiling

    2.____

3. The MAIN difference between reinforced concrete and plain concrete is that plain concrete uses _____ for reinforcing.

    A. larger aggregate
    B. high early strength cement
    C. steel
    D. a low water-cement ratio

    3.____

4. Of the following types of wood, the one that would MOST likely be used in form work for concrete is

    A. oak   B. maple   C. fir   D. birch

    4.____

5. The size that SEPARATES the fine aggregate from the coarse aggregate in a concrete mix is _____ inch.

    A. 1/8   B. 1/4   C. 3/8   D. 1/2

    5.____

6. The MINIMUM thickness of sidewalk pavements for pedes-trian use should be _____ inches.

    A. 4   B. 5   C. 6   D. 7

    6.____

7. An ADVANTAGE of using sand instead of salt on concrete roadway surfaces when snow and ice settle on them is that sand

    A. is easier to remove than salt when the snow disappears
    B. will harm catch basins less than salt when the materials are washed into the catch basin
    C. will not harm the concrete surface whereas salt is harmful to the surface
    D. will help melt the surface ice whereas salt will have no effect on the ice on the surface

    7.____

8. Sidewalks should be pitched toward the street at a MINIMUM of _____ inch per _____.

    A. 1/8; foot
    B. 1/8; yard
    C. 5/8; foot
    D. 1; foot

9. A freshly poured concrete sidewalk is usually finished with a

    A. screed
    B. wood float
    C. steel trowel
    D. darby

10.

    The shape of the roadway section shown above is USUALLY a(n)

    A. circle   B. ellipse   C. parabola   D. hyperbola

11. The MAIN advantage of using large coarse aggregate in a concrete mix is that

    A. the mix is more workable
    B. the mix is stronger
    C. there is a saving in cement
    D. less water is required

12. In building a new street, sidewalk, and curb in a previously unpaved area, the order of construction practically ALWAYS followed is that the

    A. sidewalk precedes the road pavement
    B. sidewalk follows the road pavement
    C. curb precedes the road pavement
    D. road pavement precedes the curb

13. The USUAL range of depth of a curb from top surface of road at curb to top of curb is _____ inches to _____ inches.

    A. 4; 8   B. 8; 12   C. 12; 16   D. 16; 20

14. The dimensions of common brick are GENERALLY

    A. 2 1/4" x 2 3/4" x 12"
    B. 2 1/4" x 3 3/4" x 8"
    C. 2 3/4" x 3 3/4" x 8"
    D. 2 3/4" x 4 3/4" x 12"

15. Common brick is made of

    A. limestone   B. sand   C. clay   D. loess

16. Carbon black is added to concrete to

    A. give the concrete a black color
    B. accelerate the setting of the concrete
    C. retard the setting of the concrete
    D. improve the workability of the concrete

17. When steel curb angles are used for curbs, anchors are attached, to the curb angles. The MAIN purpose of the anchors is to

    A. hold the curb in place when the curb is being poured
    B. bond the curb angle into the concrete curb
    C. anchor the curb angle into the soil
    D. anchor the curb angle into the sidewalk

17.____

18. Wire mesh is specified in pounds per

    A. square foot
    B. square yard
    C. hundred square feet
    D. hundred square yards

18.____

19. An asphalt pavement consists of three layers.
    The layer marked E in the sketch above is the _____ course.

    A. tack   B. binder   C. base   D. wearing

19.____

20. The BASE course of a sheet asphalt pavement is usually made of

    A. sheet asphalt
    B. concrete
    C. tar
    D. bituminous binder

20.____

21. In asphalt paving, the tack coat is USUALLY applied

    A. on the finished wearing surface
    B. on the surface of the soil to receive the pavement
    C. on hard dense impervious surfaces
    D. along the curb

21.____

22. The specification for a pavement states that the penetration of asphalt is measured in units of mm.
    This stands for

    A. micrometer
    B. macrometer
    C. manometer
    D. millimeter

22.____

23. In an asphalt pavement, the LIQUID part of the asphalt mix is

    A. bitumen   B. water   C. gasoline   D. benzene

23.____

24. The terms liquid limit, plastic limit, and plasticity index refer to tests on

    A. asphalt   B. soil   C. concrete   D. gravel

24.____

25. For a bituminous paving material, sieves and sieve analysis are used to analyze the

    A. cement   B. aggregate   C. clay   D. silt

25.____

26. The size of sidewalk panels is USUALLY

    A. 2' x 2'   B. 3' x 3'   C. 5' x 5'   D. 6' x 6'

26.____

27. The slope of a sidewalk is designated as 2 inches in 5 feet.
    The drop in elevation of the sidewalk in 30' is _____ foot.

    A. one   B. 1/2 of a   C. 3/4 of a   D. 1/4 of a

28. In placing temporary asphaltic pavement upon completion of the backfill in a street opening, a 3 inch thick pavement should be laid one inch above the adjoining asphalt permanent pavement.
    The MAIN reason for making the temporary pavement one inch above the finished pavement is to

    A. provide adequate drainage
    B. allow for settlement
    C. identify the temporarily paved area
    D. save excavation when the permanent pavement is placed

29. A maintenance bond for a roadway pavement is in an amount of 10% of the estimated cost.
    If the estimated cost is $80,000, the maintenance bond is

    A. $80   B. $800   C. $8,000   D. $80,000

30. Specifications require that a core be taken every 700 square yards of paved roadway or fraction thereof.
    A 100 foot by 200 foot rectangular area would require _____ core(s).

    A. 1   B. 2   C. 3   D. 4

31. An applicant must file a map at a scale of 1" = 40'.
    Six inches on the map represents _____ feet on the ground.

    A. 600   B. 240   C. 120   D. D, 60

32. A 100' x 110' lot has an area of MOST NEARLY _____ acre.

    A. 1/8   B. 1/4   C. 3/8   D. 1/2

33. 1 inch is MOST NEARLY equal to _____ feet.

    A. .02   B. .04   C. .06   D. .08

34. The area of the triangle EFG shown at the right is MOST NEARLY _____ sq.ft.
    A. 36
    B. 42
    C. 48
    D. 54

35. Specifications state: As further security for the faith-ful performance of this contract, the comptroller shall deduct, and retain until the final payment, 10% of the value of the work certified for payment in each partial payment voucher, until the amount so deducted and retained shall equal 5% of the contract price or in the case of a unit price contract, 5% of the estimated amount to be paid to the contractor under the contract.
    For a $300,000 contract, the amount to be retained at the end of the contract is

    A. $5,000   B. $10,000   C. $15,000   D. $20,000

KEY (CORRECT ANSWERS)

1.	A	16.	A
2.	A	17.	B
3.	A	18.	C
4.	C	19.	B
5.	B	20.	B
6.	A	21.	C
7.	C	22.	D
8.	A	23.	A
9.	B	24.	B
10.	C	25.	B
11.	C	26.	C
12.	C	27.	A
13.	A	28.	B
14.	B	29.	C
15.	C	30.	D

31. B
32. B
33. D
34. A
35. C

TEST 3

DIRECTIONS: Each question or incomplete statement is followed by several suggested answers or completions. Select the one that BEST answers the question or completes the statement. *PRINT THE LETTER OF THE CORRECT ANSWER IN THE SPACE AT THE RIGHT.*

Questions 1-4.

DIRECTIONS: Questions 1 through 4, inclusive, refer to the plan of a sewer shown below.

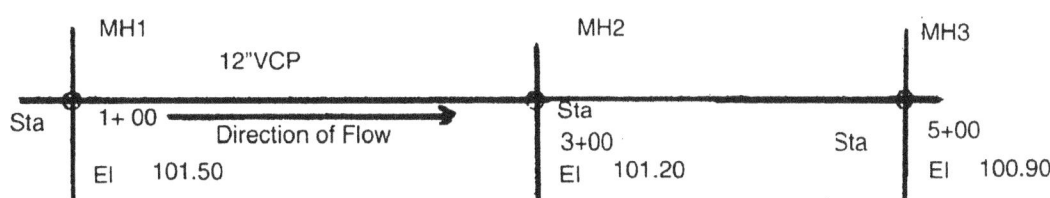

PLAN - SEWER

1. The distance, in feet, between MH1 and MH3 is _____ feet.

   A. 200　　　B. 300　　　C. 400　　　D. 500

2. The drop in elevation between MH1 and MH3 is

   A. 0.60'　　　B. 0.50'　　　C. 0.40'　　　D. 0.30'

3. If the scale of the drawing is 1 inch = 40 feet, the length of the line on the plan between MH1 and MH2 should be, in inches,

   A. 3　　　B. 4　　　C. 5　　　D. 6

4. A vertical section taken along the length of the sewer would be called a

   A. cross section　　　B. development
   C. partial plan　　　D. profile

5. A line joining points of equal elevation on a plan is known as a(n)

   A. profile　　　B. contour　　　C. elevation　　　D. isobar

6. The Federal agency concerned with safety on a construction site is

   A. OSHA　　　B. FIDC　　　C. FEMA　　　D. NHOC

7. A Federal safety requirement on construction sites is that

   A. a nurse must be present at all times
   B. a safety inspector, whose only duty is safety, be assigned full time to construction sites
   C. safety hats must be worn
   D. metal scaffolds are not permitted on the job site

8. Safety shoes are shoes that have a(n)

   A. extra heavy sole
   B. extra heavy heel
   C. metal covering the toe
   D. special leather covering over the ankles

9. A material whose use has been curtailed in building and heavy construction is

   A. poured cut asphalt
   B. lightweight concrete aggregate
   C. latex paint
   D. sprayed-on asbestos

10. In making a field report, it is POOR practice to erase information on the report in order to make a change because

    A. there is a question of what was changed and why it was changed
    B. you are liable to erase through the paper and tear the report
    C. the report will no longer look neat and presentable
    D. the duplicate copies will be smudged

11. It is PREFERABLE to print information on a field report rather than write it out longhand mainly because

    A. printing takes less time to write than writing long-hand
    B. printing is usually easier to read than longhand writing
    C. longhand writing on field reports is not acceptable in court cases
    D. printing occupies less space on a report than long hand writing

12. Where the length of roadway pavement is less than 100 lineal feet, the requirement of cores may be waived.
    The term waived in the above statement means MOST NEARLY

    A. eliminated   B. enforced
    C. considered   D. postponed

13. Inspectors are provided with standardized forms, and they have to fill in information as requested on the form.
    Of the following, the MAIN advantage of this type of form is that

    A. the inspector will be less likely to omit important information
    B. it is cheap to print
    C. it is confidential and only authorized people will see it
    D. it is easy to make copies of the form

14. Where only part of the sidewalk is to be relaid, the concrete shall match the predominant color of the existing sidewalk.
    The word predominant in the above sentence means MOST NEARLY

    A. lightest   B. darkest
    C. main   D. contrasting

15. All stands must be substantially built so as not to create any <u>hazard</u> to passersby or other persons.
    The word <u>hazard</u> in the above sentence means MOST NEARLY

    A. delay
    B. danger
    C. obstruction
    D. inconvenience

16. The lights shall be lighted and remain lighted every night during the hours <u>prescribed</u> for public street lamps.
    The word <u>prescribed</u> in the above sentence means MOST NEARLY

    A. required
    B. not needed
    C. before midnight
    D. of darkness

17. The Department of Highways in its <u>discretion</u> may direct that certain regulations be waived.
    In the above sentence, the word <u>discretion</u> means MOST NEARLY

    A. jurisdiction
    B. operation
    C. organization
    D. judgment

18. A sidewalk that abuts a curb _____ the curb.

    A. is above
    B. is below
    C. touches
    D. is integral with

19. All canopy permits shall be posted in a <u>conspicuous</u> place at the entrance for which the permit is issued.
    The word <u>conspicuous</u> means MOST NEARLY

    A. well known
    B. inaccessible
    C. easily observed
    D. obscure

20. Where a street opening is made by a licensed plumber, a plunber's bond may be filed <u>in lieu of</u> a street obstruction bond.
    The words <u>in lieu of</u> mean MOST NEARLY

    A. in addition to
    B. instead of
    C. immediately as
    D. appurtenant to

21. Of the following characteristics of a written report, the one that is MOST important is its

    A. length
    B. accuracy
    C. organization
    D. grammar

22. A written report to your superior contains many spelling errors.
    Of the following statements relating to spelling errors, the one that is MOST NEARLY correct is that

    A. this is unimportant as long as the meaning of the report is clear
    B. readers of the report will ignore the many spelling errors
    C. readers of the report will get a poor opinion of the writer of the report
    D. spelling errors are unimportant as long as the grammar is correct

23. Written reports to your superior should have the same general arrangement and layout.   23.____
The BEST reason for this requirement is that the

    A. report will be more accurate
    B. report will be more complete
    C. person who reads the report will know what the subject of the report is
    D. person who reads the report will know where to look for information in the report

24. The first paragraph of a report usually contains detailed information on the subject of the   24.____
report.
Of the following, the BEST reason for this requirement is to enable the

    A. reader to quickly find the subject of the report
    B. typist to immediately determine the subject of the report so that she will understand what she is typing
    C. clerk to determine to whom copies of the report shall be routed
    D. typist to quickly determine how many copies of the report will be needed

Questions 25-26.

DIRECTIONS: Questions 25 and 26 refer to the girder shown in the sketch below.

25. A report speaks of stiffeners on girders.   25.____
The stiffener would be the part shown as

    A. A   B. B   C. C   D. D

26. The flange would be the part shown as   26.____

    A. E   B. B   C. C   D. D

27. When an inspector is writing a report about a problem your agency handles, the report   27.____
should contain four major parts: a description of the problem, the location, the details of the problem, and

    A. your recommendation
    B. references to the drawings that pertain to the problem
    C. the borough in which the problem is located
    D. the agency to whom the problem should be referred

28. A report refers to a Pratt truss.   28.____
The material composition of the truss is MOST likely

    A. wood   B. concrete   C. steel   D. aluminum

29. A plumb bob is USUALLY used to

    A. check grades
    B. establish a vertical line
    C. hold down equipment
    D. check the grading of sand

30. As a general rule, any time a measurement is made in the field, the number of quantity should be immediately recorded.
    Of the following, the BEST reason for immediately recording this information is that

    A. the office is interested in receiving this information as quickly as possible
    B. this enables the inspector to complete his report more quickly
    C. this information may be needed for computations
    D. it is easy to forget or mistake numbers if they are not immediately recorded

KEY(CORRECT ANSWERS)

1.	C	16.	A
2.	A	17.	D
3.	C	18.	C
4.	D	19.	C
5.	B	20.	B
6.	A	21.	B
7.	C	22.	C
8.	C	23.	D
9.	D	24.	A
10.	A	25.	D
11.	B	26.	B
12.	A	27.	A
13.	A	28.	C
14.	C	29.	B
15.	B	30.	D

EXAMINATION SECTION
TEST 1

DIRECTIONS: Each question or incomplete statement is followed by several suggested answers or completions. Select the one that BEST answers the question or completes the statement. *PRINT THE LETTER OF THE CORRECT ANSWER IN THE SPACE AT THE RIGHT.*

1. A mass diagram is used in water supply computations to determine the
   A. size of the area that will be flooded when a dam is built
   B. capacity of reservoir required to supply the demand for water
   C. volume of excavation required to clear the site for a reservoir
   D. rate of flow of water into a reservoir

2. The velocity head in a pipe is equal to
   A. $\frac{v^2}{2g}$ B. $\frac{v^2}{g}$ C. $\frac{v}{2g}$ D. $\frac{v}{g}$

3. A force of 200 lbs. and a force of 300 lbs. make an angle of 30° with each other. The value of the resultant force is, in lbs., MOST NEARLY
   A. 483   B. 48   C. 493   D. 513

4. A chemical commonly used for coagulation in a water purification plant is
   A. alum   B. caustic ash   C. potash   D. saltpeter

5. The consistency of a concrete mix is measured with a
   A. water meter
   B. viscosimeter
   C. slump cone
   D. vicat needle

6. The term *4000 pound concrete* commonly means
   A. one cubic yard of concrete weighs approximately 4000 pounds
   B. the allowable stress in compression in the concrete is 400 lb./sq.in.
   C. the concrete has a minimum ultimate strength in compression of 4000 lb./sq.in. at 28 days
   D. the concrete can carry a bond stress of 4000 lb./sq.in.

Questions 7-9.

DIRECTIONS: Questions 7 through 9 refer to the sketch of a reinforced concrete beam.

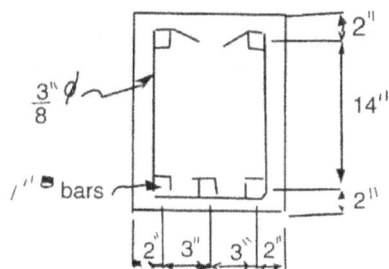

7. The effective width of the beam is, in inches, MOST NEARLY
   A. 5 B. 8 C. 9 D. 10

8. The ³⁄₈" diameter bar is _____ reinforcement.
   A. temperature
   B. tension
   C. compression
   D. shear

9. Provided no 1" bars are bent up, the upper two square bars are _____ reinforcement.
   A. temperature
   B. tension
   C. compression
   D. shear

10. The sine of 120° is the same as the sine of
    A. 45°
    B. 60°
    C. 45°, but with a negative sign
    D. 60° but with a negative sign

11. The formula for the area of a triangle is
    A. ½ab sin A   B. ½bc sin A   C. ½ac cos A   D. ½ab cos A

12. The logarithm of 7 is approximately 0.845.
    The logarithm of $(0.007)^{1/4}$ is APPROXIMATELY
    A. 9.343-10   B. 9.567-10   C. 9.461-10   D. 9.561-10

13. The center of gravity of a triangle is located at the intersection of the
    A. angle bisectors
    B. medians
    C. perpendicular bisectors of the sides
    D. radians

14. The distance between two stations was measured six times and the average distance found to be 346.215 ft.
    If one measurement of 351.205 ft. is deleted from the data as being inconsistent with the other measurements, then the average of the remaining five measurements is, in ft.,
    A. 345.217   B. 345.221   C. 345.227   D. 345.235

15. A ma of an area 380 ft. x 740 ft. is to be plotted on a sheet of drawing paper. The SMALLEST sheet of paper required to plot this map to a scale of 1" = 50', leaving a one inch margin all around, is, in inches,
    A. 8½ x 11   B. 10 x 17   C. 12 x 17   D. 10 x 15

16. On a topographic map, widely spaced contour lines indicate
    A. a gentle slope
    B. a steep slope
    C. an overhanging cliff
    D. the bank of a stream

17. The scale to which a map is drawn is 1" = 800'.
Of the following, the MOST common method by which this scale would be indicated on the map is
   A. 1/800
   B. 1" = 9600"
   C. 8.0" = one mile
   D. 1/9600

18. The angle formed between one line and the prolongation of the preceding line in a closed traverse is known as a(n) _____ angle.
   A. split   B. obtuse   C. direction   D. deflection

19. When laying out a horizontal circular curve, the deflection angle for a 100 ft. chord is equal to
   A. one-quarter of the degree of curvature
   B. one-half of the degree of curvature
   C. three-quarters of the degree of curvature
   D. the degree of curvature

20. For a given intersection angle, tables of the functions of a one degree curve show the tangent distance to be 1062.0 ft.
For the same intersection angle and a curvature of 4°, the tangent distance is, in feet, MOST NEARLY
   A. 265.5   B. 437.9   C. 649.3   D. 1153.4

21. The bending moment diagram for the beam shown in the diagram at the right is
   A. A
   B. B
   C. C
   D. D

22. The bending moment at the center of a simple beam supporting a uniform load of w pounds per foot throughout its entire length, l, is
   A. $\frac{wl^2}{2}$ B. $\frac{wl^2}{4}$ C. $\frac{3wx^2}{8}$ D. $\frac{wl^2}{8}$

23. A simple beam on a 16'0" span carries a concentrated load of 10,000 pounds. If the maximum bending moment in the beam is 465,000 inch pounds, the distance from the load to the nearer support is, in feet, MOST NEARLY
   A. 6.1   B. 6.3   C. 6.6   D. 6.9

24. The section modulus of a rectangular beam 6 inches wide and 12 inches deep is, in inches cubed,
   A. 24   B. 48   C. 96   D. 144

25. A 6" x 8" timber (actual size) is to be used as a beam on a simple span. 25.____
If the 8-inch side is vertical rather than the 6-inch side, the beam is NOT
   A. stronger in bending   B. stronger in shear
   C. stiffer   D. more efficient

26. A 6" x 8" timber (actual size) is being used as a gin pole. 26.____
The radius of gyration of this column which would be used in a column formula
to determine safe load for the gin pole is, in inches, MOST NEARLY
   A. 1.73   B. 1.87   C. 1.93   D. 2.13

27. A steel rod 25'0" long and 1 inch square in cross-section, fastened to solid 27.____
supports, is under a tension of 18,000 lb./sq.in.
If one of the supports yields 0.14 inches, the resultant tension in the bar will be,
in pounds per square inch, MOST NEARLY ($E = 30 \times 10^6$ lb./sq.in.)
   A. 3800   B. 4000   C. 4200   D. 4400

28. A round steel bar, one inch in diameter and three feet long, is elongated 28.____
.022 inches by a load applied at one end of the bar.
The magnitude of the load is, in lbs., MOST NEARLY ($E = 30 \times 10^6$ lb./sq.in.)
   A. 14,200   B. 14,400   C. 14,600   D. 14,940

29. A short hollow steel cylinder with a wall thickness of 1.5 inches is to carry a 29.____
compressive load, applied uniformly on the end, of 1,750,000 lb.
If the allowable working stress in steel in comparison is 20,000 lb./sq.in., then
the minimum outside diameter of the cylinder required to safely support this
load is, in inches, MOST NEARLY
   A. 19.4   B. 19.8   C. 20.0   D. 20.2

Questions 30-31.

DIRECTIONS: Questions 30 and 31 are to be answered on the basis of the following frame.

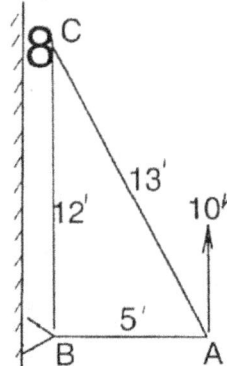

30. The reaction at joint C of the frame is, in kips, MOST NEARLY 30.____
   A. 4.17   B. 4.29   C. 4.37   D. 4.63

31. The stress in member BC of the frame is, in kips, MOST NEARLY 31.____
   A. 10.0   B. 10.6   C. 10.8   D. 11.2

32. The modulus of elasticity of aluminum is one-third that of steel. 32._____
This means that
A. steel is three times as strong as aluminum
B. aluminum is lighter than steel
C. aluminum is three times as strong as steel
D. for equal stress intensities, the unit strain in aluminum is three times that in steel

Questions 33-35.

DIRECTIONS: Questions 33 through 35 are to be answered on the basis of the following stress-strain diagram.

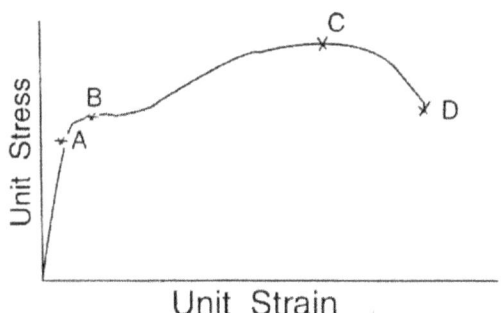

33. The stress-strain diagram is for 33._____
A. high-carbon steel B. low-carbon steel
C. cast iron D. concrete

34. The yield point is marked 34._____
A. A B. B C. C D. D

35. The ultimate strength is marked 35._____
A. A B. B C. C D. D

Questions 36-37.

DIRECTIONS: Questions 36 and 37 are to be answered on the basis of the following sketch.

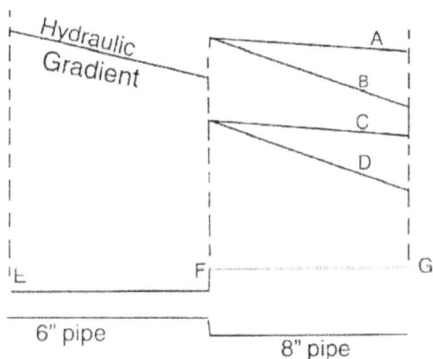

36. The velocity of flow in section EF is 6'/sec.
    The velocity of flow in section FG is, in feet per second, MOST NEARLY
    A. 3.36　　　　B. 3.38　　　　C. 3.40　　　　D. 3.44

37. If the hydraulic gradient as shown from E to F, the hydraulic gradient from F to G is marked
    A. A　　　　B. B　　　　C. C　　　　D. D

38. A 6-inch pipe line is horizontal from point A to point B, the distance AB being 2000 feet. At A, the hydraulic gradient is 10 feet above the pipe; at B it is 2 feet below the pipe.
    The head lost per thousand feet is, in feet,
    A. 1　　　　B. 3　　　　C. 7　　　　D. 6

39. A canal is to have a cross-sectional area of 60 square feet.
    If a square cross-section is used, the hydraulic radius of the canal when flowing full will be, in feet, MOST NEARLY
    A. 2.41　　　　B. 2.45　　　　C. 2.51　　　　D. 2.58

40. If one cubic foot of cement weighs 94 pounds and the specific gravity of the cement particles is 3.10, the void ratio (ratio of volume of voids to volume of solids) is MOST NEARLY
    A. 0.89　　　　B. 0.96　　　　C. 1.03　　　　D. 1.06

KEY (CORRECT ANSWERS)

1.	B	11.	B	21.	C	31.	A
2.	A	12.	C	22.	D	32.	D
3.	A	13.	B	23.	C	33.	B
4.	A	14.	A	24.	D	34.	B
5.	C	15.	B	25.	B	35.	C
6.	C	16.	A	26.	A	36.	B
7.	D	17.	D	27.	B	37.	A
8.	D	18.	D	28.	B	38.	D
9.	C	19.	B	29.	C	39.	D
10.	B	20.	A	30.	A	40.	D

SOLUTIONS TO PROBLEMS

3. **CORRECT ANSWER: A**

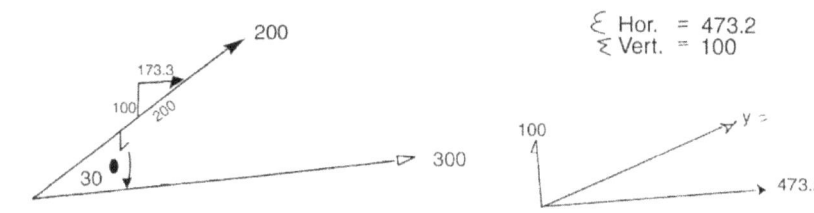

$r = \sqrt{100^2 + 473.2^2} = 483$ lbs.

10. **CORRECT ANSWER: B**

sin A = sin(π-A); sin 120° = sin 60°

11. **CORRECT ANSWER: B**

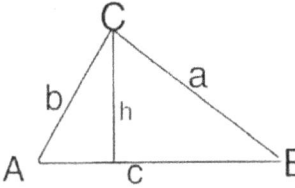

sin A = h/b
Area = $(\frac{1}{2})(c)(h) = \frac{1}{2}bc \sin A$

12. **CORRECT ANSWER: C**

Log $(0.007)\frac{1}{4} = \frac{1}{4}\log 7 \times 10^{-3} = \frac{1}{4}(-3+0.845) = 0.539$ or 9.461-10

14. **CORRECT ANSWER: A**

[(6)(346.215) – 351.205]/5 = 1826.085/5 = 365.217

15. **CORRECT ANSWER: A**
Each dimension on paper must be increased by two inches (one inch margin on each side); 380/50 ~ 8, 740/50 ~ 15 or 10 × 17

19. **CORRECT ANSWER: B**
Deflection angles for 100 ft. lengths are multiples of ½ degree of curvature.

20. **CORRECT ANSWER: A**
Since degree of curve is described by the angle subtended by a chord or are of 100 ft. length, the tangent distance is a direct measure of the degree of curve. For 4°, (1062.0)(¼) = 265.5 ft.

22. CORRECT ANSWER: D

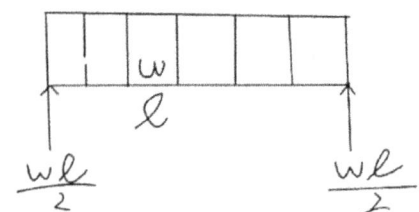

Moment @ $\frac{1}{2} = \frac{wl}{2} \frac{(1)}{(2)} - \frac{wl}{2} \frac{(1)}{(4)}$

from the rt.

$= \frac{wl^2}{4} - \frac{wl^2}{8}$

$= \frac{wl^2}{8}$

23. CORRECT ANSWER: C

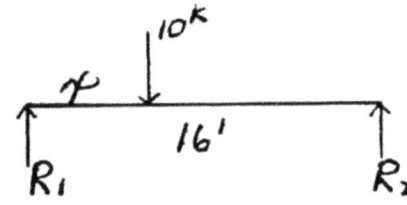

$M = \frac{465000}{12} = 38.750$ ft.-k

$R_1 = \frac{(16-x)}{(16)} 10$

$38.75 = R_1 x = \frac{(16-x)}{(16)} (10)(x) = \frac{160x - 10x^2}{16}$

$10x^2 - 160x + 38.75(16) = 0$

$x^2 - 16x + 62 = 0$

$x = \frac{-b \pm \sqrt{b^2 - 4ac}}{2a}$

$x = \frac{16 \pm \sqrt{256 - 248}}{2} = \frac{16 \pm \sqrt{8}}{2}$

$x = 8 \pm \sqrt{2}$

It must be less than 8 to be the distance to the nearer support ∴ 8 − 1.4 = 6.6

24. CORRECT ANSWER: D

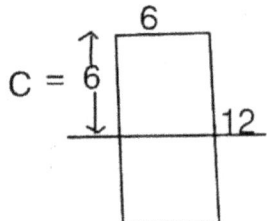

Section Modulus $= \frac{1}{c}$

$I = \frac{bh^3}{12} = \frac{6 \times 12^3}{12} = 6 \times 12^2$

$c = 6$

$\frac{1}{c} = \frac{6 \times 12^2}{6}$ $12^2 = 144$

9 (#1)

25. CORRECT ANSWER: B
By having the 8-inch side vertical rather than the 6-inch side, it becomes stronger in bending, stiffer and more efficient, but the shear strength remains the same.

26. CORRECT ANSWER: A

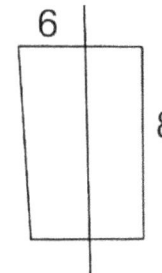

(taken about the weak axis)

$r = \dfrac{d}{\sqrt{12}}$

$d = 6$

$r = \dfrac{6}{\sqrt{12}}$ 1.73

27. CORRECT ANSWER: B
$E = 30 \times 10^6$
$A = \pi/4$
$\varepsilon = \dfrac{\sigma}{E} = \dfrac{18000}{30 \times 10^6} = 600 \times 10^{-6}$

Support yield = 0.14 inches = $\dfrac{0.14}{25 \times 12} = 467 \times 10^{-6}$

$(600-467) \times 10^{-6} = 133$ in/in

$\sigma = E\varepsilon = 30 \times 10^6 \times 133 \times 10^{-6} = 3990$ psi

28. CORRECT ANSWER: B
$E = 30 \times 10^6$ psi

$A = \dfrac{\pi D^2}{4} = \pi/4$ in²

$\varepsilon = .022/36 = 611 \times 10^{-6}$ in/in

$\sigma = \dfrac{P}{A} = P/\pi/4$

$E = \dfrac{\sigma}{\varepsilon}$

p = $E\varepsilon \pi/4 = 30 \times 10^6 \times 611 \times 10^6 \times \pi/4 = 14{,}400$ lbs.

29. CORRECT ANSWER: C

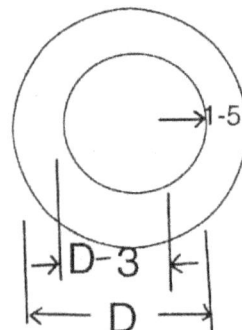

$A = \dfrac{P}{\sigma} = \dfrac{1{,}750{,}000 \text{ lbs.}}{20{,}000 \text{ psi}} = 87.5 \text{ in}^2$

$\dfrac{\pi D^2}{4} - \dfrac{\pi(D-3)^2}{4} = 87.5$

$D^2 - (D^2 - 6D + 9) = 8.75(4/\pi)$

$6D = 111.4 + 9$
$D = 20.07$

30. CORRECT ANSWER: A
Horizontal reaction C from ΣM about B =
$C(12) = 10 \times 5$
$C\rightarrow = 4.17$

31. CORRECT ANSWER: A
$\Sigma V = 0$; BC takes only the vertical loading because of the roller at B.

32. CORRECT ANSWER: D
$E = \dfrac{\sigma}{\varepsilon}$

Steel E ≈ 30
AlE ≈ 10

$\varepsilon \text{steel} = \dfrac{\sigma \text{const}}{30} = 1/30$

$\varepsilon \text{al} = \dfrac{\sigma \text{const}}{10} = 1/10$

$\dfrac{1 \text{ al}}{10} = 3\left(\dfrac{1 \text{ st}}{30}\right)$

33. CORRECT ANSWER: B
Low carbon steel because of the ductility

36. CORRECT ANSWER: B
Q = flow (ft 3/sec.)   Q = Av
A = area (ft^2)   Av = A'v
v = velocity (ft/sec) $(9\pi)(6) = (16\pi)v$
                           v = 3.38

37. CORRECT ANSWER: A
The hydraulic gradient is a line drawn through a series of points to which water would rise in piezometer tubes attached to a pipe through which water flows. The head loss in the larger pipe due to friction will be at a lesser rate than the smaller pipe because of the larger diameter and lower velocity of flow.

39. CORRECT ANSWER: D

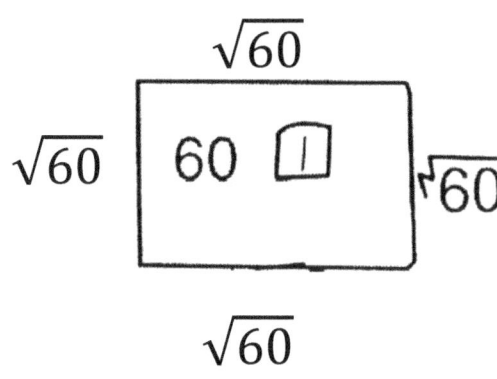

hydraulic radius = $\dfrac{\text{cross-section area of water}}{\text{wetted perimeter}}$

$= \dfrac{60}{3\sqrt{60}} = 2.58$

40. CORRECT ANSWER: D
If there were no voids, the weight of one cubic ft. would be 3.10 × 62.4 = 193.44

Volume of voids = $\dfrac{193.44 - 94}{193.44}$ ft³ = $\dfrac{99.44}{193.44}$

Volume of solids = $\dfrac{94}{193.44}$ ft³

Void ratio = $\dfrac{99.44}{94.00}$ = 1.06

TEST 2

DIRECTIONS: Each question or incomplete statement is followed by several suggested answers or completions. Select the one that BEST answers the question or completes the statement. *PRINT THE LETTER OF THE CORRECT ANSWER IN THE SPACE AT THE RIGHT.*

1. A *plane table* is MOST commonly used to
    A. determine trigonometric functions of angles
    B. plot large maps in the office from data taken in the field
    C. plot maps directly in the field
    D. adjust distances from slope measurements to horizontal measurements

   1.____

2. Of the following formulas used in taping, the one that gives the correction for sag is
    A. $\dfrac{h^2}{2s}$ B. $\dfrac{0.204W\sqrt{AE}}{\sqrt{Pn-Po}}$ C. $\dfrac{(P-Po)l}{AE}$ D. $\dfrac{W^2L}{24P^2}$

   2.____

3. Recorded distances will be less than the actual horizontal distances when measurements are taken
    A. with the tape on a slope
    B. at a temperature lower than that at which the tape was standardized
    C. with the center of the tape out of line
    D. with a tension greater than that at which the tape was standardized

   3.____

4. A 100 ft. steel tape is standardized fully supported under a 10 pound pull when the temperature is 59°F and found to be 100.17 feet long. A distance of 70.00 feet is to be laid out with this tape under the standardization conditions.
   The tape distance to lay out, in feet, is
    A. 69.88   B. 69.99   C. 70.01   D. 70.12

   4.____

5. In the closed traverse ABC, the bearings of lines AB and BC are N45°-00'E and N60°00'E, respectively. The lengths of these lines are 200 ft. and 300 ft., respectively. The bearing of line CA is MOST NEARLY
    A. S54°-00'W   B. S56°-00'W   C. S58°-00'W   D. S60°-00'W

   5.____

6. A transit is so designed that the stadia constant C is negligible. The stadia interval factor is 200. When the telescope if level,
    A. readings must be taken on the stadia red every 100 ft.
    B. the distance from the instrument to the rod is 100 times the difference between the readings of the upper and lower crosshairs on the rod
    C. the scale used to read the stadia rod is divided into 100 parts
    D. the difference of elevation from the instrument to the point on which the rod is held is equal to the stadia reading plus 1.00 ft.

   6.____

Questions 7-11.

DIRECTIONS: In Questions 7 through 11, the plan and front elevation of an object are shown on the left, and on the right are shown four figures, one of which, and only one, represents the right side elevation. Indicate the letter which represents the right side elevation.

SAMPLE QUESTION: In the sample shown below, which figure correctly represents the right side elevation?

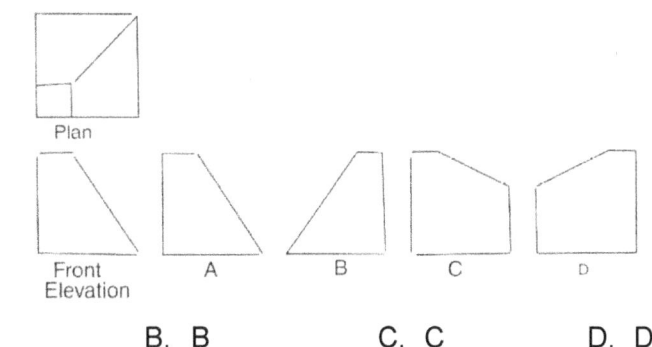

A. A B. B C. C D. D

The correct answer is A.

7.

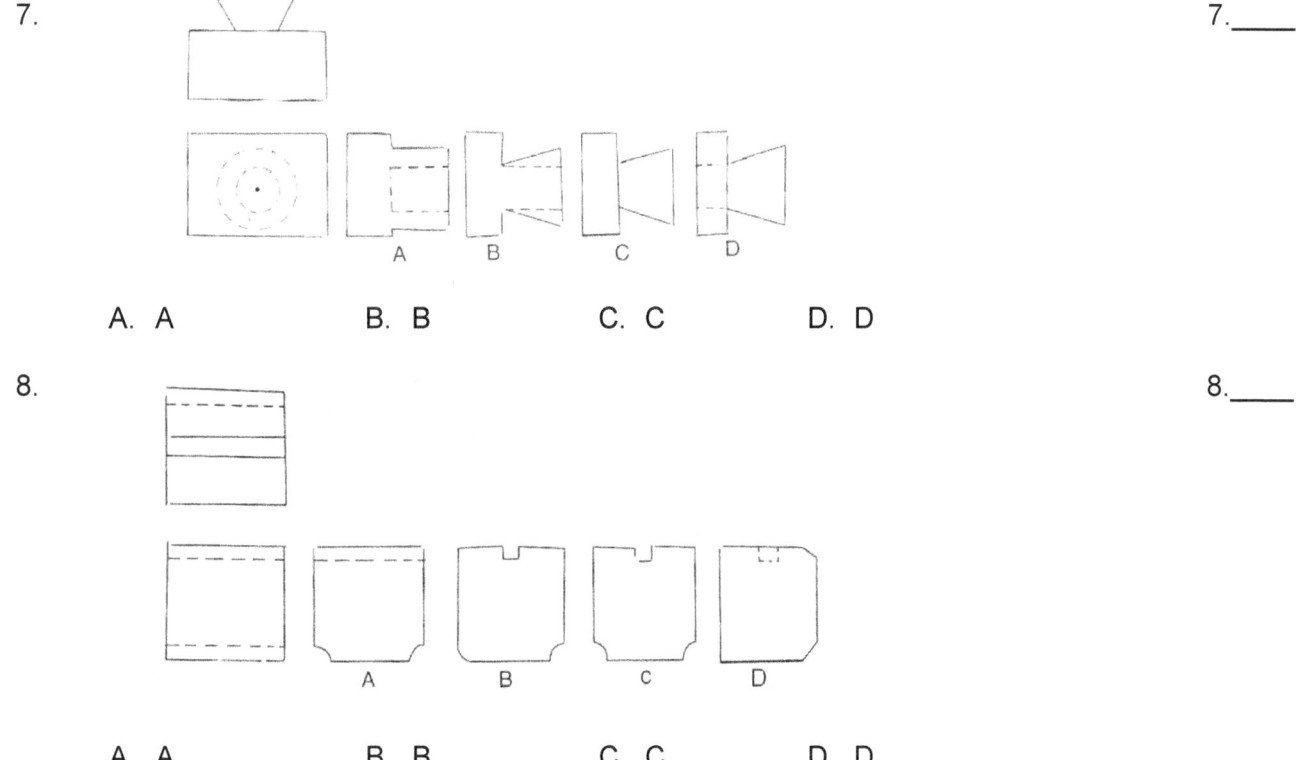

A. A B. B C. C D. D

8.

A. A B. B C. C D. D

9.

| A | B | C | D |

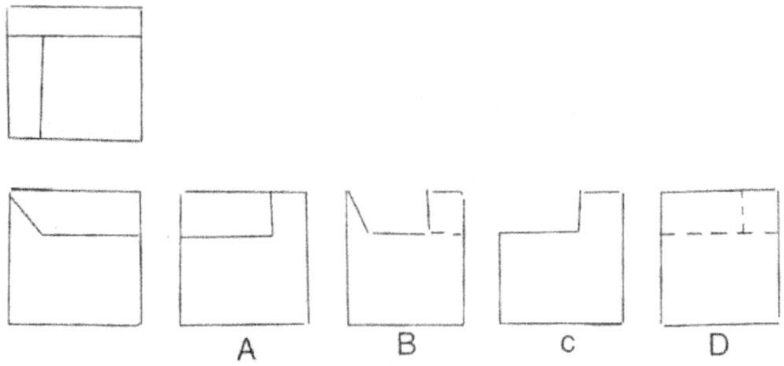

A. A   B. B   C. C   D. D

10.

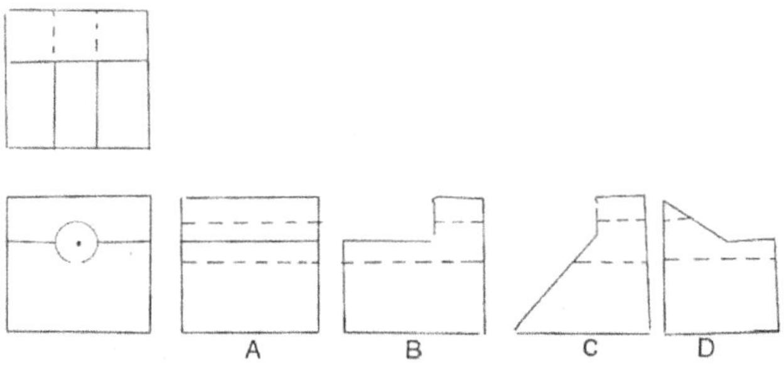

A. A   B. B   C. C   D. D

11.

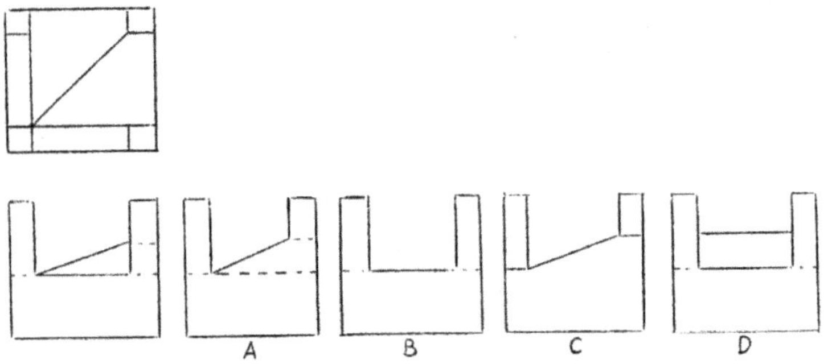

A. A   B. B   C. C   D. D

Questions 12-14.

DIRECTIONS: Questions 12 through 14 are to be answered on the basis of the following sketch.

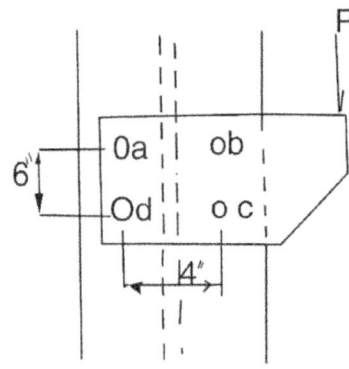

12. Maximum rivet stress occurs in rivet
    A. a only   B. b only   C. c only   D. b and c

13. The plate carrying the load is known as a _____ plate.
    A. gusset   B. flange   C. web   D. shear

14. The plate carrying the load is attached to a(n) _____ column.
    A. built-up   B. H
    C. channel   D. none of the above

15. A 3 x 3 x ³/₈ angle in a structural frame is in tension. It is connected at each end by one ⁷/₈" rivet to a gusset plate.
    The net section of the angle is equal to the gross minus _____ square inches.
    A. 0.339   B. 0.347   C. 0.375   D. 0.389

16. A formula commonly used to determine the allowable unit stresses in columns is s =

    A. $\dfrac{\pi^2 EI}{4l^2}$

    B. $17000 - .485(\dfrac{1}{r})^2$

    C. $\dfrac{22500}{1+\dfrac{l^2}{1800r^2}}$

    D. $\dfrac{P+Mc}{A \pm I}$

17. A rectangular footing 6'0" long by 4'0" wide carries a vertical load of 20,000 pounds located on the long axis 5 inches from the center of the footing.
    The maximum soil pressure under the footing due to this load is, in pounds per square inch, MOST NEARLY
    A. 1250   B. 1350   C. 1450   D. 1550

18. *Special anchorage* in concrete work commonly refers to
    A. reinforcement in concrete bolted to steel girders
    B. wing walls on a retaining wall to provide extra support
    C. a hook at the end of a reinforcing rod in continuous beam construction
    D. additional steel dowels connecting a concrete column with a concrete footing

Questions 19-20.

DIRECTIONS: Questions 19 and 20 are to be answered on the basis of the following sketch.

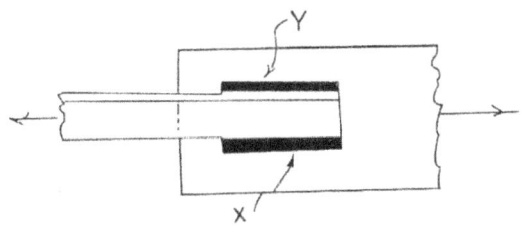

5 (#2)

19. In the welded section shown, the length of weld x should be _____ that of y.   19.____
    A. equal to   B. greater than
    C. less than   D. independent of

20. The welds shown are _____ welds.   20.____
    A. single V   B. double V   C. plug   D. fillet

21. The slope at any point on the bending moment diagram for a beam is equal   21.____
    to the _____ the beam at that point.
    A. load on   B. shear on
    C. deflection of   D. slope of

22. The shear diagram for the beam shown in the   22.____
    diagram at the right is
    A. A
    B. B
    C. C
    D. D

23. Vertical curves in highway work are usually parts of   23.____
    A. circles   B. ellipses   C. hyperbolas   D. parabolas

24. In laying out an angle with a transit, an error of one minute will result in   24.____
    locating a point 1000 ft. from the transit off the true line by APPROXIMATELY
    _____ ft.
    A. 0.1   B. 0.2   C. 0.3   D. 0.5

25. The sum of the positive departures of a closed traverse exceeds that of the   25.____
    negative departures by 0.31 ft. The sum of the negative latitudes exceeds that
    of the positive latitudes by 0.67 ft.
    The linear error of closure is, in feet, MOST NEARLY
    A. 0.39   B. 0.47   C. 0.58   D. 0.74

26. The balanced latitudes and departures of the sides of a closed traverse are   26.____
    as follows:

Line	Lat.	Dep.
AB	+152.27	+212.06
BC	+316.19	+ 83.92
CD	-522.34	+119.30
DA	+ 53.88	-415.28

    The DMD of line CD referred to a meridian through A is
    A. 567.89   B. 635.46   C. 711.26   D. 819.77

Questions 27-31.

DIRECTIONS: Questions 27 through 31 are to be answered on the basis of the following closed traverse which is drawn to scale.

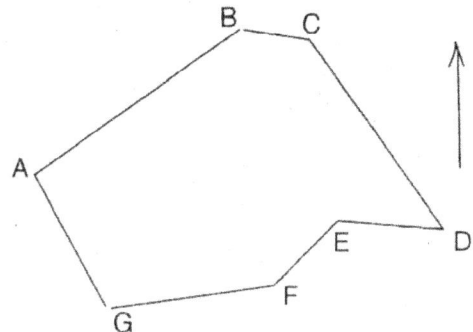

27. The sum of the interior angles of the traverse is
    A. 760°   B. 844°   C. 900°   D. 920°

    27.____

28. The arithmetical sum of the deflection angles, i.e., the sum without regard to sign, is
    A. 160°
    C. 330°
    B. 240°
    D. greater than 360°

    28.____

29. When balancing a survey of a closed traverse, the functions of angles most commonly used are
    A. sin and tan   B. cos and tan   C. sin and cos   D. tan and cot

    29.____

30. Of the following lines, the one with the LARGEST departure is
    A. AB   B. CD   C. AG   D. GF

    30.____

31. The area of the traverse could not be computed if all sides and angles were measured EXCEPT
    A. angles A, B, and C   B. sides AB and CD and angle B
    C. side AB and angles A and B   D. sides AB, BC, and CD

    31.____

32. The notes for a level run are as follows:

    32.____

Sta.	BS	HI	FS	Elev.
BM1	3.26			100.23
A	2.13		1.19	
B	4.05		3.20	
C	2.26		4.03	
BM2			4.22	

    The elevation of BMS is
    A. 99.17   B. 99.21   C. 99.25   D. 99.29

33. The foot of a leveling rod has been worn through hard use so that the rod is now .02 ft. short.
The elevation of any point found, using this rod, will be
A. .02 ft. low   B. correct   C. .02 ft. high   D. .04 ft. high

33._____

34. The correction to be applied to high rod readings on a Philadelphia rod is -0.004. In running a level circuit with this rod,
A. 0.004 should be subtracted from all high rod readings before entering them
B. the error should be ignored as it will cancel itself
C. the error should be ignored until all elevations are computed and then corrections should be made to elevations as required
D. the total error will be 0.004 times the square root of the number of high rod readings

34._____

Questions 35-40.

DIRECTIONS: Questions 35 through 40 are to be answered on the basis of the following sketch of a transit.

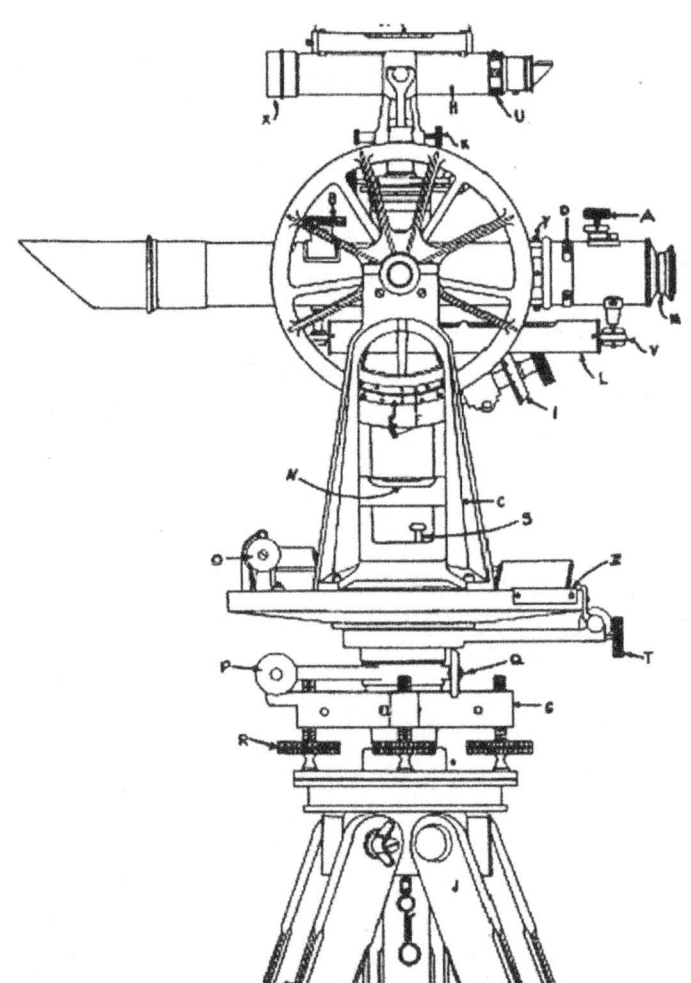

35. The vertical circle is marked
    A. D	B. E	C. F	D. I

36. A prism would be attached at
    A. M	B. U	C. X	D. Z

37. The lower motion clamp is marked
    A. K	B. P	C. Q	D. T

38. The bubble which would normally be centered to make the line of sight truly horizontal is marked
    A. L	B. N	C. O	D. W

39. The needle lifting or needle release screw is marked
    A. D	B. K	C. R	D. S

40. A peg test for this transit has been performed, and the line of sight reads 4.085 on the far rod. The far rod reading is computed to be 4.060. In making the adjustment, the first thing to move is the
    A. bubble adjusting screws
    B. capstan-headed screws on the reticule
    C. vertical slow motion
    D. vertical Vernier adjusting screws

KEY (CORRECT ANSWERS)

1.	C	11.	A	21.	B	31.	D
2.	D	12.	D	22.	D	32.	D
3.	D	13.	A	23.	D	33.	B
4.	A	14.	B	24.	C	34.	C
5.	A	15.	C	25.	D	35.	C
6.	B	16.	B	26.	C	36.	A
7.	C	17.	A	27.	C	37.	C
8.	B	18.	C	28.	D	38.	A
9.	A	19.	C	29.	C	39.	D
10.	B	20.	D	30.	A	40.	C

SOLUTIONS TO PROBLEMS

3. **CORRECT ANSWER: D**
The tapes' lengths are based on a standardized tension. If extra tension is applied, a short reading will result.

4. **CORRECT ANSWER: A**
The correction to be applied is:
70/100 × .17 = 0.12
∴ 70.00 − 0.12 = 69.88

5. **CORRECT ANSWER: A**
200 ft. @ N45°E = 2 × 45 = 90°
300 ft. @ N60°E = $\frac{3}{5}$ × 60 = $\frac{180°}{270°}$

AC = $\frac{270°}{5}$ = N54°E
CA = S54°W

6. **CORRECT ANSWER: B**
This is the definition of the stadia interval factor.

12. **CORRECT ANSWER: D**
The rivet stress is derived from the vertical load and the moment derived thereof. In this case, the vertical load is equal and the stresses due to moment are equal and additive to the vertical load. The moment stress is subtractive from the stresses on a and d.

15. **CORRECT ANSWER: C**
The net section = the gross minus the area taken by the rivet 1/8" larger than the rivet used.

The area subtracted = (8/8+1/8) × 3/8 = 0.375 in².

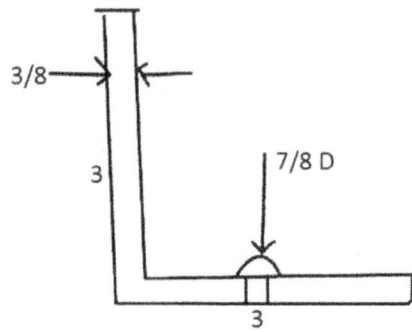

17. **CORRECT ANSWER: A**
Max. stress = P/A + $\frac{MC}{I}$ C = 3
I = bh³/12

= $\frac{20}{6 \times 4}$ + $\frac{(20 \times \frac{1}{2})(3)}{\frac{4 \times 6^3}{12}}$

= $\frac{20}{24}$ + $\frac{15}{36}$ = .83 + .42 = 1.25K psf = 1250 psf

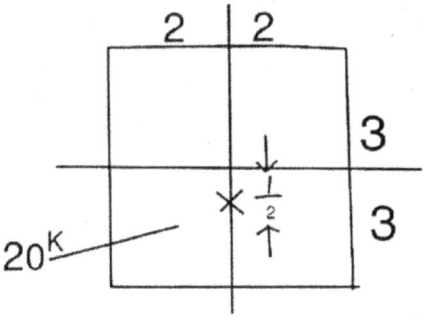

10 (#2)

23. **CORRECT ANSWER: D**
Parabolic arc is ideally suited for changes in vertical grade since slope varies at constant rate with respect to horizontal distance.

24. **CORRECT ANSWER: C**
tan 1 minute = 0.00029

α = 1 minute
b = 1000 ft.
$\frac{a}{b} = \tan\alpha$

a = tanα × b = .00029 × 1000 ft. = 0.29 ft.

25. **CORRECT ANSWER: D**

Linear error of closure $= \sqrt{(\Sigma \text{Lat})^2 + (\Sigma \text{Dep})^2}$

$= \sqrt{(0.31)^2 + (.67)^2}$

$= \sqrt{5450}$

= 0.74 ft.

26. **CORRECT ANSWER: C**
AB DMD = 212.06
BC DMD = 212.06 + 212.06 + 83.92 = 508.04
CD DMD = 508.04 + 83.92 + 119.30 = 711.26

The DMD of the first line equals the departure of the first line. The DMD of any other line is equal to the DMD of the preceding line plus the departure of the preceding line, plus the departure of the line itself.

27. **CORRECT ANSWER: C**
(n-2) × 180° = sum of the interior angles
n = number of sides
(7-2) × 180 = 900°

31. **CORRECT ANSWER: D**
There is no way to determine the lengths of these sides. All other missing data could be computed by trigonometry and geometry.

32. CORRECT ANSWER: D
    The complete notes should read as follows:

Sta.	BS	HI	FS	Elev.
BM1	3.26	103.49		100.23
A	2.13	104.43	1.19	102.30
B	4.05	105.28	3.20	101.23
C	2.26	103.51	4.03	101.25
BM2			4.22	99.29

33. CORRECT ANSWER: B
    Elevations are determined by differences of rod readings; therefore, a short rod does not affect the final data.

TEST 3

DIRECTIONS: Each question or incomplete statement is followed by several suggested answers or completions. Select the one that BEST answers the question or completes the statement. *PRINT THE LETTER OF THE CORRECT ANSWER IN THE SPACE AT THE RIGHT.*

1. A wooden beam is a rectangle 6" x 12".
   On a simple span, the ratio of the uniform load it can carry with the 6" sides vertical to that with the 12" sides vertical is as one is to
   A. 2   B. 5   C. 7   D. 9

2. A moving load consists of a 4-kip and an 8-kip concentrated load spaced 8 feet apart.
   The maximum bending moment caused by this moving load on a simple span of 16 feet is, in kip-feet,
   A. 33.3   B. 31.9   C. 27.6   D. 23.9

3. A canal with a trapezoidal cross-section is 6'0" wide at the bottom and has side slopes of one on one.
   When the depth of water is 4'6", the hydraulic radius is
   A. 2.43   B. 2.52   C. 2.55   D. 2.67

4. The minimum amount of cover required for water mains in city streets is NOT affected by
   A. depth of frost   B. consideration of shock loads
   C. depth of rock   D. any of the above

5. A vertical steel tank, 10'0" diameter, wall thickness ¼", is subjected to a hydrostatic pressure of 100 feet of water. The maximum tensile stress in the tank, in lb./sq.in., is MOST NEARLY
   A. 10,200   B. 10,400   C. 10,600   D. 10,800

6. Three eye bars, 6" x 1" x 25'0", jointly, are to carry a load of 200,000 lbs. The middle bar is .03 inch too short. Assuming the pins through the eyes to be parallel, the cross-section of the bars to be uniform throughout their entire length, and E = 30 × 10^6 #/sq.in., the stress in the outer bars in lb./sq.in. will be MOST NEARLY
   A. 10,100   B. 10,300   C. 10,500   D. 10,800

7. A property of steel NOT usually determined in the ordinary commercial tensile test of steel is
   A. modulus of rupture   B. percent reduction in area
   C. yield point   D. ultimate stress

8. In the activated sludge process, *seeding* is carried on in the
   A. grit chamber   B. aeration tank
   C. sand filter   D. sedimentation tank

9. The hydraulic radius is defined as
   A. the distance from the center of gravity of cross-sectional area of flow to the point of minimum velocity
   B. the cross-sectional area of waterway divided by the wetted perimeter
   C. half the depth of flow
   D. the depth from the free surface to the point of maximum velocity

10. Water flowing from an orifice in the side of a tank strikes the ground at a point 10 feet, below the orifice and 5 feet from the tank.
    If the coefficient of velocity is 1.00, the height of water above the orifice, in feet, is MOST NEARLY
    A. .63 B. 1.73 C. 3.5 D. 7.9

11. Of the following formulas, the one that is MOST commonly used in determining the runoff from a watershed is Q =
    A. $A\frac{1.486}{M}R^{2/3}S^{1/2}$ B. Aci C. $CLH^{3/2}$ D. $AC\sqrt{RS}$

12. Maximum discharge in a circular sewer occurs when the ratio of the depth of flow to the diameter of the pipe is MOST NEARLY
    A. .5 B. .6 C. .9 D. 1.1

13. Of the following items, the one that is LEAST important in the design of a concrete pier is
    A. corrosion B. erosion C. scour D. elutriation

14. Of the following items, the one which is LEAST related to the others is
    A. extensometer B. weir
    C. piezometer D. hook gauge

15. In a through truss bridge, a horizontal longitudinal member acting as a beam to support loads is known as a
    A. floor beam B. portal brace
    C. lower chord D. stringer

16. Using pipe A alone, a given tank is filled with water in 5 minutes. When pipe B is used alone, the same tank is filled in 7 minutes.
    If both pipes are used at the same time, the length of time required to fill this tank is, in minutes, MOST NEARLY
    A. 2.87 B. 2.92 C. 2.99 D. 3.05

17. In plane surveying, double meridian distances are used to compute the _____ of a traverse.
    A. latitudes and departures
    B. area
    C. error of closure
    D. corrections for magnetic declination for the sides

18. The deflection angle required to lay out a 50 ft. chord of a 3°00' circular curve is MOST NEARLY
    A. 0°45' B. 1°45' C. 2°30' D. 3°45'

19. Of the following, the one that is NOT a method of locating details for topography is
    A. offset distance
    B. range line
    C. tie line
    D. string line

20. *Blocking in* is a practice followed when it is necessary to
    A. set up a transit on line between two stations
    B. prolong a line around an obstacle
    C. project a high point to the ground
    D. set a point on line by double centering

21. Of the following terms, the one that is LEAST related to the others is
    A. five level section
    B. slope stake
    C. mass diagram
    D. hydraulic fill

22. Using a given 100 foot tape, the slope distance between two points on a 2% grade is found to be 250.26. When checked later, the tape is found to be 100.02 ft. long.
    The horizontal distance between the two points is MOST NEARLY
    A. 250.21 B. 250.26 C. 250.29 D. 250.32

23. When it is impossible to balance the foresight and backsight distances, precise difference in elevations may be obtained by _____ leveling.
    A. trigonometric
    B. reciprocal
    C. stadia
    D. barometric

24. Specifications usually require that controlled concrete develop its design strength
    A. when forms are stripped
    B. in 28 days
    C. in 7 days
    D. in 2 months

25. Horizontal reinforcing in the exposed face of a cantilever retaining wall is necessary PRIMARILY to reinforce against _____ stress.
    A. tensile
    B. compressive
    C. shearing
    D. shrinkage

KEY (CORRECT ANSWERS)

1.	A	11.	B
2.	A	12.	C
3.	B	13.	D
4.	C	14.	A
5.	B	15.	D
6.	A	16.	B
7.	A	17.	B
8.	B	18.	A
9.	B	19.	D
10.	A	20.	A

21. D
22. B
23. B
24. C
25. D

EXAMINATION SECTION
TEST 1

DIRECTIONS: Each question or incomplete statement is followed by several suggested answers or completions. Select the one that BEST answers the question or completes the statement. *PRINT THE LETTER OF THE CORRECT ANSWER IN THE SPACE AT THE RIGHT.*

1. Dowels connecting adjacent roadway slabs are used primarily to

    A. transmit compressive stress to adjacent slabs
    B. reinforce against temperature stress
    C. reinforce against shrinkage stress
    D. prevent differential settlement of slabs

2. Good practice requires that the minimum overhead clearance at the crown for an underpass at the intersection of two highways be MOST NEARLY _____ feet.

    A. 10　　　B. 14　　　C. 17　　　D. 19

3. A simple beam on an 18'0" span carries a uniformly distributed load including its own weight of 200 pounds per foot.
If a jack is placed under the midspan and the midpoint jacked up so it is at the same elevation as the ends, the load on the jack, in pounds, will be

    A. 960　　　　　　　　B. 1600
    C. 1800　　　　　　　 D. more than 1800

4. Of the following, the one which is NOT the symbol for a standard beam connection is

    A. A3　　　B. B3　　　C. H3　　　D. T3

5. Of the following items, the one that is NOT important in determining the minimum length of vertical curve required to connect two intersecting grades is

    A. maximum speed of vehicle
    B. grades of tangents
    C. whether intersection is at a summit or a sag
    D. crown of road

6. For an angle of intersection of 16°30', tables of the functions of a one-degree curve show the middle ordinate to be 59.30 feet.
For the same angle of intersection, the middle ordinate for a curve whose radius is 1433 feet is MOST NEARLY

    A. 14.83　　　B. 24.94　　　C. 67.35　　　D. 183.72

7. The *Proctor Test* is used in testing

    A. asphalt　　　B. concrete　　　C. soils　　　D. mortar

8. Within the cross-section of a WF beam, the horizontal shearing stress is a maximum at the

A. midpoint of the beam
B. outermost fiber of the compression flange
C. outermost fiber of the tension flange
D. point of intersection of web and flange

9. The maximum load allowed on a 3/8" fillet weld, 6" long, when the allowable shearing stress is 13,000 #/sq.in. is MOST NEARLY, in pounds,

   A. 20,700   B. 21,900   C. 24,300   D. 26,370

10. A closed level circuit was run starting at BM A. The elevation of A on closing the circuit was found to be 0.097 lower than at the start.
    Of the following, the MOST logical reason for this error, barring mistakes, is the

    A. length of the rod was not standard due either to a uniform expansion or contraction
    B. level settled after the backsights had been read
    C. turning points settled after the foresights had been read
    D. line of sight was inclined upward and each foresight distance exceeded the corresponding backsight distance

11. The sensitivity of the bubble tube of an engineer's level can best be measured by

    A. measuring the distance between etched lines on the vial
    B. taking readings on a rod a known distance away with bubble in two different positions
    C. making a two-peg test
    D. measuring the curvature of the etched surface of the vial

12. Of the following, the MOST important source of accidental error in ordinary leveling work is

    A. change in length of leveling rod due to change in temperature
    B. axis of level tube not perpendicular to vertical axis
    C. eye piece is not focused accurately
    D. failure to wave rod

13. When taking a single measure of the horizontal angle between two points which differ greatly in elevation, the MOST important of the following relationships in the transit is

    A. axis of long bubble parallel to line of sight
    B. transverse axis perpendicular to vertical axis
    C. index correction of vertical arc equal to zero
    D. vertical cross-hair in plane perpendicular to transverse axis

14. Of the following factors, the one that is LEAST important in determining the total amount of superelevation required at the edge of pavement on a horizontal curve is

    A. speed of vehicle   B. weight of vehicle
    C. radius of curve   D. width of pavement

15. If the horizontal circle of a transit is graduated to 20' and 39 divisions on the limb equal 40 civisions on the vernier, then the LEAST count of the vernier is

    A. 14"   B. 28"   C. 30"   D. 1'6"

16. The slump test for concrete is used to determine the 16.____

    A. strength B. consistency
    C. water ratio D. segregation

17. The following notes are taken from the survey of a closed traverse with five sides: 17.____

    ∠ at   Deflection Angles
    A   R 65° 25'
    B   L 45° 14'
    C   R 135° 42'
    D   R 92° 17'
    E

    The value of the deflection angle at E is MOST NEARLY
    A. 111°22' B. 111°34' C. 111°46' D. 111°50'

18. A Williot-Mohr diagram is used to determine 18.____

    A. deflection in trusses
    B. wind stress in framed bents
    C. diagonal shear in beams
    D. uplift pressure on the base of a cam

19. A reinforced concrete beam is 10" wide by 16" effective depth. If fs = 20,000 lb./sq.in., fc = 1350 lb./sq.in. and n = 10, then the value of k is MOST NEARLY 19.____

    A. .367 B. .373 C. .403 D. .419

20. Of the following concrete structures, the one in which gunite is MOST likely to be used is 20.____

    A. footings B. piles C. walls D. beams

21. For soil sampling in hardpan, the BEST method to use is 21.____

    A. jet probing B. wash boring
    C. auger boring D. core boring

22. The bending moment at the ends of a beam fully restrained at both ends which supports a uniform load of w pounds per foot throughout its entire length l is 22.____

    A. $\frac{wl^2}{8}$ B. $\frac{wl}{10}$ C. $\frac{wl^2}{10}$ D. $\frac{wl^2}{12}$

23. A reinforced concrete beam 10" wide by 16" effective depth is subjected to an end shear of 15,000 lbs. 23.____
    If fs = 20,000 #/sq.in., fc = 2500 #/sq.in., u = 187 #/sq.in., and j = .857, the perimeter of steel required to reinforce against the shear, in inches, is MOST NEARLY

    A. 2.38 B. 3.72 C. 5.85 D. 6.94

24. A precast reinforced concrete beam 20'0" long, weight 50 #/ft. is to be lifted by two slings symmetrically placed. 24.____
    For minimum bending stress in the beam, the distance from an end to a point of support, in feet, is MOST NEARLY

A. 3.98   B. 4.15   C. 4.35   D. 5.15

25. For maximum stress in *ab*, the distance the load *P* should be from the wall is MOST NEARLY
    A. 10'7"
    B. 11'9"
    C. 13'3"
    D. 15'0"

25._____

KEY (CORRECT ANSWERS)

1. D	11. B
2. B	12. C
3. D	13. B
4. D	14. B
5. D	15. C
6. A	16. B
7. C	17. D
8. A	18. A
9. A	19. C
10. D	20. C

21. D
22. D
23. C
24. B
25. D

TEST 2

DIRECTIONS: Each question or incomplete statement is followed by several suggested answers or completions. Select the one that BEST answers the question or completes the statement. *PRINT THE LETTER OF THE CORRECT ANSWER IN THE SPACE AT THE RIGHT.*

1. The rod reading at Sta. 100+27 is 4.26. With the same H.I., the rod reading at Sta. 103+16 is 6.34.
   The grade between the two stations is MOST NEARLY

   A. +0.72%   B. +0.79%   C. -0.72%   D. -0.79%

   1._____

2. In taping a distance known to be 2000 ft. long, the distance is found to be 1900.02 ft. The error is MOST probably caused by

   A. neglecting temperature correction
   B. neglecting to record one tape length
   C. tension on tape not standard
   D. wind blowing tape out of line

   2._____

3. The sum of the deflection angles for a closed traverse, where *n* equals the number of sides of the traverse, is

   A. (n-2)180°   B. 180°n   C. (n-l)360°   D. 360°

   3._____

4. When a level rod is *waved,* the correct reading is the

   A. largest reading
   B. smallest reading
   C. average of the largest and the smallest reading
   D. difference between the largest and the smallest reading

   4._____

5. A topographic map to a scale of 1:2400 has a 5-foot vertical interval. A straight line on the map connecting two adjacent contours is 0.437 inches long.
   The slope of this line is, in percent, MOST NEARLY

   A. 5.6   B. 5.7   C. 5.8   D. 6.0

   5._____

6. A Philadelphia rod is fully extended and the distance from the 1-foot mark to the 11-foot mark is measured and found to be 10.005.
   In a level circuit, a high-rod reading on this rod is

   A. 0.005 too large
   B. 0.005 too small
   C. considered correct since the errors will balance out
   D. correct if the rod is waved

   6._____

7. A differential leveling circuit without sideshots was run between two bench marks. The level was set up x times.
   The number of turning points used was

   A. 2x   B. x-2   C. x-1   D. x

   7._____

8. A closed traverse is usually preferred to an open traverse because

   8._____

A. more ground can be covered
B. a mathematical check on the work is provided
C. the area can be determined
D. the computations are easier

9. The difference in elevation between two points on the hydraulic gradient of a pipe of uniform diameter is a measure of the loss of _____ head.

   A. potential   B. pressure   C. velocity   D. total

10. Of the following values of f in the formula $h = f \dfrac{l}{d} \dfrac{V^2}{2g}$, the one which would MOST probably apply to a smooth pipe is

    A. 0.02   B. 0.11   C. 0.31   D. 0.41

11. The required cross-sectional area of a culvert is a function of

    A. width of roadway   B. depth of fill
    C. drainage area served   D. headwall area

12. The value of k for a particular reinforced concrete beam is 0.400. The value of j for this beam is MOST NEARLY

    A. 0.873   B. 0.870   C. 0.867   D. 0.865

13. A steel bar one inch in diameter is imbedded a distance of 30 inches in a mass of concrete.
    If the bar is subjected to axial pull of 10,000#, the bond stress is, in pounds per square inch, MOST NEARLY

    A. 106   B. 108   C. 112   D. 116

14. The slump test for concrete is a measure of

    A. water-cement ratio   B. consistency
    C. strength   D. size of aggregate

15. The term *special anchorage* in concrete construction refers to

    A. an anchor bolt to tie a beam to a wall
    B. tieing the reinforcement to a steel beam
    C. a *U*-shaped bar to take care of shearing stresses
    D. a hook at the end of a reinforcing bar

16.
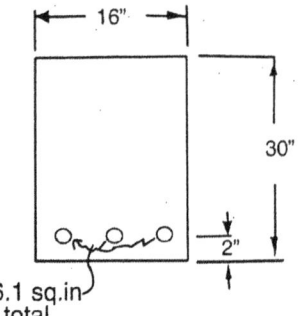

$k = \dfrac{1}{2} f_c k_2 j = 236$

Assuming exactly balanced design, the maximum bending moment that can be carried by the reinforced concrete beam in the accompanying sketch is, in inch pounds, MOST NEARLY
A. 2,960,000   B. 3,420,370   C. 4,160,500   D. 5,180,600

17. The maximum deflection of a simple beam on a span l carrying a uniformly distributed load of w per unit length is $\dfrac{5}{384}\dfrac{w}{EI}$ multiplied by

    A. l^2 B. l^3 C. l^4 D. l^7

18. The section modulus of a beam is

    A. $\int y^2 dA$ B. $\dfrac{V}{Ib}A\bar{y}$ C. $\dfrac{\sqrt{I}}{A}$ 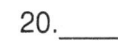   D. $\dfrac{I}{c}$

19. A timber beam 3" x 12" (actual dimensions) is simply supported on a clear span of 9'0" and carries a uniform load of 1000 #/ft. throughout its entire length.
    The maximum bending stress in the beam is, in lbs./sq.in., MOST NEARLY

    A. 1570   B. 1690   C. 1745   D. 1860

20. A wooden beam 8 inches wide by 12 inches deep (actual dimensions) carries a uniform load of 600 pounds per foot including its own weight on a simple span of 16'0".
    The MAXIMUM shear stress intensity in the beam is, in pounds per square inch,

    A. 70   B. 71   C. 72    D. 75

21. The horizontal component of the reaction at joint B in the accompanying diagram is MOST NEARLY
    A. 32K
    B. 36K
    C. 40K
    D. 44K

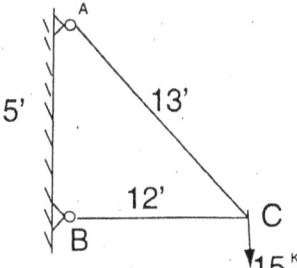

22. The yield point of a ductile metal is that unit stress at which

    A. the stress ceases to be proportional to the strain
    B. there is an increase in deformation with no increase in stress
    C. the material ruptures
    D. the metal ceases to act as an elastic material

Questions 23-27.

DIRECTIONS: Questions 23 through 27 refer to the sketch of the beam and girder connection shown below.

4 (#2)

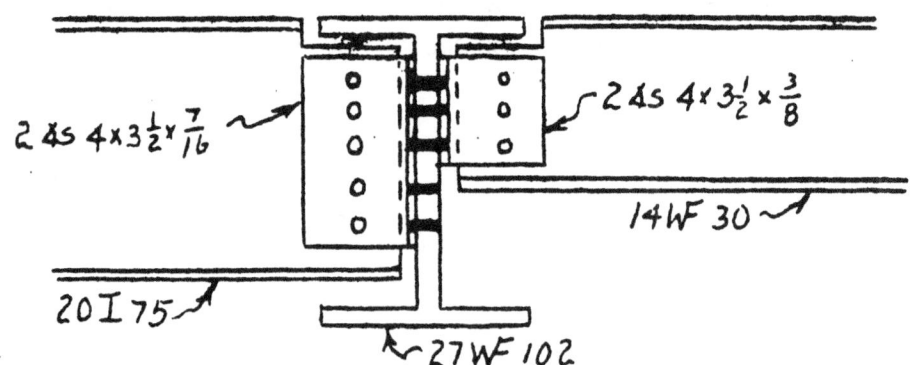

23. The diameter of the rivets used would MOST likely be

   A. 5/8"   B. 7/8"   C. 1 3/16"   D. 1 5/8"

24. Of the following allowable stresses, the only one that would be used in determining the number of rivets connecting the angles to the 20 I 75 is the allowable stress in

   A. single shear
   B. end bearing
   C. web shear
   D. enclosed bearing

25. The allowable load on rivet A is determined by the allowable stress in

   A. double shear
   B. single shear
   C. tension
   D. torsion

26. Both beams shown are

   A. chased   B. blocked   C. squared   D. clipped

27. The number of field rivets required in the connection is

   A. 4   B. 6   C. 9   D. 10

28. The term *batter* in concrete work refers to

   A. bracing of forms
   B. slope of finished surface
   C. consistency of concrete
   D. pressure of wet concrete in forms

29. Of the following items, the one that is LEAST related to the others is

   A. B.O.D.
   B. Imhoff tank
   C. effluent
   D. liquid limit

30. A beam on a simple span of 16'0" carries a concentrated load of 20 kips 5'0" from the left support and a uniform load of 3 kips per foot over the entire span.
   The distance from the left support to the point of maximum moment is, in feet, MOST NEARLY

   A. 5.92   B. 5.97   C. 6.02   D. 6.07

31. A beam has a trapezoidal cross-section which is symmetrical about a vertical axis. The top width is 4 inches, the bottom width 8 inches, and the depth 6 inches.
   The distance from the bottom of the beam to the neutral axis is, in inches,

A. 2.83   B. 2.75   C. 2.67   D. 2.59

32. The ends of a steel bar 1 inch square are set in rigid walls spaced 4'0" in the clear. Another square steel bar 2 inches on a side is set in rigid walls spaced 8'0" in the clear. The ratio of the unit stress in the longer bar to that in the shorter bar due to an increase in temperature is

   A. 3/8   B. 5/8   C. 1   D. 3/2

Questions 33-35.

DIRECTIONS: Questions 33 through 35 refer to the truss shown below.

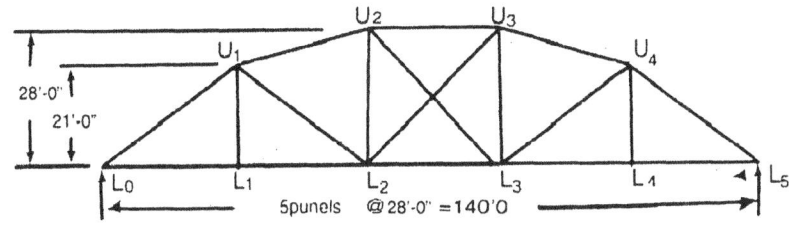

33. To obtain the stress in U_1L_2, the truss should be cut between U_1L_1 and U_2L_2 and moments taken about

   A. U_2
   B. L_1
   C. L_0
   D. a point to the left of L_0

34. The stress in member L_1L_2 for a load of one kip per foot extending over the entire span is, in kips, MOST NEARLY

   A. 74.67   B. 75.33   C. 75.67   D. 76.00

35. The stress in member U_2U_3 for a load of one kip per foot extending over the entire span is, in kips, MOST NEARLY

   A. 83.15   B. 83.30   C. 83.45   D. 84.00

36. In taping a distance on a 6% slope, the slope distance was measured. The correction per hundred feet to be applied to the measured distance is, in feet,

   A. 0.09   B. 0.12   C. 0.15   D. 0.18

37. The linear error of closure of a traverse is computed to be 0.04 feet. The sum of the lengths of the sides is 793.26 ft. The precision of the survey should be recorded as

   A. $\dfrac{0.04}{600}$ B. $\dfrac{4}{79326}$ C. $\dfrac{4}{793.26}$ D. $\dfrac{1}{19800}$

38. Errors due to eccentricity in the plates of a transit can be eliminated by   38.___
    A. reading the angle twice, once with the telescope normal, the second time with the telescope inverted
    B. using the averaged reading of the A and B verniers
    C. accurate leveling of the transit
    D. using two observers

39. A transit is set up at Sta. B and the deflection angle to Sta. C is measured (backsight on   39.___
    Sta. A) and found to be 22°15' R.
    The value of the angle ABC, measured clockwise from A to C, is

    A. 69°30'   B. 108°45'   C. 144°15'   D. 202°15'

40. The elevations of the P.V.C., P.V.I., and P.V.T. of a symmetrical vertical curve are 100.26,   40.___
    103.26, and 98.76, respectively.
    The elevation of the midpoint of the vertical curve is MOST NEARLY

    A. 98.63   B. 99.72   C. 101.38   D. 103.17

KEY (CORRECT ANSWERS)

1. C	11. C	21. B	31. C
2. B	12. C	22. B	32. C
3. D	13. A	23. B	33. D
4. B	14. B	24. D	34. A
5. B	15. D	25. B	35. D
6. A	16. A	26. B	36. D
7. C	17. C	27. D	37. D
8. B	18. D	28. B	38. B
9. D	19. B	29. D	39. D
10. A	20. D	30. A	40. C

TEST 3

DIRECTIONS: Each question or incomplete statement is followed by several suggested answers or completions. Select the one that BEST answers the question or completes the statement. *PRINT THE LETTER OF THE CORRECT ANSWER IN THE SPACE AT THE RIGHT.*

1. In highway work, the degree of curve is commonly defined as the angle

    A. at the center subtended by an arc 100 ft. in length
    B. at the center subtending the entire curve
    C. at which the two tangents to the curve intersect
    D. between a tangent and a chord 100 ft. in length

    1.____

2. The term *magnetic declination* refers to the

    A. attraction on a magnetic needle of nearby metallic objects
    B. dip of a magnetic needle
    C. angle between a given line and the meridian
    D. angle between true north and magnetic north

    2.____

3. The bearings of the sides of a closed quadrilateral are:
    AB - N12°15'W
    BC - N15°10'E
    CD - S60°20'E
    DA - S18°30'W
    The interior angle CDA of the quadrilateral is

    A. 87°25'   B. 10°110'   C. 126°40'   D. 154°15'

    3.____

4. In a given triangle, side a = 220 ft. and the angle opposite is 30°00'.
    If angle B = 45°00', then the side opposite angle B, in feet, is MOST NEARLY

    A. 311   B. 327   C. 346   D. 411

    4.____

5. Of the following statements, the one that is CORRECT is:

    A. Blue ink is used when making tracings for blueprint work
    B. If ink lines on a tracing do not dry quickly, they should be blotted
    C. Vertical dimensions should be lettered so that they read from the right side of the sheet
    D. Dimension lines should be of the same weight as lines used in the views

    5.____

6. A common method of lengthening the life of a wooden pile is by impregnating it with

    A. white lead   B. red lead
    C. sodium silicate   D. creosote

    6.____

7. The MOST common unit for measuring excavation is

    A. cubic yard   B. cubic foot
    C. ton   D. pound

    7.____

8. The width of each lane in a modern two-lane highway would MOST likely be

   A. 8'   B. 12'   C. 16'   D. 20'

Questions 9-11.

DIRECTIONS: Questions 9 through 11 refer to the figure shown below. (Any trigonomatic computation required is to be done by slide rule.)

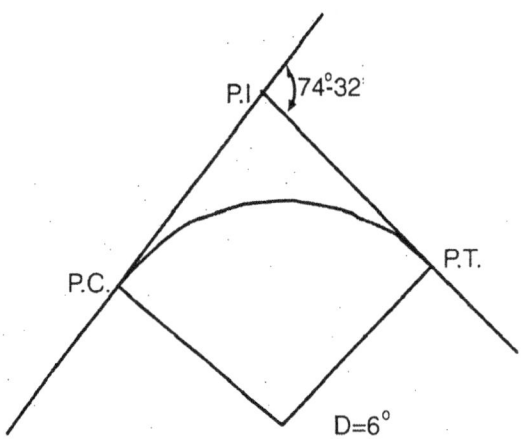

9. The station of the P.C. is 17+57.2.
   The deflection angle from the P.C. to Sta. 19 is MOST NEARLY

   A. 2°39'   B. 3°17'   C. 4°17'   D. 6°17'

10. The radius of the curve is, in feet, MOST NEARLY

    A. 955   B. 960   C. 970   D. 980

11. The station of the P.T. is MOST NEARLY

    A. 29+99.2   B. 29+99.4   C. 29+99.6   D. 30+00.4

12. Two cylindrical tanks with vertical axes lie one above the other. The lower tank is 8'0" in diameter and 8'0" high. The upper tank is 4'0" in diameter and 40'0" high with its base at the level of the top of the lower tank. The lower tank is full of water, and the upper tank is empty.
    The energy, in foot-pounds, required to pump the water from the lower to the upper tank is MOST NEARLY

    A. 502,000   B. 505,000   C. 508,000   D. 511,000

Questions 13-18.

DIRECTIONS: Questions 13 through 18 refer to the sketch of the plate girder shown below.

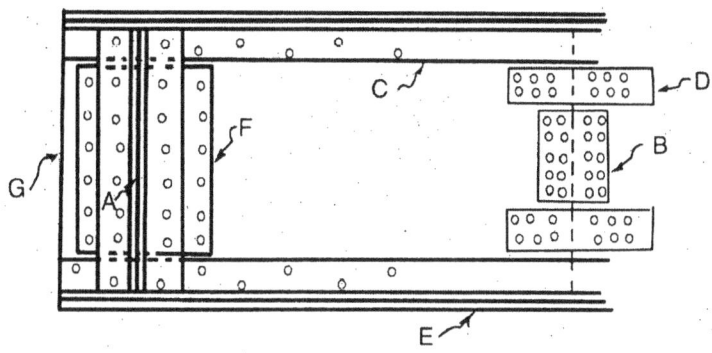

For each of the parts of the plate girder listed below in Questions 13 through 18, select the letter representing that part in the sketch above. For each of questions 13 through 18, the correct answer is

A. A   B. B   C. C   D. D   E. E   F. F   G. G

13. Flange angle   13._____

14. Shear splice   14._____

15. Stiffener   15._____

16. Cover plate   16._____

17. Web   17._____

18. Filler plate   18._____

19. Of the following symbols, the one that represents the ratio of the modulus of elasticity of steel to the modulus of elasticity of concrete in concrete design is   19._____

    A. k   B. v   C. p   D. n

20. A rectangular gate 4'0" wide by 6'0" high is submerged in water with the 4'0" side parallel to and 2'0" below the water surface. The gate is in a vertical plane.
The total pressure on the gate is, in pounds, MOST NEARLY   20._____

    A. 7480   B. 7590   C. 7660   D. 7720

21. The distance from the top of the gate to the center of pressure of the water on one side of the gate described in the preceding question is, in feet, MOST NEARLY   21._____

    A. 3.60   B. 3.70   C. 3.80   D. 3.90

22. Reservoir A is connected to Reservoir B by two parallel pipes, one 6 inches in diameter, the other 12 inches in diameter. The friction factor, f, is the same for each pipe.
If the flow in the 12-inch pipe is 6 cubic feet per second, the flow in the 6-inch pipe is, in cubic feet per second, MOST NEARLY   22._____

    A. 1.01   B. 1.03   C. 1.05   D. 1.06

23. The hydraulic radius of a rectangular channel 6'0" wide with, a 4'0" depth of water is, in feet, MOST NEARLY   23._____

A. 1.71 B. 1.75 C. 1.79 D. 1.83

24. On a transit, the tangent screw is used to

    A. clamp the telescope in either erect or inverted position
    B. adjust the level bubbles
    C. focus the objective lens
    D. rotate the telescope small distances

25. The tangent of angle A is equal to

    A. $\sqrt{1-\cos^2 A}$
    B. $\dfrac{\sec A}{\cos A}$
    C. $\sin A \cos A$
    D. $\dfrac{\sin A}{\cos A}$

26. If two stations on a mass diagram for earthwork have equal ordinates, the

    A. elevations of the two stations are the same
    B. end areas at the two stations are equal
    C. volume of cut equals the volume of fill between the two stations
    D. volume of fill between the two stations may be moved with equal economy to either station

27. The primary cause of parallax in a telescope is

    A. atmospheric disturbances
    B. maladjustment of the cross hairs
    C. improper focusing of the objective
    D. improper focusing of the eyepiece

28. The notes for a three level section for a roadway 20 ft. wide are as follows:

    $$\dfrac{c12}{16} \quad \dfrac{c13}{0} \quad \dfrac{c16}{18}$$

    The side slopes of the embankment are _____ horizontal to _____ vertical.
    A. 1; 2 B. 1; 1 C. 2; 1 D. 2; 3

29. Various combinations of the known parts of a triangle are given below. The combination which does NOT describe a unique triangle (i.e., one triangle and one only) is

    A. three sides
    B. two sides and the included angle
    C. one side and two angles
    D. two sides and an acute angle opposite one of the sides

30. To permit easier operation of vehicles, a tangent is MOST frequently connected to a horizontal circular curve by means of a

    A. reversed curve   B. spiral
    C. parabola   D. hyperbola

31. An alidade is MOST commonly used in conjunction with a

    A. transit   B. plane table
    C. barometer   D. tide gauge

32. The increase in length of a 100-foot stool tape due to a temperature rise of 15°F is, in feet, MOST NEARLY

   A. 0.0001   B. 0.0005   C. 0.01   D. 0.05

33. An instrument used to measure the area of a closed traverse, plotted to scale, is a

   A. integraph
   B. clinometer
   C. planimeter
   D. pantograph

Questions 34-35.

DIRECTIONS: Questions 34 and 35 refer to the following diagrams on the following page.

(Diagram for question 34.)   (Diagram for question 35.)

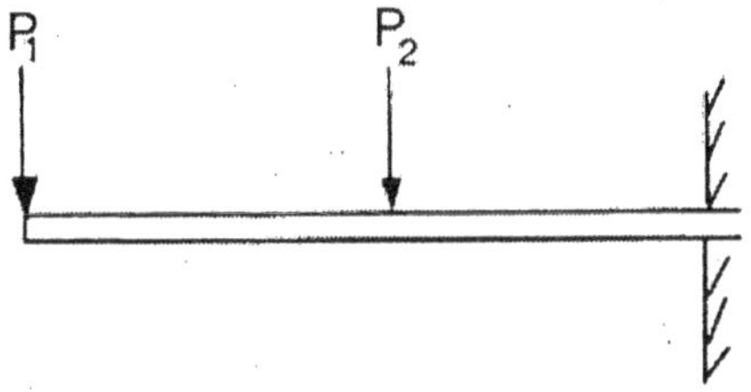

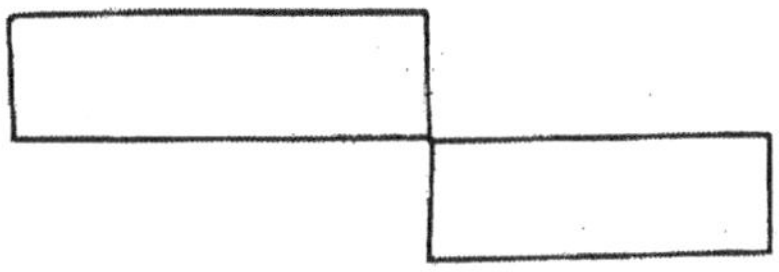

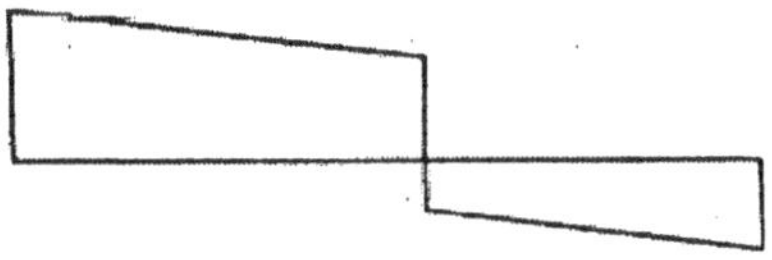

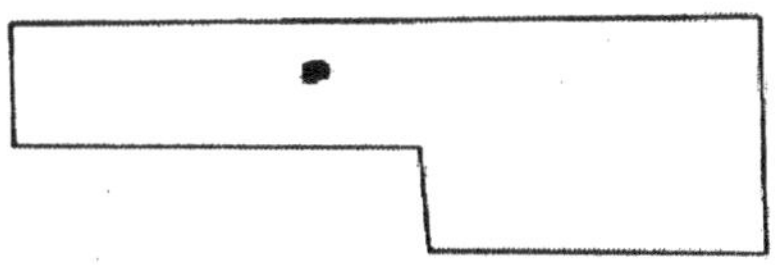

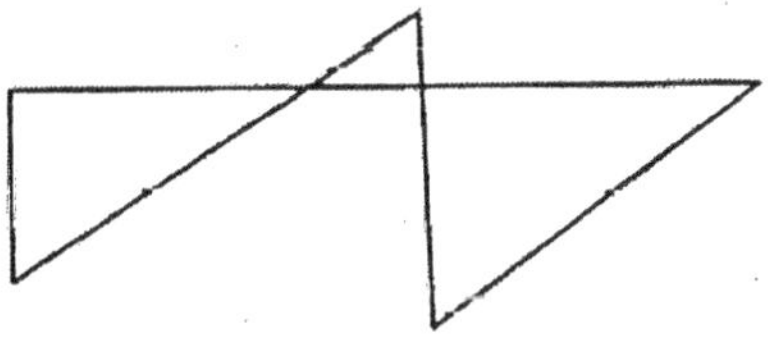

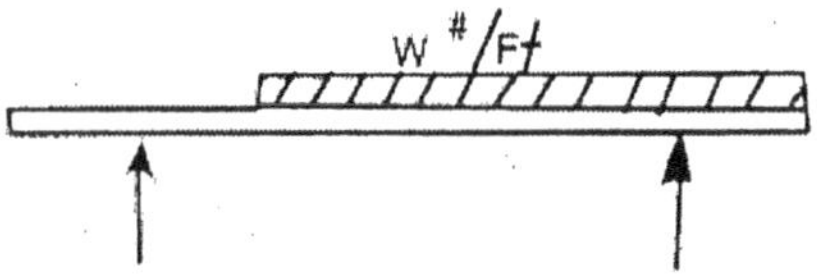

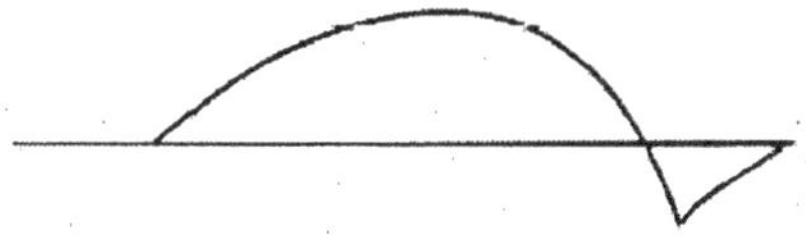

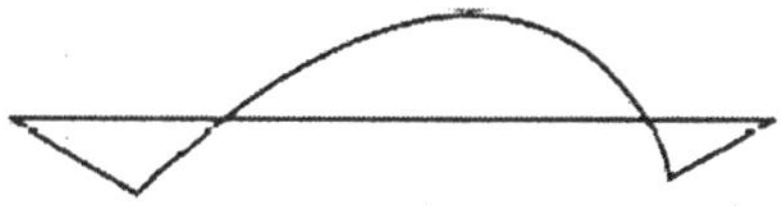

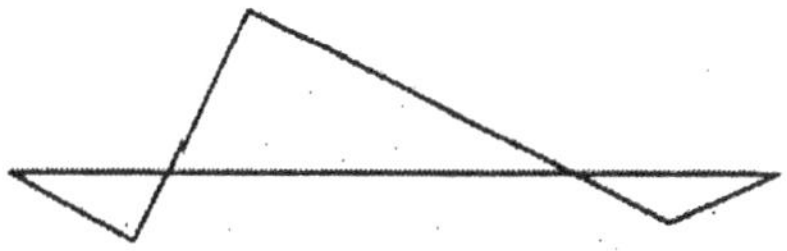

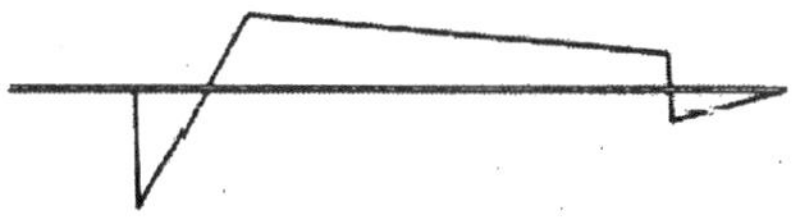

34. The shear diagram for the beam shown in the above diagram is (neglecting the weight of the beam)

   A. A   B. B   C. C   D. D

35. The moment diagram for the beam shown in the above diagram is (neglecting the weight 35.___
    of the beam)

    A. A   B. B   C. C   D. D

Questions 36-40.

DIRECTIONS: In Questions 36 through 40, the plan and front elevation of an object are shown on the left, and on the right are shown four figures, one of which, and only one, represents the right side elevation. Print in the space at the right the letter which represents the right side elevation. In the sample shown below, which figure correctly represents the right side elevation?

    A. A   B. B   C. C   D. D

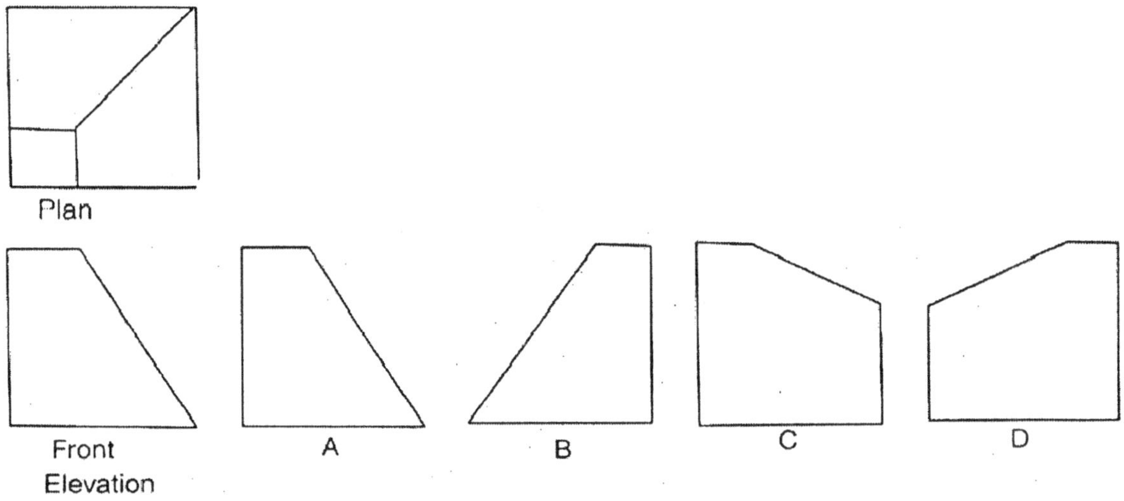

The correct answer is A.

In Questions 36 through 40, which figure correctly represents the right side elevation?
    A. A   B. B   C. C   D. D

36.   36.___

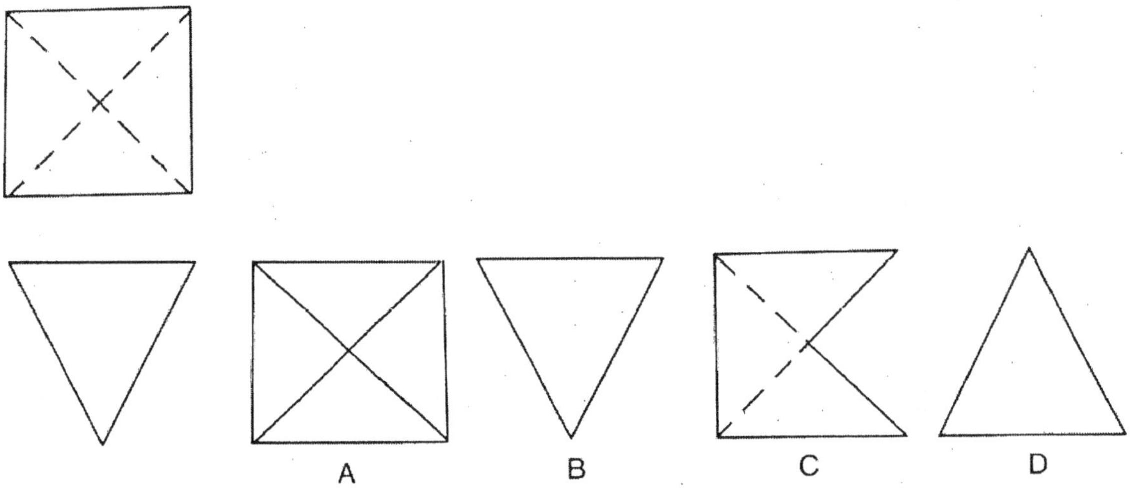

37. Questions 37-40.

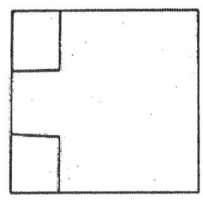
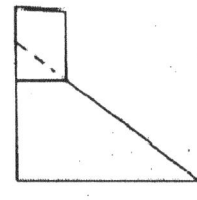 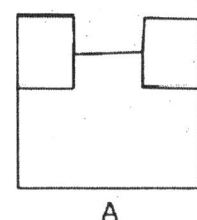 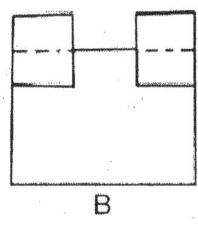 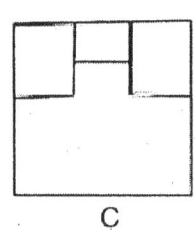 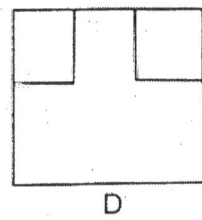
A B C D

38.

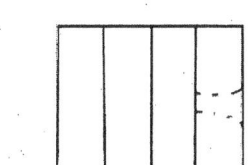
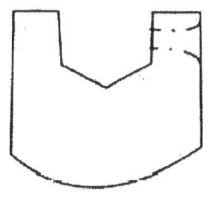 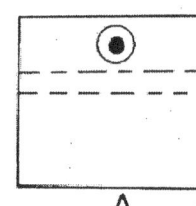 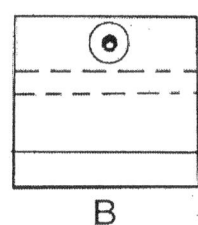 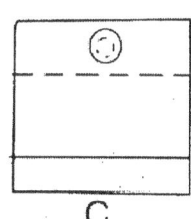 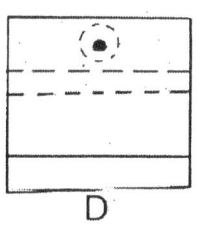
A B C D

39.

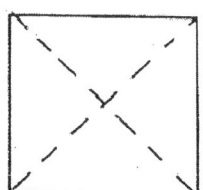
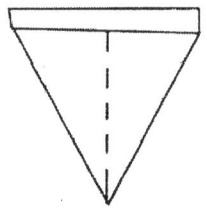 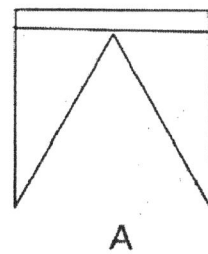 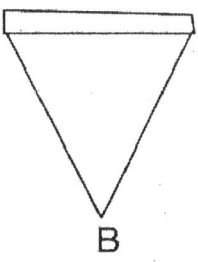 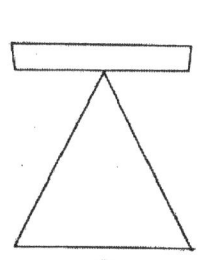 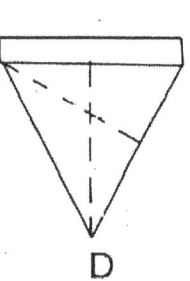
A B C D

8 (#3)

40.

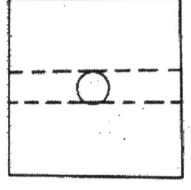

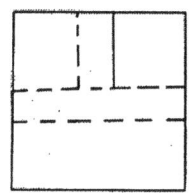 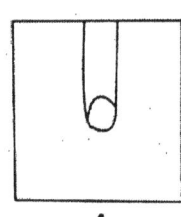 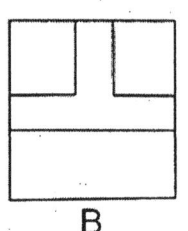 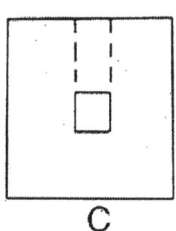 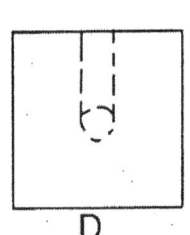
    　　　　　　　A　　　　　　　B　　　　　　　C　　　　　　　D

KEY (CORRECT ANSWERS)

1. A	11. B	21. A	31. B
2. D	12. A	22. D	32. C
3. B	13. C	23. A	33. C
4. A	14. B	24. D	34. C
5. C	15. A	25. D	35. A
6. D	16. E	26. C	36. B
7. A	17. G	27. D	37. A
8. B	18. F	28. A	38. B
9. C	19. D	29. D	39. A
10. A	20. A	30. B	40. C

EXAMINATION SECTION
TEST 1

DIRECTIONS: Each question or incomplete statement is followed by several suggested answers or completions. Select the one that BEST answers the question or completes the statement. *PRINT THE LETTER OF THE CORRECT ANSWER IN THE SPACE AT THE RIGHT.*

1. In pipe laying, the required width of trench in sand is less than that in clay because

    A. of the dilatancy of the sand
    B. the sand gives the pipe a more uniform support
    C. sand backfill puts less load upon the pipe
    D. of backfilling requirements
    E. it is easier to enlarge the trench for bell holes in sand

2. A short post, 12 inches in diameter, is subjected to 75K applied 1" from the center. The maximum stress in the post, in lbs./sq.in., is MOST NEARLY

    A. 290   B. 995   C. 1,100   D. 1,260   E. 1,340

3. Of the following, the geological feature which will have the LEAST effect on a foundation is

    A. stratification   B. foliation or cleavage
    C. striation   D. dip and strike
    E. faults

4. In tall steel frame buildings, the columns are usually erected in lengths of

    A. 16 feet   B. 20 feet
    C. one story   D. two stories
    E. three stories

5. The P.C. of a 7° curve is at Sta. 16+25.0. The deflection angle to Sta. 17+00 is

    A. 4° 29'   B. 3° 18'   C. 2° 38'   D. 1° 97'   E. 0° 42'

6. Reverse curves on highways are customarily separated by tangents. Of the following, the BEST reason for this separation is

    A. to increase sight-distance
    B. to increase the radii of the curves
    C. to improve the appearance of the highway
    D. to avoid sudden changes in curvature
    E. concerned with superelevation

7. The modulus of rupture of a wooden beam is

    A. greater than the ultimate strength in tension
    B. less than the ultimate strength in tension
    C. a function of the shearing strength if the beam is long
    D. less than the ultimate strength in compression
    E. independent of the cross-section of the beam

8. Plain sedimentation is usually preferred to chemical precipitation in sewage treatment because

   A. disposition of the sludge resulting from chemical precipitation is difficult
   B. it removes a greater percentage of total suspended matter
   C. it removes a greater percentage of organic matter
   D. chemical precipitation always increases the pH concentration
   E. the resulting sludge is not putrescible

9. The strength of clay sewer pipe is NOT usually determined by a(n) _____ test.

   A. two-edge bearing
   B. three-edge bearing
   C. sand bearing
   D. *knife-edge*
   E. Izod or impact

10. The maximum moment that three moving loads of 6, 8, and 10 kips, from left to right, respectively, spaced 6 feet apart, can cause on a span of 30 feet is, in K feet,

    A. 110   B. 120.4   C. G. 152.6   D. 132.2   E. 95.1

11. In stream flow, a curve of rate of discharge versus gage height is known as a

    A. rating curve
    B. mass diagram
    C. Rippl diagram
    D. flood curve
    E. calibration curve

12. An inverted syphon carries a canal from one side of a valley at Elev. 100 to the other at Elev. 95. Assuming the coefficient of pipe friction is independent of diameter, the required diameter of pipe varies as

    A. $Q^{9/10}$ B. $Q^{4/5}$ C. $Q^{3/5}$ D. $Q^{2/5}$ E. $Q^{1/5}$

13. Two pipe lines carrying water are at the same elevation. Each is connected to a Bourdon Gage, the center of which is 4 feet vertically above the pipe center.
    If one gage registers 10 feet and the other minus 2 feet, the difference in pressure between the two pipes, in pounds per square inch, is about

    A. 6.9   B. 6.7   C. 5.9   D. 4.7   E. 3.9

14. The reason wooden beams bearing on brick walls are cut at the end with a mitre is

    A. a precaution in the event of fire
    B. so the inspector can be sure the beam is well seated
    C. to expose a fresh surface so that faulty wood may be detected
    D. that beams so cut may be placed more easily
    E. to make fire-stopping easier

15. Of the following conditions, shearing stress in the web of rolled steel beams is MOST likely to influence the choice of section when

    A. headroom requires the use of a section shallower than the most economical section
    B. the span is long and carries several uniformly spaced concentrated loads
    C. the deflection is small
    D. the span is long and carries two heavy concentrated loads, one near each support
    E. the span is long and uniformly loaded

16. The gridiron system of water distribution is

    A. preferable to the branching system with regard to fire protection
    B. only used in the largest cities
    C. less advantageous than the branching system because it requires a superimposed high pressure system
    D. being replaced by the branching system
    E. impractical in developments with many curved streets

17. An advantage of reinforced concrete beam and girder construction, as compared to flat slab construction, is

    A. greater fire resistance
    B. cheaper form work
    C. sprinkler layout is easier
    D. ventilation of rooms is easier
    E. none of the above

18. Activated sludge is sludge that

    A. is mixed mechanically
    B. has been *seeded*
    C. is stirred by air currents which give it a spiral motion
    D. is agitated in any one of several ways
    E. has been removed from a drying bed

19. In water purification, *aeration* is used to remove

    A. turbidity   B. dissolved oxygen
    C. sediment   D. organic material
    E. objectionable gases

20. The maximum unit stress to which a material may be subjected without suffering permanent deformation is known as the

    A. elastic limit   B. yield strength
    C. proportional limit   D. yield point
    E. commercial elastic limit

21. The distance in inches from the back of the short leg to the center of gravity of a 5" x 4" x 1/2" steel angle is APPROXIMATELY

    A. 0.80   B. 1.15   C. 1.40   D. 1.55   E. 1.60

22. A symmetrical triangular roof truss of four panels at 10 feet having a span of 40 feet between end supports and a rise of 10 feet carries a vertical load at the top center of 20,000 pounds.
    The stress in the upper chord of the end panel, in pounds, is APPROXIMATELY

    A. 15,500   B. 19,500   C. 22,500   D. 26,500   E. 28,500

23. A short concrete column with an effective cross-section 30 inches square has two percent vertical steel reinforcing with proper tie.
    Assuming f_c = 500 pounds per square inch, n = 15, the live load that can safely be carried by this column is
    MOST NEARLY _____ pounds.

    A. 550,000   B. 575,000   C. 650,000   D. 675,000   E. 700,000

4 (#1)

24. A welded cylindrical horizontal steel tank 36 inches in diameter is subjected to an internal pressure caused by 72-foot head of water. The ends of the tank are capped with hemispherical heads extending outward.
If the allowable tensile strength of the steel be taken as 18,000 lbs. per sq. in., the theoretical thickness of the heads should be, in inches,

   A. 0.735   B. 0.015   C. 0.475   D. 0.625   E. 0.375

25. Water flows from reservoir A, elev. 178, to reservoir B, elev. 106, through 3220 feet of 6" pipe; f = .02.
The velocity in the pipe, in ft./sec., is MOST NEARLY

   A. 1   B. 2   C. 3.5   D. 4.5   E. 6

26. Water is flowing through an open channel of triangular cross-section. The side slopes of the channel are 1:1. The water is 8 feet deep.
The hydraulic radius is

   A. 7.65   B. 6.40   C. 4.37   D. 3.59   E. 2.82

27. The building code of the large city specifies that bearing piles of wood shall not be spaced closer center to center, in inches, than

   A. 20   B. 24   C. 28   D. 32   E. 36

28. The four sides of a rectangular pier have a uniform batter of 2 inches per foot.
If the top of the pier is 4 feet by 10 feet and the pier is 12 feet high, the volume, to the NEAREST cubic foot, is

   A. 668   B. 880   C. 992   D. 745   E. 858

29. To lay out a line 170.00 feet long with a 100-foot tape which is actually 100.03 feet long, the taped distance should be

   A. 169.03   B. 169.95   C. 170.45   D. 170.50   E. 170.65

30. Of the following, the LEAST satisfactory method of preventing electrolysis in underground pipe lines near street railways is

   A. applying an insulating coat to the pipe
   B. using track joint bonds
   C. using track joint bonds and cross bonds
   D. using insulating joints on the pipe
   E. providing drains for the road bed

31. A uniformly loaded beam is continuous over four uniformly spaced supports, A, B, C, and D, reading from left to right.
If the support B settles slightly, the

   A. reaction at D decreases   B. reaction at C decreases
   C. moment at C decreases   D. moment at B increases
   E. reaction at A decreases

32. A flanged shaft coupling uses four 1-inch bolts equispaced on a circle 6 inches in radius. When the shaft is transmitting 300 horsepower at 200 r.p.m., the stress in the bolts, in pounds per square inch, is MOST NEARLY

    A. 5000   B. 4500   C. 4000   D. 3500   E. 3000

33. A simple beam on a 16 foot span carries a concentrated load of 5000 pounds at the midpoint.
    If E is 1,600,000 pounds per square inch and I is 1728 inches fourth, the center deflection, in inches, is MOST NEARLY

    A. 0.27   B. 0.39   C. 0.47   D. 0.59   E. 0.67

34. The tensile efficiency of a riveted butt joint with adequate straps is a function of

    A. rivet diameter and plate width
    B. rivet diameter and plate thickness
    C. rivet diameter, plate width, and plate thickness
    D. plate width and thickness
    E. rivet value in double shear and in bearing

35. A 24-inch beam is made up of two 12-inch steel I-beams, the flanges in contact being riveted.
    If the moment of inertia of a single 12-inch beam is 300 inches fourth and the cross-sectional area 15 square inches, the moment of inertia of the 24-inch beam is, in inches fourth, MOST NEARLY

    A. 2390   B. 1680   C. 1540   D. 920   E. 580

36. A distance taped on a 3 percent slope is 231.24 feet. The length, in feet, of the horizontal projection is

    A. 231.14   B. 231.07   C. 231.00   D. 230.93   E. 230.86

37. In running a closed level circuit, 50 set-ups were made. If each of the rod readings varied accidentally by plus or minus 0.003 feet from its correct value, the probable error of closure of the circuit is, in feet,

    A. 0.405   B. 0.325   C. 0.030   D. 0.015   E. 0.005

38. The dry weight of a cubic foot of sand is 104 pounds. The specific gravity of the sand grains is 2.60.
    The submerged weight of a cubic foot of this sand in fresh water is, in pounds,

    A. 56   B. 60   C. 64   D. 68   E. 72

39. A street 40 feet wide with a parabolic cross-section has a crown of 6 inches at the center. The elevation of a point on the street surface 4 feet from the gutter is below the crown a distance, in inches, of

    A. 1.29   B. 2.73   C. 3.84   D. 4.51   E. 5.19

40. Line AB is extended to C with the transit set at A, a single, careful sight being taken. Subsequently, the transit is set at B, and C checked by a *double reverse*. All three points are at the same elevation.
    If C fails to check the average of the *double reverse*, the transit is not in adjustment in that

    A. the horizontal axis is not perpendicular to the vertical axis
    B. the line of sight is not perpendicular to the horizontal axis
    C. either *a* or *b* or both may be the cause
    D. the axis of the objective slide does not coincide with the optical axis
    E. the line of sight is not parallel to the long bubble

41. The BEST material to use for a hydraulic-fill dam is a well-graded mixture ranging from

    A. gravel to fine silt
    B. sand to clay
    C. coarse sand to silt
    D. gravel to fine sand
    E. chips to ash

42. A round steel bar, one inch in diameter, is embedded 40 inches in concrete.
    The unit tensile stress in the bar which will develop a bond stress of 100 pounds per square inch is, in pounds per square inch, about

    A. 19,000   B. 17,000   C. 16,000   D. 15,000   E. 13,000

43. The MOST important advantage of the Invar tape over the ordinary steel tape is it(s)

    A. will not rust
    B. high modulus of elasticity
    C. low coefficient of thermal expansion
    D. greater strength
    E. cheapness

44. Two clean steel pipes, one 12 inches in diameter, the other 6 inches in diameter, run from one reservoir to another in parallel.
    If the slope of the hydraulic gradient is the same for the two pipes, the ratio of the discharge of the larger pipe to that of the smaller is about

    A. 5.6   B. 4.7   C. 3.9   D. 2.3   E. 1.1

45. The use of steel pipe to convey water is desirable because it

    A. never requires an inside coating
    B. can be fabricated by unskilled labor
    C. is not subject to electrolysis
    D. can carry large external loads
    E. does not have to be caulked

46. Reinforcing steel is usually shaped on the job

    A. by heating in a forge
    B. by cutting and welding
    C. by hand bending
    D. never
    E. on a bar-bending table

47. *Bulking* of sand

    A. is a maximum with a water content of about 6%
    B. is of no importance in concrete proportioning
    C. varies directly as the moisture content
    D. is greater for a coarse sand than a fine sand
    E. does not occur unless the sand contains over one-half gallon of water per cubic foot

48. The cinders used in *cinder concrete* should be

    A. thoroughly wetted down at least 24 hours before mixing
    B. thoroughly dry before mixing
    C. fine and powdery
    D. at least 50 percent uncombined carbon
    E. at least 50 percent combined carbon

49. Bank-run gravel ordinarily

    A. contains no sand
    B. contains too much sand to make a well-proportioned aggregate for concrete
    C. makes a well-proportioned aggregate for concrete
    D. contains too little sand to make a well-proportioned aggregate for concrete
    E. makes a good binder for macadam roads

50. The practical limit on the depth below water level to which the pneumatic caisson process may be carried is, in feet,

    A. 75   B. 85   C. 95   D. 110   E. 125

KEY (CORRECT ANSWERS)

1. D	11. A	21. D	31. A	41. B
2. C	12. D	22. C	32. A	42. C
3. C	13. A	23. B	33. A	43. C
4. D	14. A	24. B	34. A	44. A
5. C	15. D	25. E	35. B	45. E
6. E	16. A	26. E	36. A	46. E
7. A	17. E	27. B	37. C	47. A
8. A	18. B	28. B	38. C	48. A
9. E	19. E	29. B	39. C	49. B
10. D	20. A	30. A	40. D	50. D

TEST 2

DIRECTIONS: Each question or incomplete statement is followed by several suggested answers or completions. Select the one that BEST answers the question or completes the statement. *PRINT THE LETTER OF THE CORRECT ANSWER IN THE SPACE AT THE RIGHT.*

1. In earthwork, if two stations on a mass diagram have equal ordinates of like sign

    A. between the two stations, the volume of cut equals the volume of fill
    B. elevation of surface at the two stations is the same
    C. depth of cut or fill at the two stations is the same
    D. the distance between two stations equals the limit of economical haul

2. In the design of a reinforced concrete footing, which carries a reinforced concrete column, the distance from the face of the column to the critical section for shear is, in inches,

    A. kd   B. jd   C. d   D. zero

3. A major city building code permits reduction in the design live load of columns below the top floor as computed on the basis of design floor load because

    A. loads on lower floors offset moments created by loads on upper floors
    B. side sway is less when all floors are fully loaded
    C. lower columns are better braced
    D. it is unreasonable to expect all floors to be fully loaded at the same time

4. The term S2S means _____ two sides.

    A. shellac   B. sandpaper
    C. surfaced   D. split

5. The term *drop panel* is commonly used in

    A. plastering walls   B. plywood forms
    C. prefabricated housing   D. flat slab construction

6. In controlled concrete, the water-cement ratio is selected on the basis of

    A. consistency desired   B. proportion of aggregates
    C. type of aggregates   D. strength desired

7. A surcharge is usually MOST closely associated with

    A. highway superelevation   B. very long piles
    C. allowable fluid pressure D. retaining walls

8. Steam at 300 lb./sq.in. flows through a 1 ft. diameter pipe. The pipe walls are 1 in. thick. The unit circumferential stress is, in pounds per square inch,

    A. 900   B. 1800   C. 3200   D. 4800

9. On a topographic map, the symbol shown at the right represents
    A. tidal flat
    B. cultivated land
    C. orchard
    D. salt marsh

10. A square steel plate, 8 ft. on a side, is submerged in water with the top edge parallel to the water surface and 10 ft. below the surface.
   If the plate makes an angle of 30 with the water surface, the total pressure on the plate is, in pounds,

   A. 2688 B. 8649 C. 31,560 D. 47,900

11. The stress in a steel bar 8 feet long, cross-sectional area 4 sq.in., rigidly set in a wall at both ends, due to a temperature rise of 30° F is, in pounds per square inch, ($E = 30 \times 10^6$ lb./sq.in.; coefficient of expansion = 645×10^{-8})

   A. 628 B. 2775 C. 5800 D. 12,235

12. The maximum unit stress up to which a material may be stressed without suffering permanent deformation when the stress is removed is called

   A. proportional limit   B. yield point
   C. elastic limit   D. ultimate stress

13. The elongation of a steel bar, 100 feet long, cross-sectional area 1 sq.in., supported at one end and hanging vertically, due to its own weight is, in inches,
   (Steel weighs 490 lb./cu.ft.; $E = 30 \times 10^6$ lb./sq.in.)

   A. .0019 B. .0068 C. .0077 D. .1586

14. Lehoann's solution is used to determine

   A. orientation of a plane table
   B. longitude of station
   C. elevation of B.M. by method of least squares
   D. distances in a triangulation net

15. In laying out a circular curve, the formula $R \text{ vers } \frac{1}{2} I$ is used to determine the

   A. middle ordinate   B. tangent distance
   C. long chord   D. external distance

16. The results of a survey of a closed traverse are as follows:

Line	Lat.	Dep.
AB	100.62	272.21
BC	153.27	422.16
CD	-322.14	19.23
DA	68.33	-713.50

   The magnitude of the linear error of closure is, in feet,
   A. .04 B. .07 C. .13 D. .15

17. The notes for a three level section for a 20 feet wide roadway are

   $\frac{c\,7.5}{15}$ $\frac{c\,9}{0}$ $\frac{c\,12}{18}$

   The cross-sectional area of cut is, in square feet,
   A. 198 B. 246 C. 327 D. 415

18. To determine the elevation of a point on the face of a building, a level was set up, a sight of 1.487 taken with a rod on the cap bolt of a hydrant, Elev. 39.470, and another sight taken on a tape with its zero end at the point (the tape stretching downward from the point).
    If the reading on the tape was 1.212, the elevation of the point is

    A. 42.169   B. 41.353   C. 40.457   D. 39.899

19. In taping, an accidental error may result from

    A. the tapeman unintentionally making a mistake
    B. the temperature being greater than that at which tape was standardized
    C. causes beyond control of the tapeman
    D. assuming slope distances to be horizontal distances

20. The maximum shearing stress in a wood joist 3 in. by 10 in., actual dimensions, simply supported at its ends on a 14 feet span, and sustaining a uniform load, including its own weight of 150 lb./ft. over the entire length is, in pounds per square inch,

    A. 39   B. 52   C. 68   D. 126

21. If the moment of inertia of a section is 1500 in. 4, and its area is 12 sq.in., the radius of gyration of the section is, in inches, APPROXIMATELY

    A. 11   B. 27   C. 49   D. 101

22. Of the following types of wall, which one is LEAST like the others in function? _____ wall.

    A. Curtain   B. Retaining   C. Spandrel   D. Wing

23. The bending moment at the ends of a beam rigidly supported at both ends and carrying a uniform load of w #/ft. throughout its entire length 1 ft. is, in ft.lbs.,

    A. $\dfrac{w1^2}{8}$ B. $\dfrac{w1}{10}$ C. $\dfrac{w1^2}{10}$ D. $\dfrac{w1^2}{12}$

24. The hydraulic radius of a rectangular canal 4 feet wide is 1.20.
    The depth of flow, in feet, is

    A. 1.6   B. 2.1   C. 2.6   D. 3.0

25. The dynamic pressure into which the kinetic energy of water is transformed when the valve at the outlet of a pipe is suddenly closed is called

    A. velocity head   B. static head
    C. water hammer   D. hydraulic gradient

26. The length of a 3/8" fillet weld required to resist a shear of 12,000 lbs., if the allowable shearing stress is 13,000 lb./sq.in., is, in inches,

    A. 1.97   B. 2.31   C. 2.77   D. 3.48

27. Bridge trusses are built with a slight camber in order to 27.___

    A. make erection easier
    B. avoid sag under load
    C. eliminate secondary stresses
    D. reduce tension in lower chord

28. The formula for determining the value of *n* in concrete design, as given by the A.C.I. and a major city building code is 28.___

    A. $\dfrac{3000}{f'c}$ B. $\dfrac{fs}{f'c}$ C. $\dfrac{fs}{fc}$ D. $\dfrac{Es}{fc \times 10^3}$

29. In reinforced concrete design with fs = 18,000 lb./sq.in., fc = 1000 lb./sq.in. and n = 12, the value of k is 29.___

    A. .389   B. .396   C. .400   D. .420

30. Water flows through a 2" ⌀ orifice in the side of a tank under a head of 20 ft. If Cd = .60, the quantity of discharge is, in cfs, 30.___

    A. .47   B. .91   C. 1.27   D. 239.4

31. Water discharges through a turbine at the rate of 60,000 cfm under a head of 100 ft. If the efficiency of the turbine is 70%, the horsepower developed by the turbine is 31.___

    A. 646   B. 7,950   C. 21,300   D. 44,440

32. Stirrups are used in concrete construction to 32.___

    A. support reinforcing rods
    B. reinforce concrete for the diagonal tension component of shear
    C. hold forms together
    D. prevent cracking of concrete due to changes of temperature

33. In the design of a steel member in tension, rivet holes must be deducted to obtain the net section. 33.___
This is not done when the member is in compression because

    A. rivet holes are smaller
    B. formulae for design of compression members reduce allowable stress
    C. rivets can be placed more efficiently
    D. rivets are assumed to fill the holes

34. In a specific gravity determination, the weight of a flask full of water is 390.0 grams. The weight of the same flask filled with water and 96.2 grams of sand is 450.0 grams. The specific gravity of the sand is 34.___

    A. 2.58   B. 2.66   C. 2.74   D. 2.82

35. A soil has a void ratio of 0.80 and a specific gravity of solids of 2.67. The total weight (including the water) of a saturated cubic foot of this soil is, in pounds, 35.___

    A. 173.4   B. 120.4   C. 111.1   D. 72.7

36. The loss in head per 1,000 feet in a 12-inch water pipe is 9 feet, and the friction factor, f, is 0.0161.
    The velocity of flow in the pipe is, in feet per second,

    A. 6.0   B. 8.1   C. 13.9   D. 18.3

Questions 37-40.

DIRECTIONS: Questions 37 through 40 refer to the truss shown below.

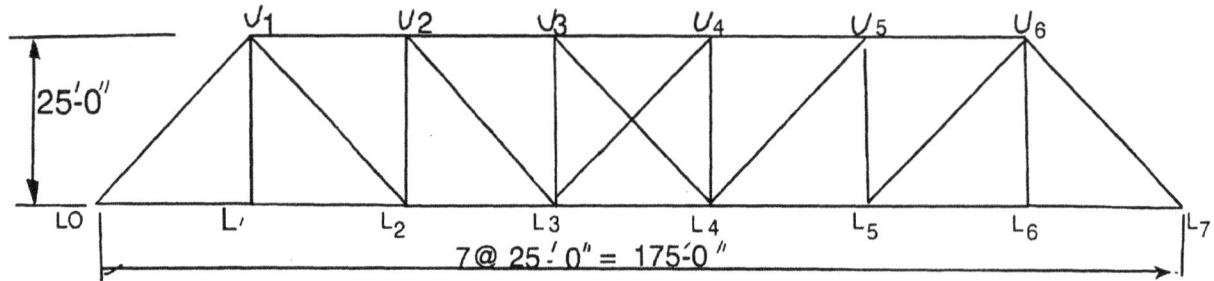

37. If a uniformly distributed live load of 2 kips per foot extends over the entire length of the truss, the live load shear in panel L_2L_3 is, in kips,

    A. 150   B. 100   C. 50   D. 0

38. If the stress in U_2L_2 is -150 kips (compression) and in L_1L_2 +300 kips (tension), the stress in L_2L_3 is, in kips,

    A. +619   B. +450   C. +324   D. +108

39. For a uniformly distributed live load, the maximum tensile stress in member U_2L_3 will occur when the truss is loaded from the

    A. right up to panel point L_3
    B. right up to a point between L_3 and L_2
    C. left up to panel point L_2
    D. left up to a point between L_2 and L_3

40. For a uniformly distributed live load, the maximum tensile stress in member U_2L_2 will occur when the truss is loaded from the left up to

    A. panel point L_3
    B. panel point L_2
    C. a point midway between L_2 and L_3
    D. a point 8'4" from L_2 in panel L_2L_3

KEY (CORRECT ANSWERS)

1. A	11. C	21. A	31. B
2. C	12. C	22. A	32. B
3. D	13. B	23. D	33. D
4. C	14. A	24. D	34. B
5. D	15. A	25. C	35. B
6. D	16. C	26. D	36. A
7. D	17. B	27. B	37. C
8. B	18. A	28. A	38. B
9. D	19. C	29. C	39. B
10. D	20. B	30. A	40. D

TEST 3

DIRECTIONS: Each question or incomplete statement is followed by several suggested answers or completions. Select the one that BEST answers the question or completes the statement. *PRINT THE LETTER OF THE CORRECT ANSWER IN THE SPACE AT THE RIGHT.*

1. A grit chamber is an enlarged channel through which sewage flows   1.___

    A. while being screened
    B. with a velocity of from 0.6 to 2.6 feet per minute
    C. with a velocity reduced to cause heavy solids to be deposited
    D. depositing grit which decomposes in the bottom
    E. in recessed chambers

2. An end post is   2.___

    A. a long column
    B. a diagonal compression member
    C. a short column
    D. the end member of a compression chord on a through truss
    E. the outside vertical member of a bent

3. A strut is   3.___

    A. a long column
    B. a diagonal compression member
    C. a wide column
    D. the end member of a compression chord on a through truss
    E. the outside vertical member of a bent

4. Of the following items, the one which has NOTHING to do with stadia computations is   4.___

    A. Cox computer   B. Beaman arc
    C. stadia slide rule   D. stadia tables
    E. gradienter

5. In laying up a brick wall, bond refers to the   5.___

    A. adhesive property of the mortar
    B. anchors or ties which hold a brick veneer wall to a building
    C. beam anchors
    D. use of bats or half bricks
    E. use of headers and stretchers

6. In a reinforced concrete building of the slab beam and girder type, architectural considerations limit the size of one beam to such an extent that the concrete stress in that beam is excessive.   6.___
   The MOST practical solution is to

    A. ignore the architectural considerations
    B. use a better quality concrete throughout the building
    C. use a better quality concrete in the beam under consideration
    D. increase the required tension steel
    E. provide compression steel

92

7. A reinforced concrete beam 10" wide x 12" effective depth, on a simple span of 12'0", is reinforced in tension only with three 1/2" square rods.
   If the allowable steel and concrete stresses are 18,000 and 600 p.s.i., respectively, and K is 1/3, the maximum uniform load that the beam can carry (including its own weight) is, in pounds per foot,
   A. 592   B. 623   C. 667   D. 689   E. 714

8. A statically indeterminate structure
   A. is one to which the equations of static equilibrium do not apply
   B. is statically indeterminate because of secondary stresses
   C. requires more material than an equivalent statically determinate structure because of the uncertainty of the exact values of the stresses in the former
   D. is statically indeterminate because of rigid joints
   E. requires at least one equation in addition to those of static equilibrium, for a solution

9. A masonry wall with a rectangular cross-section is 14 feet high.
   If water stands behind the wall two feet below its top and if the masonry weighs 150 pounds per cubic foot, the required width of the wall to just prevent overturning is, in feet,
   A. 4.14   B. 4.54   C. 5.24   D. 5.84   E. 6.04

10. If the hydraulic radius of a stream is close to unity, the cross-section of the stream is
    A. semi-circular
    B. square
    C. triangular
    D. deep and narrow
    E. wide and shallow

11. In column formulae, allowance for accidental eccentricity
    A. is made in the factor of safety
    B. is a function of length
    C. is not made
    D. depends only on the section of the column
    E. must be estimated by the designer

12. An emergency pipe line connecting two reservoirs consists of 3,000 feet of 16" pipe followed by 6,000 feet of 24" pipe which leads into the lower reservoir.
    The hydraulic grade line for this pipe
    A. does not drop continuously in the direction of flow
    B. drops continuously in the direction of flow
    C. is affected by the ground profile
    D. is affected by the pipe profile
    E. never rises in the direction of flow

13. The use of several pipes rather than one pipe in an inverted syphon carrying a sewer under a subway is considered good practice because

    A. it helps prevent deposition in the syphon
    B. it reduces the headroom required
    C. several small pipes are cheaper than one big one
    D. the resultant head loss is smaller
    E. it reduces the velocity of flow

14. If the objective lens of a transit telescope is focused to give an observer the clearest possible view of an object,

    A. no parallax can exist
    B. the proper way to eliminate parallax would involve refocusing of both objective and eyepiece
    C. parallax should be ignored
    D. any error due to parallax can be eliminated by a direct and a reversed sight
    E. nothing can be done to eliminate any parallax that may exist

15. The ground rod at Sta. 18+00 is 6.2. If the grade rod is 8.8,

    A. the fill is 3.7
    B. the cut is 14.8
    C. the fill is 15.0
    D. there is no way of telling whether there is cut or fill of 14.8
    E. there is no way of telling whether there is cut or fill of 3.7

16. In a circular curve of radius R and central angle I, the distance $R(\frac{1}{\cos \frac{1}{2}} - 1)$ is used to locate the

    A. point of curvature
    B. point of intersection or vertex
    C. center of the curve from the vertex
    D. midpoint of the chord of the circular curve
    E. midpoint of the long chord

17. A line 442.25 feet long is to be laid out with a 100-foot steel tape which is 100.07 feet long.
    The taped length which should be laid out in the field is

    A. 441.94   B. 441.99   C. 442.04   D. 442.09   E. 442.14

18. Water flows from reservoir A, Elev. 100, to reservoir B through 16,100 feet of 12-inch pipe.
    If the friction factor, f, is 0.02 and the flow 3.14 cubic feet per second, the elevation of the water surface in reservoir B is MOST NEARLY

    A. 32   B. 28   C. 24   D. 20   E. 16

19. The area bounded by the X-axis, the ordinates x = 1 and x = 4, and the curve $y = x^2-6x-7$ is

    A. 45   B. 41   C. 37   D. 33   E. 29

20. A tie rod 20'0" long and one inch in diameter, fastened to rigid supports at its ends, is under a tension of 10,000 p.s.i. when the temperature is 68° F.
    If the temperature rises to 98° F, the tension in the rod will be MOST NEARLY, in p.s.i.,

    A. 4140   B. 5960   C. 7235   D. 10,800   E. 13,444

21. A 14 WF 246 section has a cross-sectional area, in square inches, of about

    A. 63.5   B. 72.5   C. 76.5   D. 80.5   E. 84.5

22. A load of lumber consists of 25 pieces 4" x 6" x 15'3". The total F.B.M. is MOST NEARLY

    A. 8160   B. 6640   C. 762   D. 868   E. 2155

23. In concrete work, the slump test

    A. is used to determine time of initial set
    B. may be used as a rough check of the water-cement ratio
    C. could give identical results for two concrete mixes of entirely different water-cement ratios
    D. is used in the field only after the concrete has proper workability
    E. is gradually being replaced by the Vicat apparatus

24. A gusset plate is attached to one flange of an H-section column by four rivets which lie at the corners of a 6" x 8" rectangle with the 6" side horizontal. The plate carries a vertical concentrated load with action line 20 inches to the right of the center of the rivet group. Lettering the rivets a, b, c, and d in clockwise order starting at the upper lefthand corner, the maximum total rivet stress occurs in

    A. a and b   B. b and d   C. b *only*
    D. b and c   E. c and d

25. A steel I-beam with a section modulus of 120 inches cubed is to carry a uniformly-distributed load including its own weight on a simple span of 12'0". The maximum allowable fibre stress is 16,000 p.s.i.
    Of the following loads, in pounds per foot (including the weight of the beam), the largest load the beam can carry is

    A. 767   B. 2890   C. 8800   D. 19,705   E. 24,664

26. A flat plate carrying a tensile load of 24,000 pounds is to be connected to a gusset plate by means of 5/16" fillet welds.
    If the allowable unit shearing stress on welds is 11,300 p.s.i., the total length of weld required, in inches, is MOST NEARLY

    A. 27.4   B. 17.3   C. 9.6   D. 7.7   E. 6.6

27. The latitudes and departures of a closed traverse are as follows:

Line	Latitude	Departure
AB	+1000	0
BC	0	+1000
CA	-998	-998

    The error of closure is MOST NEARLY

    A. 1:1200   B. 1:1000   C. 1:800   D. 1:500   E. 1:300

28. The flanges and web of an H-section 12" wide by 12" deep are each 1" thick. The moment of inertia of the section about an axis through the center of gravity and parallel to the flanges is, in inches fourth,

    A. 263 B. 387 C. 595 D. 811 E. 929

29. A circular gate 4' in diameter lies in a vertical plane with its top 4' below the water surface.
    The total water pressure on one side of the gate, in pounds, is MOST NEARLY

    A. 800 B. 3200 C. 3700 D. 4700 E. 4500

30. Two 3/8" plates under a tension of 50,000 lbs. are lap riveted with 7/8" rivets. Allowable unit values of rivets are 15,000 lbs. p.s.i. for shear and 32,000 lbs. p.s.i. for bearing. The number of 7/8" rivets required for this joint is

    A. 1 B. 2 C. 3 D. 4 E. 6

31. A Warren-type deck truss with a span of 60' 0" has 3 panels at 20' 0" and is 20' 0" deep. Under a uniform load of one kip per foot per truss, the maximum stress in the compression chord is, in kips,

    A. 40 B. 35 C. 30 D. 20 E. 10

32. The allowable tensile and bond stresses in reinforcing bars for concrete are 16,000 and 100 p.s.i., respectively. The depth of embedment, in inches, required to develop the allowable tensile strength of a 3/4" diameter bar is

    A. 50 B. 30 C. 20 D. 10 E. 5

33. A sedimentation tank is an enlarged channel through which sewage flows

    A. while being screened
    B. with a velocity of from 0.5 to 2.5 feet per minute
    C. with a velocity reduced to cause heavy solids to be deposited
    D. depositing grit which decomposes in the bottom
    E. in recessed chambers

34. A level is set up so that a Philadelphia rod reads 4.00 on B.M.A., elev. 90.00. A tape rod is then set to read 0.00 at B.M.A. and reads 0.84 at point B.
    The elevation of point B is

    A. computed from the H.I. B. 90.84
    C. 90.37   D. 88.74
    E. 87.14

35. A Proctor compaction test is usually MOST closely associated with the use in the field of a

    A. drag line   B. bulldozer
    C. pile driver   D. sheep's-foot roller
    E. post-hole digger

36. The MOST important consideration in the design of a building foundation resting on a deep clay layer is concerned with

    A. minimum settlement
    B. differential settlement
    C. length of construction period
    D. weather conditions during construction
    E. shape of footing

37. The discharge of a stream varies from 0.1 to 10.0 cubic feet per second, with a mean discharge of about 0.3 c.f.s. The BEST type of weir to measure flow in this stream is

    A. suppressed rectangular
    B. contracted rectangular
    C. trapezoidal
    D. submerged
    E. triangular

38. A peg test on a transit has been completed.
    The first step in the actual adjustment based on the result of the test involves movement of

    A. a diagonally-opposite pair of foot screws
    B. the cross-hair ring
    C. the long bubble by means of the bubble-adjusting screw
    D. the telescope about the horizontal axis
    E. the plate bubbles

39. A steel specimen was tested to destruction in a tension test in which no extensometer was used.
    Results which could be reported would include

    A. elastic limit
    B. yield point
    C. modulus of elasticity
    D. proportional limit
    E. initial set

40. Of the five items following, which one bears the LEAST relationship to the other four?

    A. Shore
    B. Needle
    C. Pretest pile
    D. Underpinning
    E. Pile loading test

KEY (CORRECT ANSWERS)

1. C	11. B	21. B	31. D
2. D	12. A	22. C	32. B
3. B	13. A	23. C	33. B
4. E	14. B	24. D	34. B
5. E	15. C	25. C	35. D
6. E	16. C	26. C	36. B
7. A	17. A	27. A	37. E
8. E	18. D	28. D	38. D
9. A	19. A	29. D	39. B
10. E	20. A	30. E	40. E

EXAMINATION SECTION
TEST 1

DIRECTIONS: Each question or incomplete statement is followed by several suggested answers or completions. Select the one that BEST answers the question or completes the statement. *PRINT THE LETTER OF THE CORRECT ANSWER IN THE SPACE AT THE RIGHT.*

1. The most common approach used by a prime contractor to hold its subcontractors to their initial bids is the doctrine of promissory estoppel. In order to bind a subcontractor to its bid price, the prime contractor must prove each of the following EXCEPT that the

    A. prime contractor relied on the subcontractor's offer when making its own bid
    B. subcontractor submitted a clear and definite offer
    C. subcontractor's bid was formally accepted by the prime contractor
    D. subcontractor could have expected the prime contractor to rely on the subcontractor's offer when making its own bid

1.____

2. Which type of specification in a construction contract is intended to invite the greatest amount of competition?

    A. Base bid   B. Closed
    C. Open   D. Bidder's choice

2.____

3. Written or graphic instruments issued prior to the execution of a contract, which modify or interpret the bidding documents by additions, deletions, clarifications, or corrections, are generally referred to as

    A. contract modifications   B. addenda
    C. reference documents   D. supplementary conditions

3.____

4. What type of warranty is used to limit the manufacturer's responsibility in a construction contract?

    A. Service agreement   B. Correction of work
    C. Limited term   D. Material-only

4.____

5. Which of the following statements represents the most important difference between drawings and specifications?

    A. Specifications constitute one of the contract documents.
    B. Specifications segregate information in order to aid in forming subcontracts.
    C. Drawings are used to show which materials are to be used.
    D. Drawings name the quantity of materials to be used.

5.____

6. The usual fidelity bond arrangement used in construction contracts is used to protect the contractor against

    A. loss, damage or excessive wear of rented equipment
    B. catastrophic damage to completed elements of the construction project
    C. dishonest acts of an employee such as theft, forgery or embezzlement
    D. bid stability of subcontractors

6.____

7. Each of the following is a common purpose of an agreement in construction contract documents EXCEPT to

   A. state the work to be done and the price to be paid for it
   B. specifically formalize the construction contract
   C. act as a single instrument that brings together all of the contract segments by reference
   D. list the technical specifications that must be adhered to in the construction project

8. Which of the following is an attribute that might be considered for the ceiling subsystem in a performance specification?

   A. Maximum claim spread 25
   B. Fire safety
   C. Smoke development shall not exceed 75
   D. ASTM E84

9. Of the following types of hold-harmless clauses, _____ indemnification used in construction contracts indemnifies the owner and/or architect engineer even when the party indemnified is solely responsible for the loss.

   A. limited-form   B. intermediate-form
   C. broad-form   D. omnibus

10. Unit kitchens are an item that would be described under the _____ Division heading in the CSI Masterformat of specifications.

    A. Equipment   B. Special Construction
    C. Furnishings   D. Specialties

11. Which of the following information is usually described in contract specifications?

    A. Test and code requirements
    B. Size of component parts
    C. Overall dimensions
    D. Schedules of finishes, windows, and doors

12. The PRIMARY advantage associated with unit-price construction contracts is

    A. open competition on projects involving quantities of work that cannot be accurately forecast at the time of bidding or negotiation
    B. fully completed drawings and specifications at the time of bidding or negotiation
    C. greater-than-usual flexibility with regard to special reimbursable costs
    D. flexibility in negotiating a unit price for agreed-upon work items

13. Which of the following information is typically shown by drawings?

    A. Methods of fabrication, installation, and erection
    B. Alternates and unit prices
    C. Interrelation of materials, equipment, and space
    D. Gages of manufacturer's equipment

14. Which of the following is/are typical purposes of a changed-condition clause in a construction contract?
    I. To protect the owner from unforeseen increases in project costs
    II. To reduce the contractor's liability for the unexpected
    III. To alleviate the need for including large contingency sums in the bid
    The CORRECT answer is:

    A. I only   B. II only   C. I, II   D. II, III

15. In construction contracts, a special warranty most frequently applies to the work of a(n)

    A. architect   B. subcontractor
    C. engineer   D. contractor

16. The MAIN advantage associated with the use of bid bonds as security for submitted proposals is that they

    A. will hold subcontractors accountable for their subbids
    B. don't require an annual service charge
    C. are estimated according to the minimum bid price
    D. don't immobilize appreciable sums of a contractor's money

17. Under most statutes governing construction contract law, a prime contractor may be relieved from its bid at any time after the opening of bids by the *doctrine of mistake.* Which of the following are conditions that would support an argument for applying the doctrine of mistake?
    The
    I. mistake relates to a material feature of the contract
    II. mistake is one of judgment, rather than fact
    III. owner is put in a status quo position, to the extent that he suffers no serious prejudice except the loss of his bargain
    IV. mistake is of a mechanical or clerical nature
    The CORRECT answer is:

    A. I only   B. III only   C. II, IV   D. I, III, IV

18. Which of the following is NOT typically a disadvantage associated with the use of retainage arrangements in construction contracts?

    A. Reduced bidding competition
    B. Higher construction costs for owners
    C. Tends to sacrifice workmanship for speed of completion
    D. Cash-flow problems for contractors

19. What is the term for a detailed compilation of the quantity of each elementary work item that is called for on the project?

    A. Specification   B. Takeoff
    C. Bid invitation   D. Summary sheet

20. Which of the following is NOT one of the general types of specifications used in construction contracts?

    A. Proprietary   B. Surety
    C. Descriptive   D. Performance

21. When negotiating a cost-plus contract, the owner and contractor must pay particular attention to each of the following considerations EXCEPT

   A. a list of job costs to be reimbursable to the contractor
   B. a common understanding regarding the accounting methods to be used
   C. the number of work units to be performed in executing the project
   D. a definite and mutually agreeable subcontract-letting procedure

22. According to construction contract law, what is the term for a promise by a party called the guarantor to make good the mistake, debt, or default of another party?

   A. Guaranty   B. Warranty   C. Guarantee   D. Surety

23. In a technical section that has been written according to the CSI standard format, which of the following descriptions would be sequenced FIRST?

   A. Warranty
   B. Summary
   C. Project/site conditions
   D. Maintenance

24. In a construction contract, addendum changes to _____ are typically sequenced first.

   A. drawings
   B. bid form
   C. prior addenda
   D. general conditions

25. Which of the following is typically added to a construction contract as a means of providing financial protection to a contractor?
   I. Value engineering clause
   II. Escalation clause
   III. Escape clause
   The CORRECT answer is:

   A. I only   B. I, II   C. I, III   D. II, III

KEY (CORRECT ANSWERS)

1. C
2. C
3. B
4. D
5. B

6. C
7. D
8. B
9. C
10. A

11. A
12. A
13. C
14. D
15. B

16. D
17. D
18. C
19. B
20. B

21. C
22. A
23. B
24. C
25. D

TEST 2

DIRECTIONS: Each question or incomplete statement is followed by several suggested answers or completions. Select the one that BEST answers the question or completes the statement. *PRINT THE LETTER OF THE CORRECT ANSWER IN THE SPACE AT THE RIGHT.*

1. Which type of specification is most commonly used for public work? 1.____

    A. Open
    B. Closed
    C. Restricted
    D. Bidder's choice

2. Changes in the general conditions of a contract are expressed in the form of 2.____

    A. contract modifications
    B. change orders
    C. supplementary conditions
    D. addenda

3. The listing of subcontractors is often troublesome for contractors when it comes to bidding on projects with 3.____

    A. unbalanced bids
    B. alternates
    C. contract bonds
    D. unit pricing

4. Of the following, it is NOT a typical right assigned to an owner under the terms of a construction contract to 4.____

    A. inspect the work as it proceeds
    B. terminate the contract for cause
    C. intervene in the direction and control of the work
    D. retain a specified portion of the contractor's periodic payments

5. In most states, oral purchase agreements are NOT enforceable when 5.____

    A. they are carried out without the knowledge or consent of the prime contractor
    B. the price of goods is $500 or more
    C. the seller has not been approved by the owner
    D. the seller is not required under the agreement to deliver the goods to the site

6. Which of the following elements of a project manual is NOT usually included under the Sample Forms heading? 6.____

    A. Bid bond
    B. Supplementary conditions
    C. Performance and payment bonds
    D. Agreement

7. As part of a construction contract, a retainage arrangement can substantially serve an owner in each of the following ways EXCEPT 7.____

    A. protection against a contractor's failure to remedy defective work
    B. collection of damages from the contractor for late completion
    C. protection against breach of contract
    D. protection against damages to others caused by the contractor's performance

8. In general, the submission of *qualified* bids by a contractor is not permissible in public bidding because it

   A. is considered to be an arbitrary and unfair practice.
   B. will make the bid subject to rejection
   C. avoids fixing a total cost for the project
   D. is an illegal practice

9. Which of the following bonds is given by a self-insured contractor to the state to guarantee payment of statutory benefits to injured employees?

   A. Union wage bond
   B. License bond
   C. Workman's compensation bond
   D. Fidelity bond

10. The Divisions of the CSI Masterformat of specifications are based on four major categories. Which of the following is NOT one of these categories?

    A. Trades
    C. Place relationships
    B. Levels of specialization
    D. Materials

11. In construction contract law, what is the term for the promise that certain facts are true as represented and that they will remain so?

    A. Guaranty   B. Guarantee   C. Surety   D. Warranty

12. An owner may occasionally want a contractor to start construction operations before the formalities associated with the signing of the contract can be completed. In this case, a(n) _____ should be conveyed to authorize the start of work.

    A. letter of intent
    C. proviso of estoppel
    B. escape clause
    D. writ of mediation

13. In performance specifying, the term *criterion* refers to a(n)

    A. set of physical measurements of the materials specified
    B. qualitative statement of the desired performance
    C. evaluative procedure to assure compliance with the standard
    D. quantitative statement of the desired performance

14. A construction contract may be terminated on the grounds of the doctrine of impossibility of performance. Which of the following would be most likely to be interpreted as constituting impossibility of performance?

    A. Prolonged infirmity of prime contractor
    B. Withdrawal of subbids that make the execution of construction too costly to be profitable
    C. Unexpected site conditions found that make the construction impracticable
    D. One party finds it an economic burden to continue

15. Which of the following contracts is NOT typically defined in a contractual liability insurance policy that is included in a construction contract?

    A. Hold-harmless agreements
    C. Easement agreements
    B. Lease of premises
    D. Sidetrack agreements

16. For a contractor, the main disadvantage associated with lump-sum contracts is that   16._____
    A. they increase the likelihood of impossibility of performance
    B. the total amount of payment will be unknown until project completion
    C. they make it more difficult to hold subcontractors to their subbids
    D. adverse changes in the contractor's project costs will not be compensated

17. When a bidder's list of substitutions is used in the specifications of a construction contract, each of the following is generally true EXCEPT   17._____
    A. the bid must include the net difference in cost if the substitutions are accepted
    B. each bidder is free to submit any substitution
    C. it is the best method for achieving pure competition
    D. each of the bidders is unaware of the substitution his competitor may offer

18. In a(n) _____ contract, it is especially important that the work must be of such a nature that it can be fairly well-defined and a reasonably good estimate of cost can be approximated at the time of negotiations.   18._____
    A. incentive   B. cost-plus-fixed-fee
    C. progress payment   D. cost-plus-percentage

19. In a typical surety bond arrangement written into a construction contract, the principal is the   19._____
    A. owner   B. surety company
    C. contractor   D. architect/engineer

20. When several prime contracts are desired in a construction project, the limits of each prime contract will usually be established in the   20._____
    A. specifications   B. general conditions
    C. agreement   D. bidding requirements

21. Under the terms of a *liquidated damages* bid bond, the surety agrees to pay the _____ as damages for a contractor's default on a bid.   21._____
    A. entire bond amount
    B. difference between the contractor's defaulted low bid and the price the owner must pay to the next lowest responsible bidder
    C. agreed-upon percentage, usually 5 to 10 percent, of the minimum bid price
    D. amount of the initial progress payment plus a penalty

22. Which of the following descriptions in a technical section would appear in Part 3, according to the CSI standard format?   22._____
    A. Manufacturers   B. Installation
    C. Definitions   D. Accessories

23. Before a contract award is made, the bids must be carefully studied and evaluated by the owner and architect-engineer, a process which is typically referred to as   23._____
    A. prepping   B. polling
    C. canvassing   D. bonding

24. On small projects, office functions are usually carried out in a contractor's main office and particular items of office overhead are difficult to establish. If the contractor is working such a project on a cost-plus basis, it is common practice to

    A. agree with the owner upon a disinterested third party who will estimate the total office overhead costs of the project, and incorporate this figure into the contract
    B. eliminate office overhead altogether as a reimbursed cost and increase the contractor's fee by a reasonable amount
    C. agree in advance with the owner upon an estimated percentage of total job costs that will be named as office overhead in the accounting of the contract
    D. agree in advance with the owner upon a fixed amount that will be named as office overhead in the accounting of the contract

25. In the absence of any clause in a construction contract that addresses the point of excusable delay by a contractor, the contractor may only expect relief from delays with specified causes. Which of the following is NOT one of these causes?

    A. The architect-engineer
    B. The law
    C. Subcontractors
    D. The owner

KEY (CORRECT ANSWERS)

1.	A		11.	D
2.	C		12.	A
3.	B		13.	D
4.	C		14.	C
5.	B		15.	A
6.	B		16.	D
7.	C		17.	C
8.	B		18.	B
9.	C		19.	C
10.	B		20.	A

21. A
22. B
23. C
24. B
25. C

EXAMINATION SECTION
TEST 1

DIRECTIONS: Each question or incomplete statement is followed by several suggested answers or completions. Select the one that BEST answers the question or completes the statement. *PRINT THE LETTER OF THE CORRECT ANSWER IN THE SPACE AT THE RIGHT.*

1. Of the following, the one MOST important quality required of a good supervisor is
   A. ambition   B. leadership   C. friendliness   D. popularity

2. It is often said that a supervisor can delegate authority but never responsibility. This means MOST NEARLY that
   A. a supervisor must do his own work if he expects it to be done properly
   B. a supervisor can assign someone else to do his work, but in the last analysis, the supervisor himself must take the blame for any actions followed
   C. authority and responsibility are two separate things that cannot be borne by the same person
   D. it is better for a supervisor never to delegate his authority

3. One of your men who is a habitual complainer asks you to grant him a minor privilege.
   Before granting or denying such a request, you should consider
   A. the merits of the case
   B. that it is good for group morale to grant a request of this nature
   C. the man's seniority
   D. that to deny such a request will lower your standing with the men

4. A supervisory practice on the part of a foreman which is MOST likely to lead to confusion and inefficiency is for him to
   A. give orders verbally directly to the man assigned to the job
   B. issue orders only in writing
   C. follow up his orders after issuing them
   D. relay his orders to the men through co-workers

5. It would be POOR supervision on a foreman's part if he
   A. asked an experienced maintainer for his opinion on the method of doing a special job
   B. make it a policy to avoid criticizing a man in front of his co-workers
   C. consulted his assistant supervisor on unusual problems
   D. allowed a cooling-off period of several days before giving one of his men a deserved reprimand

6. Of the following behavior characteristics of a supervisor, the one that is MOST likely to lower the morale of the men he supervises is
   A. diligence
   B. favoritism
   C. punctuality
   D. thoroughness

6.____

7. Of the following, the BEST method of getting an employee who is not working up to his capacity to produce more work is to
   A. have another employee criticize his production
   B. privately criticize his production but encourage him to produce more
   C. criticize his production before his associates
   D. criticize his production and threaten to fire him

7.____

8. Of the following, the BEST thing for a supervisor to do when a subordinate has done a very good job is to
   A. tell him to take it easy
   B. praise his work
   C. reduce his workload
   D. say nothing because he may become conceited

8.____

9. Your orders to your crew are MOST likely to be followed if you
   A. explain the reasons for these orders
   B. warn that all violators will be punished
   C. promise easy assignments to those who follow these orders best
   D. say that they are for the good of the department

9.____

10. In order to be a good supervisor, you should
    A. impress upon your men that you demand perfection in their work at all times
    B. avoid being blamed for your crew's mistakes
    C. impress your superior with your ability
    D. see to it that your men get what they are entitled to

10.____

11. In giving instructions to a crew, you should
    A. speak in as loud a tone as possible
    B. speak in a coaxing, persuasive manner
    C. speak quietly, clearly, and courteously
    D. always use the word *please* when giving instructions

11.____

12. Of the following factors, the one which is LEAST important in evaluating an employee and his work is his
    A. dependability
    B. quantity of work done
    C. quality of work done
    D. education and training

12.____

13. When a District Superintendent first assumes his command, it is LEAST important for him at the beginning to observe
    A. how his equipment is designed and its adaptability
    B. how to reorganize the district for greater efficiency
    C. the capabilities of the men in the district
    D. the methods of operation being employed

13.____

3 (#1)

14. When making an inspection of one of the buildings under your supervision, the BEST procedure to follow in making a record of the inspection is to
    A. return immediately to the office and write a report from memory
    B. write down all the important facts during or as soon as you complete the inspection
    C. fix in your mind all important facts so that you can repeat them from memory if necessary
    D. fix in your mind all important facts so that you can make out your report at the end of the day

14.____

15. Assume that your superior has directed you to make certain changes in your established procedure. After using this modified procedure on several occasions, you find that the original procedure was distinctly superior and you wish to return to it.
    You should
    A. let your superior find this out for himself
    B. simply change back to the original procedure
    C. compile definite data and information to prove your case to your superior
    D. persuade one of the more experienced workers to take this matter up with your superior

15.____

16. An inspector visited a large building under construction. He inspected the soil lines at 9 A.M., water lines at 10 A.M., fixtures at 11 A.M., and did his office work in the afternoon. He followed the same pattern daily for weeks.
    This procedure was
    A. *good*, because it was methodical and he did not miss anything
    B. *good*, because it gave equal time to all phases of the plumbing
    C. *bad*, because not enough time was devoted to fixtures
    D. *bad*, because the tradesmen knew when the inspection would occur

16.____

17. Assume that one of the foremen in a training course, which you are conducting, proposes a poor solution for a maintenance problem.
    Of the following, the BEST course of action for you to take is to
    A. accept the solution tentatively and correct it during the next class meeting
    B. point out all the defects of this proposed solution and wait until somebody thinks of a better solution
    C. try to get the class to reject this proposed solution and develop a better solution
    D. let the matter pass since somebody will present a better solution as the class work proceeds

17.____

18. As a supervisor, you should be seeking ways to improve the efficiency of shop operations by means such as changing established work procedures.
    The following are offered as possible actions that you should consider in changing established work procedures:
    I. Make changes only when your foremen agree to them
    II. Discuss changes with your supervisor before putting them into practice

18.____

III. Standardize any operation which is performed on a continuing basis
IV. Make changes quickly and quietly in order to avoid dissent
V. Secure expert guidance before instituting unfamiliar procedures

Of the following suggested answers, the one that describes the actions to be taken to change established work procedures is

   A. I, IV, V   B. II, III, V   C. III, IV, V   D. All of the above

19. A supervisor determined that a foreman, without informing his superior, delegated responsibility for checking time cards to a member of his gang. The supervisor then called the foreman into his office where he reprimanded the foreman.
This action of the supervisor in reprimanding the foreman was
   A. *proper*, because the checking of time cards is the foreman's responsibility and should not be delegated
   B. *proper*, because the foreman did not ask the supervisor for permission to delegate responsibility
   C. *improper*, because the foreman may no longer take the initiative in solving future problems
   D. *improper*, because the supervisor is interfering in a function which is not his responsibility

20. A capable supervisor should check all operations under his control.
Of the following, the LEAST important reason for doing this is to make sure that
   A. operations are being performed as scheduled
   B. he personally observes all operations at all times
   C. all the operations are still needed
   D. his manpower is being utilized efficiently

21. A supervisor makes it a practice to apply fair and firm discipline in all cases of rule infractions, including those of a minor nature.
This practice should PRIMARILY be considered
   A. *bad*, since applying discipline for minor violations is a waste of time
   B. *good*, because not applying discipline for minor infractions can lead to a more serious erosion of discipline
   C. *bad*, because employees do not like to be disciplined for minor violations of the rules
   D. *good*, because violating any rule can cause a dangerous situation to occur

22. A maintainer would PROPERLY consider it poor supervisory practice for a foreman to consult with him on
   A. which of several repair jobs should be scheduled first
   B. how to cope with personal problems at home
   C. whether the neatness of his headquarters can be improved
   D. how to express a suggestion which the maintainer plans to submit formally

23. Assume that you have determined that the work of one of your foremen and the men he supervises is consistently behind schedule. When you discuss this situation with the foreman, he tells you that his men are poor workers and then complains that he must spend all of his time checking on their work.
The following actions are offered for your consideration as possible ways of solving the problem of poor performance of the foreman and his men:
   I. Review the work standards with the foreman and determine whether they are realistic.
   II. Tell the foreman that you will recommend him for the foreman's training course for retraining.
   III. Ask the foreman for the names of the maintainers and then replace them as soon as possible.
   IV. Tell the foreman that you expect him to meet a satisfactory level of performance.
   V. Tell the foreman to insist that his men work overtime to catch up to the schedule.
   VI. Tell the foreman to review the type and amount of training he has given the maintainers.
   VII. Tell the foreman that he will be out of a job if he does not produce on schedule.
   VIII. Avoid all criticism of the foreman and his methods.
   Which of the following suggested answers CORRECTLY lists the proper actions to be taken to solve the problem of poor performance of the foreman and his men?
   A. I, II, IV, VI   B. I, III, V, VII   C. II, III, VI, VIII   D. IV, V, VI, VIII

24. When a conference or a group discussion is tending to turn into a *bull session* without constructive purpose, the BEST action to take is to
   A. reprimand the leader of the bull session
   B. redirect the discussion to the business at hand
   C. dismiss the meeting and reschedule it for another day
   D. allow the bull session to continue

25. Assume that you have been assigned responsibility for a program in which a high production rate is mandatory. From past experience, you know that your foremen do not perform equally well in the various types of jobs given to them. Which of the following methods should you use in selecting foremen for the specific types of work involved in the program?
   A. Leave the method of selecting foremen to your supervisor
   B. Assign each foreman to the work he does best
   C. Allow each foreman to choose his own job
   D. Assign each foreman to a job which will permit him to improve his own abilities

KEY (CORRECT ANSWERS)

1.	B	11.	C
2.	B	12.	D
3.	A	13.	B
4.	D	14.	B
5.	D	15.	C
6.	B	16.	D
7.	B	17.	C
8.	B	18.	B
9.	A	19.	A
10.	D	20.	B

21. B
22. A
23. A
24. B
25. B

TEST 2

DIRECTIONS: Each question or incomplete statement is followed by several suggested answers or completions. Select the one that BEST answers the question or completes the statement. *PRINT THE LETTER OF THE CORRECT ANSWER IN THE SPACE AT THE RIGHT.*

1. A foreman who is familiar with modern management principles should know that the one of the following requirements of an administrator which is LEAST important is his ability to
    A. coordinate work
    B. plan, organize, and direct the work under his control
    C. cooperate with others
    D. perform the duties of the employees under his jurisdiction

    1.____

2. When subordinates request his advice in solving problems encountered in their work, a certain chief occasionally answers the request by first asking the subordinate what he thinks should be done.
   This action by the chief is, on the whole,
    A. *desirable*, because it stimulates subordinates to give more thought to the solution of problems encountered
    B. *undesirable*, because it discourages subordinates from asking questions
    C. *desirable*, because it discourages subordinates from asking questions
    D. *undesirable*, because it undermines the confidence of subordinates in the ability of their supervisor

    2.____

3. Of the following factors that may be considered by a unit head in dealing with the tardy subordinate, the one which should be given LEAST consideration is the
    A. frequency with which the employee is tardy
    B. effect of the employee's tardiness upon the work of other employees
    C. willingness of the employee to work overtime when necessary
    D. cause of the employee's tardiness

    3.____

4. The MOST important requirement of a good inspectional report is that it should be
    A. properly addressed   B. lengthy
    C. clear and brief   D. spelled correctly

    4.____

5. Building superintendents frequently inquire about departmental inspectional procedures.
   Of the following, it is BEST to
    A. advise them to write to the department for an official reply
    B. refuse as the inspectional procedure is a restricted matter
    C. briefly explain the procedure to them
    D. avoid the inquiry by changing the subject

    5.____

6. Reprimanding a crew member before other workers is a
   A. *good* practice; the reprimand serves as a warning to the other workers
   B. *bad* practice; people usually resent criticism made in public
   C. *good* practice; the other workers will realize that the supervisor is fair
   D. *bad* practice; the other workers will take sides in the dispute

7. Of the following actions, the one which is LEAST likely to promote good work is for the group leader to
   A. praise workers for doing a good job
   B. call attention to the opportunities for promotion for better workers
   C. threaten to recommend discharge of workers who are below standard
   D. put into practice any good suggestion made by crew members

8. A supervisor notices that a member of his crew has skipped a routine step in his job.
   Of the following, the BEST action for the supervisor to take is to
   A. promptly question the worker about the incident
   B. immediately assign another man to complete the job
   C. bring up the incident the next time the worker asks for a favor
   D. say nothing about the incident but watch the worker carefully in the future

9. Assume you have been told to show a new worker how to operate a piece of equipment.
   Your FIRST step should be to
   A. ask the worker if he has any questions about the equipment
   B. permit the worker to operate the equipment himself while you carefully watch to prevent damage
   C. demonstrate the operation of the equipment for the worker
   D. have the worker read an instruction booklet on the maintenance of the equipment

10. Whenever a new man was assigned to his crew, the supervisor would introduce him to all other crew members, take him on a tour of the plant, tell him about bus schedules and places to eat.
    This practice is
    A. *good*; the new man is made to feel welcome
    B. *bad*; supervisors should not interfere in personal matters
    C. *good*; the new man knows that he can bring his personal problems to the supervisor
    D. *bad*; work time should not be spent on personal matters

11. The MOST important factor in successful leadership is the ability to
    A. obtain instant obedience to all orders
    B. establish friendly personal relations with crew members
    C. avoid disciplining crew members
    D. make crew members want to do what should be done

12. Explaining the reasons for departmental procedure to workers tends to 12._____
    A. waste time which should be used for productive purposes
    B. increase their interest in their work
    C. make them more critical of departmental procedures
    D. confuse them

13. If you want a job done well do it yourself. 13._____
    For a supervisor to follow this advice would be
    A. *good*; a supervisor is responsible for the work of his crew
    B. *bad*; a supervisor should train his men, not do their work
    C. *good*; a supervisor should be skilled in all jobs assigned to his crew
    D. *bad*; a supervisor loses respect when he works with his hands

14. When a supervisor discovers a mistake in one of the jobs for which his crew is responsible, it is MOST important for him to find out 14._____
    A. whether anybody else knows about the mistake
    B. who was to blame for the mistake
    C. how to prevent similar mistakes in the future
    D. whether similar mistakes occurred in the past

15. A supervisor who has to explain a new procedure to his crew should realize that questions from the crew USUALLY show that they 15._____
    A. are opposed to the new practice
    B. are completely confused by the explanation
    C. need more training in the new procedure
    D. are interested in the explanation

16. A good way for a supervisor to retain the confidence of his or her employees is to 16._____
    A. say as little as possible
    B. check work frequently
    C. make no promises unless they will be fulfilled
    D. never hesitate in giving an answer to any question

17. Good supervision is ESSENTIALLY a matter of 17._____
    A. patience in supervising workers   B. care in selecting workers
    C. skill in human relations   D. fairness in disciplining workers

18. It is MOST important for an employee who has been assigned a monotonous task to 18._____
    A. perform this task before doing other work
    B. ask another employee to help
    C. perform this task only after all other work has been completed
    D. take measures to prevent mistakes in performing the task

19. One of your employees has violated a minor agency regulation.
The FIRST thing you should do is
    A. warn the employee that you will have to take disciplinary action if it should happen again
    B. ask the employee to explain his or her actions
    C. inform your supervisor and wait for advice
    D. write a memo describing the incident and place it in the employee's personnel file

20. One of your employees tells you that he feels you give him much more work than the other employees, and he is having trouble meeting your deadlines.
You should
    A. ask if he has been under a lot of non-work related stress lately
    B. review his recent assignments to determine if he is correct
    C. explain that this is a busy time, but you are dividing the work equally
    D. tell him that he is the most competent employee and that is why he receives more work

21. A supervisor assigns one of his crew to complete a portion of a job. A short time later, the supervisor notices that the portion has not been completed.
Of the following, the BEST way for the supervisor to handle this is to
    A. ask the crew member why he has not completed the assignment
    B. reprimand the crew member for not obeying orders
    C. assign another crew member to complete the assignment
    D. complete the assignment himself

22. Supposes that a member of your crew complains that you are *playing favorites* in assigning work.
Of the following, the BEST method of handling the complaint is to
    A. deny it and refuse to discuss the matter with the worker
    B. take the opportunity to tell the worker what is wrong with his work
    C. ask the worker for examples to prove his point and try to clear up any misunderstanding
    D. promise to be more careful in making assignments in the future

23. A member of your crew comes to you with a complaint. After discussing the matter with him, it is clear that you have convinced him that his complaint was not justified.
At this point, you should
    A. permit him to drop the matter
    B. make him admit his error
    C. pretend to see some justification in his complaint
    D. warn him against making unjustified complaints

24. Suppose that a supervisor has in his crew an older man who works rather slowly. In other respects, this man is a good worker; he is seldom absent, works carefully, never loafs, and is cooperative.

The BEST way for the supervisor to handle this worker is to
- A. try to get him to work faster and less carefully
- B. give him the most disagreeable job
- C. request that he be given special training
- D. permit him to work at his own speed

25. Suppose that a member of your crew comes to you with a suggestion he thinks will save time in doing a job. You realize immediately that it won't work.
Under these circumstances, your BEST action would be to
- A. thank the worker for the suggestion and forget about it
- B. explain to the worker why you think it won't work
- C. tell the worker to put the suggestion in writing
- D. ask the other members of your crew to criticize the suggestion

25.____

KEY (CORRECT ANSWERS)

1.	D		11.	D
2.	A		12.	B
3.	C		13.	B
4.	C		14.	C
5.	C		15.	D
6.	B		16.	C
7.	C		17.	C
8.	A		18.	D
9.	C		19.	B
10.	A		20.	B

21.	A
22.	C
23.	A
24.	D
25.	B

PREPARING WRITTEN MATERIAL

PARAGRAPH REARRANGEMENT
COMMENTARY

The sentences that follow are in scrambled order. You are to rearrange them in proper order and indicate the letter choice containing the correct answer at the space at the right.

Each group of sentences in this section is actually a paragraph presented in scrambled order. Each sentence in the group has a place in that paragraph; no sentence is to be left out. You are to read each group of sentences and decide upon the best order in which to put the sentences so as to form a well-organized paragraph.

The questions in this section measure the ability to solve a problem when all the facts relevant to its solution are not given.

More specifically, certain positions of responsibility and authority require the employee to discover connection between events sometimes, apparently, unrelated. In order to do this, the employee will find it necessary to correctly infer that unspecified events have probably occurred or are likely to occur. This ability becomes especially important when action must be taken on incomplete information.

Accordingly, these questions require competitors to choose among several suggested alternatives, each of which presents a different sequential arrangement of the events. Competitors must choose the MOST logical of the suggested sequences.

In order to do so, they may be required to draw on general knowledge to infer missing concepts or events that are essential to sequencing the given events. Competitors should be careful to infer only what is essential to the sequence. The plausibility of the wrong alternatives will always require the inclusion of unlikely events or of additional chains of events which are NOT essential to sequencing the given events.

It's very important to remember that you are looking for the best of the four possible choices, and that the best choice of all may not even be one of the answers you're given to choose from.

There is no one right way to solve these problems. Many people have found it helpful to first write out the order of the sentences, as they would have arranged them, on their scrap paper before looking at the possible answers. If their optimum answer is there, this can save them some time. If it isn't, this method can still give insight into solving the problem. Others find it most helpful to just go through each of the possible choices, contrasting each as they go along. You should use whatever method feels comfortable and works for you.

While most of these types of questions are not that difficult, we've added a higher percentage of the difficult type, just to give you more practice. Usually there are only one or two questions on this section that contain such subtle distinctions that you're unable to answer confidently. And you then may find yourself stuck deciding between two possible choices, neither of which you're sure about.

EXAMINATION SECTION
TEST 1

DIRECTIONS: Each question consists of several sentences which can be arranged in a logical sequence. For each question, select the choice which places the numbered sentences in the MOST logical sequence. *PRINT THE LETTER OF THE CORRECT ANSWER IN THE SPACE AT THE RIGHT.*

1.
   I. A body was found in the woods.
   II. A man proclaimed innocence.
   III. The owner of a gun was located.
   IV. A gun was traced.
   V. The owner of a gun was questioned.
   The CORRECT answer is:
   A. IV, III, V, II, I
   B. II, I, IV, III, V
   C. I, IV, III, V, II
   D. I, III, V, II, IV
   E. I, II, IV, III, V

   1.____

2.
   I. A man is in a hunting accident.
   II. A man fell down a flight of steps.
   III. A man lost his vision in one eye,
   IV. A man broke his leg.
   V. A man had to walk with a cane.
   The CORRECT answer is:
   A. II, IV, V, I, III
   B. IV, V, I, III, II
   C. III, I, IV, V, II
   D. I, III, V, II, IV
   E. I, III, II, IV, V

   2.____

3.
   I. A man is offered a new job.
   II. A woman is offered a new job.
   III. A man works as a waiter.
   IV. A woman works as a waitress.
   V. A woman gives notice.
   The CORRECT answer is:
   A. IV, II, V, III, I
   B. IV, II, V, I, III
   C. II, IV, V, III, I
   D. III, I, IV, II, V
   E. IV, III, II, V, I

   3.____

4.
   I. A train let the station late.
   II. A man was late for work.
   III. A man lost his job.
   IV. Many people complained because the train was late.
   V. There was a traffic jam.
   The CORRECT answer is:
   A. V, II, I, IV, III
   B. V, I, IV, II, III
   C. V, I, II, IV, III
   D. I, V, IV, II, III
   E. II, I, IV, V, III

   4.____

5.
   I. The burden of proof as to each issue is determined before trial and remains upon the same party throughout the trial.
   II. The jury is at liberty to believe one witness' testimony as against a number of contradictory witnesses.
   III. In a civil case, the party bearing the burden of proof is required to prove his contention by a fair preponderance of the evidence.
   IV. However, it must be noted that a fair preponderance of evidence does not necessarily mean a greater number of witnesses.
   V. The burden of proof is the burden which rests upon one of the parties to an action to persuade the trier of the facts, generally the jury, that a proposition he asserts is true.
   VI. If the evidence is equally balanced, or if it leaves the jury in such doubt as to be unable to decide the controversy either way, judgment must be given against the party upon whom the burden of proof rests.
   The CORRECT answer is:
   A. III, II, V, IV, I, VI   B. I, II, VI, V, III, IV   C. III, IV, V, I, II, VI
   D. V, I, III, VI, IV, II   E. I, V, III, VI, IV, II

6.
   I. If a parent is without assets and is unemployed, he cannot be convicted of the crime of non-support of a child.
   II. The term *sufficient ability* has been held to mean sufficient financial ability.
   III. It does not matter if his unemployment is by choice or unavoidable circumstances.
   IV. If he fails to take any steps at all, he may be liable to prosecution for endangering the welfare of a child.
   V. Under the penal law, a parent is responsible for the support of his minor child only if the parent is of *sufficient ability*.
   VI. An indigent parent may meet his obligation by borrowing money or by seeking aid under the provisions of the Social Welfare Law.
   The CORRECT answer is:
   A. VI, I, V, III, II, IV   B. I, III, V, II, IV, VI   C. V, II, I, III, VI, IV
   D. I, VI, IV, V, II, III   E. II, V, I, III, VI, IV

7.
   I. Consider, for example, the case of a rabble rouser who urges a group of twenty people to go out and break the windows of a nearby factory.
   II. Therefore, the law fills the indicated gap with the crime of *inciting to riot*.
   III. A person is considered guilty of inciting to riot when he urges ten or more persons to engage in tumultuous and violent conduct of a kind likely to create public alarm.
   IV. However, if he has not obtained the cooperation of at least four people, he cannot be charged with unlawful assembly.
   V. The charge of inciting to riot was added to the law to cover types of conduct which cannot be classified as either the crime of *riot* or the crime of *unlawful assembly*.
   VI. If he acquires the acquiescence of at least four of them, he is guilty of unlawful assembly even if the project does not materialize.
   The CORRECT answer is:
   A. III, V, I, VI, IV, II   B. V, I, IV, VI, II, III   C. III, IV, I, V, II, VI
   D. V, I, IV, VI, III, II   E. V, III, I, VI, IV, II

8. I. If, however, the rebuttal evidence presents an issue of credibility, it is for the jury to determine whether the presumption has, in fact, been destroyed.
   II. Once sufficient evidence to the contrary is introduced, the presumption disappears from the trial.
   III. The effect of a presumption is to place the burden upon the adversary to come forward with evidence to rebut the presumption.
   IV. When a presumption is overcome and ceases to exist in the case, the fact or facts which gave rise to the presumption still remain.
   V. Whether a presumption has been overcome is ordinarily a question for the court.
   VI. Such information may furnish a basis for a logical inference.
   The CORRECT answer is:
   A. IV, VI, II, V, I, III   B. III, II, V, I, IV, VI   C. V, III, VI, IV, II, I
   D. V, IV, I, II, VI, III   E. II, III, V, I, IV, VI

8.____

9. I. An executive may answer a letter by writing his reply on the face of the letter itself instead of having a return letter typed.
   II. This procedure is efficient because it saves the executive's time, the typist's time, and saves office file space.
   III. Copying machines are used in small offices as well as large offices to save time and money in making brief replies to business letters.
   IV. A copy is made on a copying machine to go into the company files, while the original is mailed back to the sender.
   The CORRECT answer is:
   A. I, II, IV, III   B. I, IV, II, III   C. III, I, IV, II   D. III, IV, II, I

9.____

10. I. Most organizations favor one of the types but always include the others to a lesser degree.
    II. However, we can detect a definite trend toward greater use of symbolic control.
    III. We suggest that our local police agencies are today primarily utilizing material control.
    IV. Control can be classified into three types: physical, material, and symbolic.
    The CORRECT answer is:
    A. IV, II, III, I   B. II, I, IV, III   C. III, IV, II, I   D. IV, I, III, II

10.____

11. I. Project residents had first claim to this use, followed by surrounding neighborhood children.
    II. By contrast, recreation space within the project's interior was found to be used more often by both groups.
    III. Studies of the use of project grounds in many cities showed grounds left open for public use were neglected and unused, both by residents and by members of the surrounding community.
    IV. Project residents had clearly laid claim to the play spaces, setting up and enforcing unwritten rules for use.
    V. Each group, by experience, found their activities easily disrupted by other groups, and their claim to the use of space for recreation difficult to enforce.

11.____

The CORRECT answer is:
A. IV, V, I, II, III
B. V, II, IV, III, I
C. I, IV, III, II, V
D. III, V, II, IV, I

12. I. They do not consider the problems correctable within the existing subsidy formula and social policy of accepting all eligible applicants regardless of social behavior.
    II. A recent survey, however, indicated that tenants believe these problems correctable by local housing authorities and management within the existing financial formula.
    III. Many of the problems and complaints concerning public housing management and design have created resentment between the tenant and the landlord.
    IV. This same survey indicated that administrators and managers do not agree with the tenants.
    The CORRECT answer is:
    A. II, I, III, IV   B. I, III, IV, II   C. III, II, IV, I   D. IV, II, I, III

12.____

13. I. In single-family residences, there is usually enough distance between tenants to prevent occupants from annoying one another.
    II. For example, a certain small percentage of tenant families has one or more members addicted to alcohol.
    III. While managers believe in the right of individuals to live as they choose, the manager becomes concerned when the pattern of living jeopardizes others' rights.
    IV. Still others turn night into day, staging lusty entertainments which carry on into the hours when most tenants are trying to sleep.
    V. In apartment buildings, however, tenants live so closely together that any misbehavior can result in unpleasant living conditions.
    VI. Other families engage in violent argument.
    The CORRECT answer is:
    A. III, II, V, IV, VI, I
    B. I, V, II, VI, IV, III
    C. II, V, IV, I, III, VI
    D. IV, II, V, VI, III, I

13.____

14. I. Congress made the commitment explicit in the Housing Act of 194, establishing as a national goal the realization of a *decent home and suitable environment for every American family*.
    II. The result has been that the goal of decent home and suitable environment is still as far distant as ever for the disadvantaged urban family.
    III. In spite of this action by Congress, federal housing programs have continued to be fragmented and grossly underfunded.
    IV. The passage of the National Housing Act signaled a few federal commitment to provide housing for the nation's citizens.
    The CORRECT answer is:
    A. I, IV, III, II   B. IV, I, III, II   C. IV, I, II, III   D. II, IV, I, III

14.____

15. I. The greater expense does not necessarily involve *exploitation*, but it is often perceived as exploitative and unfair by those who are aware of the price differences involved, but unaware of operating costs.
    II. Ghetto residents believe they are *exploited* by local merchants, and evidence substantiates some of these beliefs.
    III. However, stores in low-income areas were more likely to be small independents, which could not achieve the economies available to supermarket chains and were, therefore, more likely to charge higher prices, and the customers were more likely to buy smaller-sized packages which are more expensive per unit of measure.
    IV. A study conducted in one city showed that distinctly higher prices were charged for goods sold in ghetto stores in other areas.
    The CORRECT answer is:
    A. IV, II, I, III   B. IV, I, III, II   C. II, IV, III, I   D. II, III, IV, I

15.____

KEY (CORRECT ANSWERS)

1.	C	6.	C	11.	D
2.	E	7.	A	12.	C
3.	B	8.	B	13.	B
4.	B	9.	C	14.	B
5.	D	10.	D	15.	C

PREPARING WRITTEN MATERIAL
EXAMINATION SECTION
TEST 1

DIRECTIONS: Each of the following sentences may be classified under one of the following four categories:
  A. *Faulty* because of incorrect grammar or usage
  B. *Faulty* because of incorrect punctuation or spelling
  C. *Faulty* because of incorrect capitalization
  D. *Correct*

Examine each sentence carefully. Then, in the correspondingly numbered space on the right, print the capital letter preceding the option which is the best of the four suggested above.

(All incorrect sentences contain but one type of error. Consider a sentence correct if it contains none of the types of errors mentioned, even though there may be other correct ways of expressing the same thought.

1. They gave the poor man some food when he approached.   1.____
2. I regret the loss caused by the error.   2.____
3. The students have a new teacher for shop mantenance.   3.____
4. They sweared to bring out all the facts.   4.____
5. He decided to open a branch store on 33rd street.   5.____
6. His speed is equal and more than that of a racehorse.   6.____
7. He felt very warm on that Summer day.   7.____
8. He was assisted by his friend, who lives in the next house.   8.____
9. The climate of New York is colder than California.   9.____
10. I shall wait for you on the corner.   10.____
11. Did we see the boy whose the leader?   11.____
12. Being a modest person, John seldom takes about his invention.   12.____
13. The gang is called the smith street boys.   13.____
14. He seen the man break into the store.   14.____

15. We expected to lay still there for quite a while. 15._____
16. He is considered to be the Leader of his organization. 16._____
17. Although He received an invitation, He won't go. 17._____
18. The letter must be here some place. 18._____
19. I thought it to be he. 19._____
20. We expect to remain here for a long time. 20._____
21. The committee was agreed. 21._____
22. Two-thirds of the building are finished. 22._____
23. The water was froze. 23._____
24. Everyone of the salesmen must supply their own car. 24._____
25. Who is the author of Gone With the Wind? 25._____
26. He marched on and declaring that he would never surrender. 26._____
27. Who shall I say called? 27._____
28. Everyone has left but they. 28._____
29. Who did we give the order to? 29._____
30. Send your order in immediately. 30._____
31. I believe I paid the Bill. 31._____
32. I have not met but one person. 32._____
33. Why aren't Tom, and Fred, going to the dance? 33._____
34. What reason is there for him not going? 34._____
35. The seige of Malta was a tremendous event. 35._____
36. I was there yesterday I assure you. 36._____
37. Your ukulele is better than mine. 37._____
38. No one was there only Mary. 38._____

3 (#1)

39. The Capital city of Vermont is Montpelier.   39.____

40. Reggie Jackson may hit the largest amount of home runs this season.   40.____

KEY (CORRECT ANSWERS)

1.	B	11.	B	21.	D	31.	C
2.	D	12.	D	22.	A	32.	A
3.	B	13.	C	23.	A	33.	B
4.	A	14.	A	24.	A	34.	A
5.	C	15.	A	25.	B	35.	B
6.	A	16.	C	26.	A	36.	B
7.	C	17.	C	27.	D	37.	B
8.	D	18.	A	28.	D	38.	A
9.	A	19.	A	29.	A	39.	C
10.	D	20.	D	30.	D	40.	A

TEST 2

Questions 1-3.

DIRECTIONS: Questions 1 through 3 each consist of four sentences. Choose the one sentence in each set of four that would be BEST for a formal letter or report. Consider grammar and appropriate usage.

1. A. Most all the work he completed before he become ill.
   B. He completed most of the work before becoming ill.
   C. Prior to him becoming ill his work was mostly completed.
   D. Before he became will most of the work he had completed.

   1.____

2. A. Being that the report lacked a clearly worded recommendation, it did not matter that it contained enough information.
   B. There was enough information in the report, although it, including the recommendation, were not clearly worded.
   C. Although the report contained enough information, it did not have a clearly worded recommendation.
   D. Though the report did not have a recommendation that was clearly worded, and the information therein contained was enough.

   2.____

3. A. Having already overlooked the important mistakes, the ones which she found were not as important toward the end of the letter.
   B. Toward the end of the letter she had already overlooked the important mistakes, so that which she had found were not important.
   C. The mistakes which she had already overlooked were not as important as those which near the end of letter she had found.
   D. The mistakes which she found near the end of the letter were not so important as those which she had already overlooked.

   3.____

Questions 4-5.

DIRECTIONS: Select the correct answer.

4. The unit has exceeded _____ goals and the employees are satisfied with _____ accomplishments.
   A. their; it's   B. it's, it's   C. is, there   D. its, their

   4.____

5. Research indicates that employees who _____ no opportunity for close social relationships often find their work unsatisfying, and this _____ of satisfaction often reflects itself in low production.
   A. have, lack   B. have, excess   C. has, lack   D. has, excess

   5.____

KEY (CORRECT ANSWERS)

1. B
2. C
3. D
4. D
5. A

TEST 3

DIRECTIONS: Select the choice which BEST expresses the thought and which contains NO errors in grammar or sentence construction.

1.
   A. She, hearing a signal, the source lamp flashed.
   B. While hearing a signal, the source lamp flashed
   C. In hearing a signal, the source lamp flashed.
   D. As she heard a signal, the source lamp flashed.

   1.____

2.
   A. Every one of the time records have been initialed in the designated spaces.
   B. All of the time records has been initialed in the designated spaces.
   C. Which one of the time records was initialed in the designated spaces.
   D. The time records all been initialed in the designated spaces.

   2.____

3.
   A. If there is no one else to answer the phone, you will have to answer it.
   B. You will have to answer it yourself if no one else answers the phone.
   C. If no one else is not around to pick up the phone, you have to do it.
   D. You will have to answer the phone when nobodys here to do it.

   3.____

4.
   A. Dr. Byrnes not in his office. What could I do for you?
   B. Dr. Byrnes is not in his office. Is there something I can do for you?
   C. Since Dr. Byrnes is not in his office, might there be something I may do for you?
   D. Is there any ways I can assist you since Dr. Brynes is not in his office?

   4.____

5.
   A. She do not understand how the new console works.
   B. The way the new console works, she doesn't understand.
   C. She doesn't understand how the new console works.
   D. The new console works, so that she doesn't understand.

   5.____

KEY (CORRECT ANSWERS)

1. D
2. C
3. A
4. B
5. C

TEST 4

DIRECTIONS: The following questions each consist of a sentence which may or may not be an example of good English usage.

Consider grammar, punctuation, spelling, capitalization, awkwardness, etc.

Examine each sentence and then choose the correct statement about it from the four choices below. If the English usage in the sentence given is better than any of the changes suggested in options B, C, or D, choose option A. (Do not choose an option that will change the meaning of the sentence.)

1. The typist used an extention cord in order to connect her typewriter to the outlet nearest to her desk. 1.____
   A. This is an example of acceptable writing.
   B. A period should be placed after the word "cord" and the word "in" should have a capital "I."
   C. A comma should be placed after the word "typewriter."
   D. The word "extention" should be spelled "extension."

2. He would have went to the conference if he had received an invitation. 2.____
   A. This is an example of acceptable writing.
   B. The word "went" should be replaced by the word "gone."
   C. The word "had" should be replaced by "would have."
   D. The word "conference" should be spelled "conference."

3. In order to make the report neater, he spent many hours rewriting it. 3.____
   A. This is an example of acceptable writing.
   B. The word "more" should be inserted before the word "neater."
   C. There should be a colon after the word "neater."
   D. The word "spent" should be changed to "have spent."

4. His supervisor told him that he should of read the memorandum more carefully. 4.____
   A. This is an example of acceptable writing.
   B. The word "memorandum" should be spelled "memorandom."
   C. The word "of" should be replaced by the word "have."
   D. The word "carefully" should be replaced by the word "have."

5. It was decided that two separate reports should be written. 5.____
   A. This is an example of acceptable writing.
   B. A comma should be inserted after the word "decided."
   C. The word "be" should be replaced by the word "been."
   D. A colon should be inserted after the word "that."

6. She don't seem to understand that the work must be done as soon as possible. 6.____
   A. This is an example of acceptable writing.
   B. The word "doesn't" should replace the word "don't."
   C. The word "why" should replace the word "that."
   D. The word "as" before the word "soon" should be eliminated.

KEY (CORRECT ANSWERS)

1. D
2. B
3. A
4. C
5. A
6. B

PHILOSOPHY, PRINCIPLES, PRACTICES, AND TECHNICS OF SUPERVISION, ADMINISTRATION, MANAGEMENT, AND ORGANIZATION

TABLE OF CONTENTS

	Page
MEANING OF SUPERVISION	1
THE OLD AND THE NEW SUPERVISION	1
THE EIGHT (8) BASIC PRINCIPLES OF THE NEW SUPERVISION	1
I. Principle of Responsibility	1
II. Principle of Authority	2
III. Principle of Self-Growth	2
IV. Principle of Individual Worth	2
V. Principle of Creative Leadership	2
VI. Principle of Success and Failure	2
VII. Principle of Science	3
VIII. Principle of Cooperation	3
WHAT IS ADMINISTRATION?	3
I. Practices Commonly Classed as "Supervisory"	3
II. Practices Commonly Classed as "Administrative"	3
III. Practices Commonly Classed as Both "Supervisory" and "Administrative"	4
RESPONSIBILITIES OF THE SUPERVISOR	4
COMPETENCIES OF THE SUPERVISOR	4
THE PROFESSIONAL SUPERVISOR-EMPLOYEE RELATIONSHIP	4
MINI-TEXT IN SUPERVISION, ADMINISTRATION, MANAGEMENT, AND ORGANIZATION	5
I. Brief Highlights	5
A. Levels of Management	6
B. What the Supervisor Must Learn	6
C. A Definition of Supervision	6
D. Elements of the Team Concept	6
E. Principles of Organization	6
F. The Four Important Parts of Every Job	7
G. Principles of Delegation	7
H. Principles of Effective Communications	7
I. Principles of Work Improvement	7
J. Areas of Job Improvement	7
K. Seven Key Points in Making Improvements	8

	L.	Corrective Techniques for Job Improvement	8
	M.	A Planning Checklist	8
	N.	Five Characteristics of Good Directions	9
	O.	Types of Directions	9
	P.	Controls	9
	Q.	Orienting the New Employee	9
	R.	Checklist for Orienting New Employees	9
	S.	Principles of Learning	10
	T.	Causes of Poor Performance	10
	U.	Four Major Steps in On-the-Job Instructions	10
	V.	Employees Want Five Things	10
	W.	Some Don'ts in Regard to Praise	11
	X.	How to Gain Your Workers' Confidence	11
	Y.	Sources of Employee Problems	11
	Z.	The Supervisor's Key to Discipline	11
	AA.	Five Important Processes of Management	12
	BB.	When the Supervisor Fails to Plan	12
	CC.	Fourteen General Principles of Management	12
	DD.	Change	12
II.	Brief Topical Summaries		13
	A.	Who/What is the Supervisor?	13
	B.	The Sociology of Work	13
	C.	Principles and Practices of Supervision	14
	D.	Dynamic Leadership	14
	E.	Processes for Solving Problems	15
	F.	Training for Results	15
	G.	Health, Safety, and Accident Prevention	16
	H.	Equal Employment Opportunity	16
	I.	Improving Communications	16
	J.	Self-Development	17
	K.	Teaching and Training	17
		1. The Teaching Process	17
		a. Preparation	17
		b. Presentation	18
		c. Summary	18
		d. Application	18
		e. Evaluation	18
		2. Teaching Methods	18
		a. Lecture	18
		b. Discussion	18
		c. Demonstration	19
		d. Performance	19
		e. Which Method to Use	19

PHILOSOPHY, PRINCIPLES, PRACTICES, AND TECHNICS
OF
SUPERVISION, ADMINISTRATION, MANAGEMENT, AND ORGANIZATION

MEANING OF SUPERVISION

The extension of the democratic philosophy has been accompanied by an extension in the scope of supervision. Modern leaders and supervisors no longer think of supervision in the narrow sense of being confined chiefly to visiting employees, supplying materials, or rating the staff. They regard supervision as being intimately related to all the concerned agencies of society, they speak of the supervisor's function in terms of "growth," rather than the "improvement" of employees.

This modern concept of supervision may be defined as follows: Supervision is leadership and the development of leadership within groups which are cooperatively engaged in inspection, research, training, guidance, and evaluation.

THE OLD AND THE NEW SUPERVISION

TRADITIONAL
1. Inspection
2. Focused on the employee
3. Visitation
4. Random and haphazard
5. Imposed and authoritarian
6. One person usually

MODERN
1. Study and analysis
2. Focused on aims, materials, methods, supervisors, employees, environment
3. Demonstrations, intervisitation, workshops, directed reading, bulletins, etc.
4. Definitely organized and planned (scientific)
5. Cooperative and democratic
6. Many persons involved (creative)

THE EIGHT (8) BASIC PRINCIPLES OF THE NEW SUPERVISION

I. Principle of Responsibility
    Authority to act and responsibility for acting must be joined.
    A. If you give responsibility, give authority.
    B. Define employee duties clearly.
    C. Protect employees from criticism by others.
    D. Recognize the rights as well as obligations of employees.
    E. Achieve the aims of a democratic society insofar as it is possible within the area of your work.
    F. Establish a situation favorable to training and learning.
    G. Accept ultimate responsibility for everything done in your section, unit, office, division, department.
    H. Good administration and good supervision are inseparable.

II. Principle of Authority
The success of the supervisor is measured by the extent to which the power of authority is not used.
   A. Exercise simplicity and informality in supervision
   B. Use the simplest machinery of supervision
   C. If it is good for the organization as a whole, it is probably justified.
   D. Seldom be arbitrary or authoritative.
   E. Do not base your work on the power of position or of personality.
   F. Permit and encourage the free expression of opinions.

III. Principle of Self-Growth
The success of the supervisor is measured by the extent to which, and the speed with which, he is no longer needed.
   A. Base criticism on principles, not on specifics.
   B. Point out higher activities to employees.
   C. Train for self-thinking by employees to meet new situations.
   D. Stimulate initiative, self-reliance, and individual responsibility
   E. Concentrate on stimulating the growth of employees rather than on removing defects.

IV. Principle of Individual Worth
Respect for the individual is a paramount consideration in supervision.
   A. Be human and sympathetic in dealing with employees.
   B. Don't nag about things to be done.
   C. Recognize the individual differences among employees and seek opportunities to permit best expression of each personality.

V. Principle of Creative Leadership
The best supervision is that which is not apparent to the employee.
   A. Stimulate, don't drive employees to creative action.
   B. Emphasize doing good things.
   C. Encourage employees to do what they do best.
   D. Do not be too greatly concerned with details of subject or method.
   E. Do not be concerned exclusively with immediate problems and activities.
   F. Reveal higher activities and make them both desired and maximally possible.
   G. Determine procedures in the light of each situation but see that these are derived from a sound basic philosophy.
   H. Aid, inspire, and lead so as to liberate the creative spirit latent in all good employees.

VI. Principle of Success and Failure
There are no unsuccessful employees, only unsuccessful supervisors who have failed to give proper leadership.
   A. Adapt suggestions to the capacities, attitudes, and prejudices of employees.
   B. Be gradual, be progressive, be persistent.
   C. Help the employee find the general principle; have the employee apply his own problem to the general principle.
   D. Give adequate appreciation for good work and honest effort.
   E. Anticipate employee difficulties and help to prevent them.
   F. Encourage employees to do the desirable things they will do anyway.
   G. Judge your supervision by the results it secures.

VII. Principle of Science
Successful supervision is scientific, objective, and experimental. It is based on facts, not on prejudices.
   A. Be cumulative in results.
   B. Never divorce your suggestions from the goals of training.
   C. Don't be impatient of results.
   D. Keep all matters on a professional, not a personal, level.
   E. Do not be concerned exclusively with immediate problems and activities.
   F. Use objective means of determining achievement and rating where possible.

VIII. Principle of Cooperation
Supervision is a cooperative enterprise between supervisor and employee.
   A. Begin with conditions as they are.
   B. Ask opinions of all involved when formulating policies.
   C. Organization is as good as its weakest link.
   D. Let employees help to determine policies and department programs.
   E. Be approachable and accessible—physically and mentally.
   F. Develop pleasant social relationships.

WHAT IS ADMINISTRATION

Administration is concerned with providing the environment, the material facilities, and the operational procedures that will promote the maximum growth and development of supervisors and employees. (Organization is an aspect and a concomitant of administration.)

There is no sharp line of demarcation between supervision and administration; these functions are intimately interrelated and, often, overlapping. They are complementary activities.

I. Practices Commonly Classed as "Supervisory"
   A. Conducting employees' conferences
   B. Visiting sections, units, offices, divisions, departments
   C. Arranging for demonstrations
   D. Examining plans
   E. Suggesting professional reading
   F. Interpreting bulletins
   G. Recommending in-service training courses
   H. Encouraging experimentation
   I. Appraising employee morale
   J. Providing for intervisitation

II. Practices Commonly Classified as "Administrative"
   A. Management of the office
   B. Arrangement of schedules for extra duties
   C. Assignment of rooms or areas
   D. Distribution of supplies
   E. Keeping records and reports
   F. Care of audio-visual materials
   G. Keeping inventory records
   H. Checking record cards and books

      I.   Programming special activities
      J.   Checking on the attendance and punctuality of employees

III.   Practices Commonly Classified as Both "Supervisory" and "Administrative"
     A.   Program construction
     B.   Testing or evaluating outcomes
     C.   Personnel accounting
     D.   Ordering instructional materials

RESPONSIBILITIES OF THE SUPERVISOR

A person employed in a supervisory capacity must constantly be able to improve his own efficiency and ability. He represent the employer to the employees and only continuous self-examination can make him a capable supervisor.

Leadership and training are the supervisor's responsibility. An efficient working unit is one in which the employees work with the supervisor. It is his job to bring out the best in his employees. He must always be relaxed, courteous, and calm in his association with his employees. Their feelings are important, and a harsh attitude does not develop the most efficient employees.

COMPETENCES OF THE SUPERVISOR

    I.   Complete knowledge of the duties and responsibilities of his position.
    II.   To be able to organize a job, plan ahead, and carry through.
    III.   To have self-confidence and initiative.
    IV.   To be able to handle the unexpected situation and make quick decisions.
    V.   To be able to properly train subordinates in the positions they are best suited for.
    VI.   To be able to keep good human relations among his subordinates.
    VII. To be able to keep good human relations between his subordinates and himself and to earn their respect and trust.

THE PROFESSIONAL SUPERVISOR-EMPLOYEE RELATIONSHIP

There are two kinds of efficiency: one kind is only apparent and is produced in organizations through the exercise of mere discipline; this is but a simulation of the second, or true, efficiency which springs from spontaneous cooperation. If you are a manager, no matter how great or small your responsibility, it is your job, in the final analysis, to create and develop this involuntary cooperation among the people whom you supervise. For, no matter how powerful a combination of money, machines, and materials a company may have, this is a dead and sterile thing without a team of willing, thinking, and articulate people to guide it.

The following 21 points are presented as indicative of the exemplary basic relationship that should exist between supervisor and employee:

1. Each person wants to be liked and respected by his fellow employee and wants to be treated with consideration and respect by his superior.
2. The most competent employee will make an error. However, in a unit where good relations exist between the supervisor and his employees, tenseness and fear do not exist. Thus, errors are not hidden or covered up, and the efficiency of a unit is not impaired.

3. Subordinates resent rules, regulations, or orders that are unreasonable or unexplained.
4. Subordinates are quick to resent unfairness, harshness, injustices, and favoritism.
5. An employee will accept responsibility if he knows that he will be complimented for a job well done, and not too harshly chastised for failure; that his supervisor will check the cause of the failure, and, if it was the supervisor's fault, he will assume the blame therefore. If it was the employee's fault, his supervisor will explain the correct method or means of handling the responsibility.
6. An employee wants to receive credit for a suggestion he has made, that is used. If a suggestion cannot be used, the employee is entitled to an explanation. The supervisor should not say "no" and close the subject.
7. Fear and worry slow up a worker's ability. Poor working environment can impair his physical and mental health. A good supervisor avoids forceful methods, threats, and arguments to get a job done.
8. A forceful supervisor is able to train his employees individually and as a team, and is able to motivate them in the proper channels.
9. A mature supervisor is able to properly evaluate his subordinates and to keep them happy and satisfied.
10. A sensitive supervisor will never patronize his subordinates.
11. A worthy supervisor will respect his employees' confidences.
12. Definite and clear-cut responsibilities should be assigned to each executive.
13. Responsibility should always be coupled with corresponding authority.
14. No change should be made in the scope or responsibilities of a position without a definite understanding to that effect on the part of all persons concerned.
15. No executive or employee, occupying a single position in the organization, should be subject to definite orders from more than one source.
16. Orders should never be given to subordinates over the head of a responsible executive. Rather than do this, the officer in question should be supplanted.
17. Criticisms of subordinates should, whoever possible, be made privately, and in no case should a subordinate be criticized in the presence of executives or employees of equal or lower rank.
18. No dispute or difference between executives or employees as to authority or responsibilities should be considered too trivial for prompt and careful adjudication.
19. Promotions, wage changes, and disciplinary action should always be approved by the executive immediately superior to the one directly responsible.
20. No executive or employee should ever be required, or expected, to be at the same time an assistant to, and critic of, another.
21. Any executive whose work is subject to regular inspection should, wherever practicable, be given the assistance and facilities necessary to enable him to maintain an independent check of the quality of his work.

MINI-TEXT IN SUPERVISION, ADMINISTRATION, MANAGEMENT, AND ORGANIZATION

I. Brief Highlights

Listed concisely and sequentially are major headings and important data in the field for quick recall and review.

A. Levels of Management
Any organization of some size has several levels of management. In terms of a ladder, the levels are:

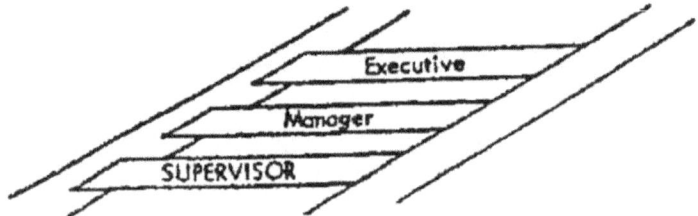

The first level is very important because it is the beginning point of management leadership.

B. What the Supervisor Must Learn
A supervisor must learn to:
1. Deal with people and their differences
2. Get the job done through people
3. Recognize the problems when they exist
4. Overcome obstacles to good performance
5. Evaluate the performance of people
6. Check his own performance in terms of accomplishment

C. A Definition of Supervisor
The term supervisor means any individual having authority, in the interests of the employer, to hire, transfer, suspend, lay-off, recall, promote, discharge, assign, reward, or discipline other employees or responsibility to direct them, or to adjust their grievances, or effectively to recommend such action, if, in connection with the foregoing, exercise of such authority is not of a merely routine or clerical nature but requires the use of independent judgment.

D. Elements of the Team Concept
What is involved in teamwork? The component parts are:
1. Members
2. A leader
3. Goals
4. Plans
5. Cooperation
6. Spirit

E. Principles of Organization
1. A team member must know what his job is.
2. Be sure that the nature and scope of a job are understood.
3. Authority and responsibility should be carefully spelled out.
4. A supervisor should be permitted to make the maximum number of decisions affecting his employees.
5. Employees should report to only one supervisor.
6. A supervisor should direct only as many employees as he can handle effectively.
7. An organization plan should be flexible.

8. Inspection and performance of work should be separate.
9. Organizational problems should receive immediate attention.
10. Assign work in line with ability and experience.

F. The Four Important Parts of Every Job
1. Inherent in every job is the *accountability* for results.
2. A second set of factors in every job is *responsibilities*.
3. Along with duties and responsibilities one must have the *authority* to act within certain limits without obtaining permission to proceed.
4. No job exists in a vacuum. The supervisor is surrounded by key *relationships*.

G. Principles of Delegation
Where work is delegated for the first time, the supervisor should think in terms of these questions:
1. Who is best qualified to do this?
2. Can an employee improve his abilities by doing this?
3. How long should an employee spend on this?
4. Are there any special problems for which he will need guidance?
5. How broad a delegation can I make?

H. Principles of Effective Communications
1. Determine the media.
2. To whom directed?
3. Identification and source authority.
4. Is communication understood?

I. Principles of Work Improvement
1. Most people usually do only the work which is assigned to them.
2. Workers are likely to fit assigned work into the time available to perform it.
3. A good workload usually stimulates output.
4. People usually do their best work when they know that results will be reviewed or inspected.
5. Employees usually feel that someone else is responsible for conditions of work, workplace layout, job methods, type of tools/equipment, and other such factors.
6. Employees are usually defensive about their job security.
7. Employees have natural resistance to change.
8. Employees can support or destroy a supervisor.
9. A supervisor usually earns the respect of his people through his personal example of diligence and efficiency.

J. Areas of Job Improvement
The areas of job improvement are quite numerous, but the most common ones which a supervisor can identify and utilize are:
1. Departmental layout
2. Flow of work
3. Workplace layout
4. Utilization of manpower
5. Work methods
6. Materials handling

7. Utilization
8. Motion economy

K. Seven Key Points in Making Improvements
1. Select the job to be improved
2. Study how it is being done now
3. Question the present method
4. Determine actions to be taken
5. Chart proposed method
6. Get approval and apply
7. Solicit worker participation

l. Corrective Techniques of Job Improvement
Specific Problems
1. Size of workload
2. Inability to meet schedules
3. Strain and fatigue
4. Improper use of men and skills
5. Waste, poor quality, unsafe conditions
6. Bottleneck conditions that hinder output
7. Poor utilization of equipment and machine
8. Efficiency and productivity of labor

General Improvement
1. Departmental layout
2. Flow of work
3. Work plan layout
4. Utilization of manpower
5. Work methods
6. Materials handling
7. Utilization of equipment
8. Motion economy

Corrective Techniques
1. Study with scale model
2. Flow chart study
3. Motion analysis
4. Comparison of units produced to standard allowance
5. Methods analysis
6. Flow chart and equipment study
7. Down time vs. running time
8. Motion analysis

M. A Planning Checklist
1. Objectives
2. Controls
3. Delegations
4. Communications
5. Resources
6. Manpower

7. Equipment
8. Supplies and materials
9. Utilization of time
10. Safety
11. Money
12. Work
13. Timing of improvements

N. Five Characteristics of Good Directions
In order to get results, directions must be:
1. Possible of accomplishment
2. Agreeable with worker interests
3. Related to mission
4. Planned and complete
5. Unmistakably clear

O. Types of Directions
1. Demands or direct orders
2. Requests
3. Suggestion or implication
4. volunteering

P. Controls
A typical listing of the overall areas in which the supervisor should establish controls might be:
1. Manpower
2. Materials
3. Quality of work
4. Quantity of work
5. Time
6. Space
7. Money
8. Methods

Q. Orienting the New Employee
1. Prepare for him
2. Welcome the new employee
3. Orientation for the job
4. Follow-up

R. Checklist for Orienting New Employees   Yes   No
1. Do you appreciate the feelings of new employees
   when they first report for work?   ___   ___
2. Are you aware of the fact that the new employee must
   make a big adjustment to his job?   ___   ___
3. Have you given him good reasons for liking the job and
   the organization?   ___   ___
4. Have you prepared for his first day on the job?   ___   ___
5. Did you welcome him cordially and make him feel needed?   ___   ___

		Yes	No
6.	Did you establish rapport with him so that he feels free to talk and discuss matters with you?	___	___
7.	Did you explain his job to him and his relationship to you?	___	___
8.	Does he know that his work will be evaluated periodically on a basis that is fair and objective?	___	___
9.	Did you introduce him to his fellow workers in such a way that they are likely to accept him?	___	___
10.	Does he know what employee benefits he will receive?	___	___
11.	Does he understand the importance of being on the job and what to do if he must leave his duty station?	___	___
12.	Has he been impressed with the importance of accident prevention and safe practice?	___	___
13.	Does he generally know his way around the department?	___	___
14.	Is he under the guidance of a sponsor who will teach the right way of doing things?	___	___
15.	Do you plan to follow-up so that he will continue to adjust successfully to his job?	___	___

S. Principles of Learning
1. Motivation
2. Demonstration or explanation
3. Practice

T. Causes of Poor Performance
1. Improper training for job
2. Wrong tools
3. Inadequate directions
4. Lack of supervisory follow-up
5. Poor communications
6. Lack of standards of performance
7. Wrong work habits
8. Low morale
9. Other

U. Four Major Steps in On-The-Job Instruction
1. Prepare the worker
2. Present the operation
3. Tryout performance
4. Follow-up

V. Employees Want Five Things
1. Security
2. Opportunity
3. Recognition
4. Inclusion
5. Expression

W. Some Don'ts in Regard to Praise
1. Don't praise a person for something he hasn't done.
2. Don't praise a person unless you can be sincere.
3. Don't be sparing in praise just because your superior withholds it from you.
4. Don't let too much time elapse between good performance and recognition of it

X. How to Gain Your Workers' Confidence
Methods of developing confidence include such things as:
1. Knowing the interests, habits, hobbies of employees
2. Admitting your own inadequacies
3. Sharing and telling of confidence in others
4. Supporting people when they are in trouble
5. Delegating matters that can be well handled
6. Being frank and straightforward about problems and working conditions
7. Encouraging others to bring their problems to you
8. Taking action on problems which impede worker progress

Y. Sources of Employee Problems
On-the-job causes might be such things as:
1. A feeling that favoritism is exercised in assignments
2. Assignment of overtime
3. An undue amount of supervision
4. Changing methods or systems
5. Stealing of ideas or trade secrets
6. Lack of interest in job
7. Threat of reduction in force
8. Ignorance or lack of communications
9. Poor equipment
10. Lack of knowing how supervisor feels toward employee
11. Shift assignments

Off-the-job problems might have to do with:
1. Health
2. Finances
3. Housing
4. Family

Z. The Supervisor's Key to Discipline
There are several key points about discipline which the supervisor should keep in mind:
1. Job discipline is one of the disciplines of life and is directed by the supervisor.
2. It is more important to correct an employee fault than to fix blame for it.
3. Employee performance is affected by problems both on the job and off.
4. Sudden or abrupt changes in behavior can be indications of important employee problems.
5. Problems should be dealt with as soon as possible after they are identified.
6. The attitude of the supervisor may have more to do with solving problems than the techniques of problem solving.
7. Correction of employee behavior should be resorted to only after the supervisor is sure that training or counseling will not be helpful.

8. Be sure to document your disciplinary actions.
9. Make sure that you are disciplining on the basis of facts rather than personal feelings.
10. Take each disciplinary step in order, being careful not to make snap judgments, or decisions based on impatience.

AA. Five Important Processes of Management
1. Planning
2. Organizing
3. Scheduling
4. Controlling
5. Motivating

BB. When the Supervisor Fails to Plan
1. Supervisor creates impression of not knowing his job
2. May lead to excessive overtime
3. Job runs itself—supervisor lacks control
4. Deadlines and appointments missed
5. Parts of the work go undone
6. Work interrupted by emergencies
7. Sets a bad example
8. Uneven workload creates peaks and valleys
9. Too much time on minor details at expense of more important tasks

CC. Fourteen General Principles of Management
1. Division of work
2. Authority and responsibility
3. Discipline
4. Unity of command
5. Unity of direction
6. Subordination of individual interest to general interest
7. Remuneration of personnel
8. Centralization
9. Scalar chain
10. Order
11. Equity
12. Stability of tenure of personnel
13. Initiative
14. Esprit de corps

DD. Change

Bringing about change is perhaps attempted more often, and yet less well understood, than anything else the supervisor does. How do people generally react to change? (People tend to resist change that is imposed upon them by other individuals or circumstances.

Change is characteristic of every situation. It is a part of every real endeavor where the efforts of people are concerned.

1. Why do people resist change?
   People may resist change because of:
   a. Fear of the unknown
   b. Implied criticism
   c. Unpleasant experiences in the past
   d. Fear of loss of status
   e. Threat to the ego
   f. Fear of loss of economic stability

2. How can we best overcome the resistance to change?
   In initiating change, take these steps:
   a. Get ready to sell
   b. Identify sources of help
   c. Anticipate objections
   d. Sell benefits
   e. Listen in depth
   f. Follow up

II. Brief Topical Summaries

   A. Who/What is the Supervisor?
      1. The supervisor is often called the "highest level employee and the lowest level manager."
      2. A supervisor is a member of both management and the work group. He acts as a bridge between the two.
      3. Most problems in supervision are in the area of human relations, or people problems.
      4. Employees expect: Respect, opportunity to learn and to advance, and a sense of belonging, and so forth.
      5. Supervisors are responsible for directing people and organizing work. Planning is of paramount importance.
      6. A position description is a set of duties and responsibilities inherent to a given position.
      7. It is important to keep the position description up-to-date and to provide each employee with his own copy.

   B. The Sociology of Work
      1. People are alike in many ways; however, each individual is unique.
      2. The supervisor is challenged in getting to know employee differences. Acquiring skills in evaluating individuals is an asset.
      3. Maintaining meaningful working relationships in the organization is of great importance.
      4. The supervisor has an obligation to help individuals to develop to their fullest potential.
      5. Job rotation on a planned basis helps to build versatility and to maintain interest and enthusiasm in work groups.
      6. Cross training (job rotation) provides backup skills.

7. The supervisor can help reduce tension by maintaining a sense of humor, providing guidance to employees, and by making reasonable and timely decisions. Employees respond favorably to working under reasonably predictable circumstances.
8. Change is characteristic of all managerial behavior. The supervisor must adjust to changes in procedures, new methods, technological changes, and to a number of new and sometimes challenging situations.
9. To overcome the natural tendency for people to resist change, the supervisor should become more skillful in initiating change.

C. Principles and Practices of Supervision
1. Employees should be required to answer to only one superior.
2. A supervisor can effectively direct only a limited number of employees, depending upon the complexity, variety, and proximity of the jobs involved.
3. The organizational chart presents the organization in graphic form. It reflects lines of authority and responsibility as well as interrelationships of units within the organization.
4. Distribution of work can be improved through an analysis using the "Work Distribution Chart."
5. The "Work Distribution Chart" reflects the division of work within a unit in understandable form.
6. When related tasks are given to an employee, he has a better chance of increasing his skills through training.
7. The individual who is given the responsibility for tasks must also be given the appropriate authority to insure adequate results.
8. The supervisor should delegate repetitive, routine work. Preparation of recurring reports, maintaining leave and attendance records are some examples.
9. Good discipline is essential to good task performance. Discipline is reflected in the actions of employees on the job in the absence of supervision.
10. Disciplinary action may have to be taken when the positive aspects of discipline have failed. Reprimand, warning, and suspension are examples of disciplinary action.
11. If a situation calls for a reprimand, be sure it is deserved and remember it is to be done in private.

D. Dynamic Leadership
1. A style is a personal method or manner of exerting influence.
2. Authoritarian leaders often see themselves as the source of power and authority.
3. The democratic leader often perceives the group as the source of authority and power.
4. Supervisors tend to do better when using the pattern of leadership that is most natural for them.
5. Social scientists suggest that the effective supervisor use the leadership style that best fits the problem or circumstances involved.
6. All four styles—telling, selling, consulting, joining—have their place. Using one does not preclude using the other at another time.

7. The theory X point of view assumes that the average person dislikes work, will avoid it whenever possible, and must be coerced to achieve organizational objectives.
8. The theory Y point of view assumes that the average person considers work to be a natural as play, and, when the individual is committed, he requires little supervision or direction to accomplish desired objectives.
9. The leader's basic assumptions concerning human behavior and human nature affect his actions, decisions, and other managerial practices.
10. Dissatisfaction among employees is often present, but difficult to isolate. The supervisor should seek to weaken dissatisfaction by keeping promises, being sincere and considerate, keeping employees informed, and so forth.
11. Constructive suggestions should be encouraged during the natural progress of the work.

E. Processes for Solving Problems
1. People find their daily tasks more meaningful and satisfying when they can improve them.
2. The causes of problems, or the key factors, are often hidden in the background. Ability to solve problems often involves the ability to isolate them from their backgrounds. There is some substance to the cliché that some persons "can't see the forest for the trees."
3. New procedures are often developed from old ones. Problems should be broken down into manageable parts. New ideas can be adapted from old one.
4. People think differently in problem-solving situations. Using a logical, patterned approach is often useful. One approach found to be useful includes these steps:
   a. Define the problem
   b. Establish objectives
   c. Get the facts
   d. Weigh and decide
   e. Take action
   f. Evaluate action

F. Training for Results
1. Participants respond best when they feel training is important to them.
2. The supervisor has responsibility for the training and development of those who report to him.
3. When training is delegated to others, great care must be exercised to insure the trainer has knowledge, aptitude, and interest for his work as a trainer.
4. Training (learning) of some type goes on continually. The most successful supervisor makes certain the learning contributes in a productive manner to operational goals.
5. New employees are particularly susceptible to training. Older employees facing new job situations require specific training, as well as having need for development and growth opportunities.
6. Training needs require continuous monitoring.
7. The training officer of an agency is a professional with a responsibility to assist supervisors in solving training problems.

8. Many of the self-development steps important to the supervisor's own growth are equally important to the development of peers and subordinates. Knowledge of these is important when the supervisor consults with others on development and growth opportunities.

G. Health, Safety, and Accident Prevention
1. Management-minded supervisors take appropriate measures to assist employees in maintaining health and in assuring safe practices in the work environment.
2. Effective safety training and practices help to avoid injury and accidents.
3. Safety should be a management goal. All infractions of safety which are observed should be corrected without exception.
4. Employees' safety attitude, training and instruction, provision of safe tools and equipment, supervision, and leadership are considered highly important factors which contribute to safety and which can be influenced directly by supervisors.
5. When accidents do occur, they should be investigated promptly for very important reasons, including the fact that information which is gained can be used to prevent accidents in the future.

H. Equal Employment Opportunity
1. The supervisor should endeavor to treat all employees fairly, without regard to religion, race, sex, or national origin.
2. Groups tend to reflect the attitude of the leader. Prejudice can be detected even in very subtle form. Supervisors must strive to create a feeling of mutual respect and confidence in every employee.
3. Complete utilization of all human resources is a national goal. Equitable consideration should be accorded women in the work force, minority-group members, the physically and mentally handicapped, and the older employee. The important question is: "Who can do the job?"
4. Training opportunities, recognition for performance, overtime assignments, promotional opportunities, and all other personnel actions are to be handled on an equitable basis.

I. Improving Communications
1. Communications is achieving understanding between the sender and the receiver of a message. It also means sharing information—the creation of understanding.
2. Communication is basic to all human activity. Words are means of conveying meanings; however, real meanings are in people.
3. There are very practical differences in the effectiveness of one-way, impersonal, and two-way communications. Words spoken face-to-face are better understood. Telephone conversations are effective, but lack the rapport of person-to-person exchanges. The whole person communicates.
4. Cooperation and communication in an organization go hand in hand. When there is a mutual respect between people, spelling out rules and procedures for communicating is unnecessary.
5. There are several barriers to effective communications. These include failure to listen with respect and understanding, lack of skill in feedback, and misinterpreting the meanings of words used by the speaker. It is also common

practice to listen to what we want to hear, and tune out things we do not want to hear.
6. Communication is management's chief problem. The supervisor should accept the challenge to communicate more effectively and to improve interagency and intra-agency communications.
7. The supervisor may often plan for and conduct meetings. The planning phase is critical and may determine the success or the failure of a meeting.
8. Speaking before groups usually requires extra effort. Stage fright may never disappear completely, but it can be controlled.

J. Self-Development
1. Every employee is responsible for his own self-development.
2. Toastmaster and toastmistress clubs offer opportunities to improve skills in oral communications.
3. Planning for one's own self-development is of vital importance. Supervisors know their own strengths and limitations better than anyone else.
4. Many opportunities are open to aid the supervisor in his developmental efforts, including job assignments; training opportunities, both governmental and non-governmental—to include universities and professional conferences and seminars.
5. Programmed instruction offers a means of studying at one's own rate.
6. Where difficulties may arise from a supervisor's being away from his work for training, he may participate in televised home study or correspondence courses to meet his self-development needs.

K. Teaching and Training
1. The Teaching Process
Teaching is encouraging and guiding the learning activities of students toward established goals. In most cases this process consists of five steps: preparation, presentation, summarization, evaluation, and application.

   a. Preparation
   Preparation is two-fold in nature; that of the supervisor and the employee. Preparation by the supervisor is absolutely essential to success. He must know what, when, where, how, and whom he will teach. Some of the factors that should be considered are:
   1) The objectives
   2) The materials needed
   3) The methods to be used
   4) Employee participation
   5) Employee interest
   6) Training aids
   7) Evaluation
   8) Summarization

   Employee preparation consists in preparing the employee to receive the material. Probably the most important single factor in the preparation of the employee is arousing and maintaining his interest. He must know the objectives of the training, why he is there, how the material can be used, and its importance to him.

b. Presentation
In presentation, have a carefully designed plan and follow it. The plan should be accurate and complete, yet flexible enough to meet situations as they arise. The method of presentation will be determined by the particular situation and objectives.

c. Summary
A summary should be made at the end of every training unit and program. In addition, there may be internal summaries depending on the nature of the material being taught. The important thing is that the trainee must always be able to understand how each part of the new material relates to the whole.

d. Application
The supervisor must arrange work so the employee will be given a chance to apply new knowledge or skills while the material is still clear in his mind and interest is high. The trainee does not really know whether he has learned the material until he has been given a chance to apply it. If the material is not applied, it loses most of its value.

e. Evaluation
The purpose of all training is to promote learning. To determine whether the training has been a success or failure, the supervisor must evaluate this learning.
In the broadest sense, evaluation includes all the devices, methods, skills, and techniques used by the supervisor to keep himself and the employees informed as to their progress toward the objectives they are pursuing. The extent to which the employee has mastered the knowledge, skills, and abilities, or changed his attitudes, as determined by the program objectives, is the extent to which instruction has succeeded or failed.
Evaluation should not be confined to the end of the lesson, day, or program but should be used continuously. We shall note later the way this relates to the rest of the teaching process.

2. Teaching Methods
A teaching method is a pattern of identifiable student and instructor activity used in presenting training material.
All supervisors are faced with the problem of deciding which method should be used at a given time.

a. Lecture
The lecture is direct oral presentation of material by the supervisor. The present trend is to place less emphasis on the trainer's activity and more on that of the trainee.

b. Discussion
Teaching by discussion or conference involves using questions and other techniques to arouse interest and focus attention upon certain areas, and by doing so creating a learning situation. This can be one of the most

valuable methods because it gives the employees an opportunity to express their ideas and pool their knowledge.

c. Demonstration
The demonstration is used to teach how something works or how to do something. It can be used to show a principle or what the results of a series of actions will be. A well-staged demonstration is particularly effective because it shows proper methods of performance in a realistic manner.

d. Performance
Performance is one of the most fundamental of all learning techniques or teaching methods. The trainee may be able to tell how a specific operation should be performed but he cannot be sure he knows how to perform the operation until he has done so.
As with all methods, there are certain advantages and disadvantages to each method.

e. Which Method to Use
Moreover, there are other methods and techniques of teaching. It is difficult to use any method without other methods entering into it. In any learning situation, a combination of methods is usually more effective than any one method alone.

Finally, evaluation must be integrated into the other aspects of the teaching-learning process.

It must be used in the motivation of the trainees; it must be used to assist in developing understanding during the training; and it must be related to employee application of the results of training.

This is distinctly the role of the supervisor.

GLOSSARY OF BRIDGE ENGINEERING AND INSPECTION TERMS

	Page
Abutment ...... Aggregate	1
Allowable Unit Stress ...... Arch, Circular	2
Arch, Multi-Centered ...... Backstay	3
Backwall ...... Batter Pile	4
Bay ...... Berm	5
Blanket ...... Bracing	6
Bracing, (cont'd) ...... Brush Curb	7
Buckle ...... Cantilever Beam, Girder, or Truss	8
Cantilever Span ...... Check Analysis	9
Chord ...... Coefficient of Thermal Expansion	10
Cofferdam ...... Coping	11
Corbel ...... Covered Bridge	12
Cracking (reflection) ...... Curves in Plan and Profile	13
Cut ...... Diaphragm	14
Diaphragm Wall ...... Double Movable Bridge	15
Dowel ...... Drip Bead	16
Drip Hole ...... Expansion Dam	17
Expansion Joint ...... Falsework	18
Fascia ...... Fixed Bearing	19
Fixed Bridge ...... Foundation	20
Consolidated Soil Foundation ...... Girder Bridge	21
Girder Span ...... Guide Roller	22
Gusset ...... Hook Belt	23
Howe Truss ...... Joint	24
Keystone ...... Lateral Bracing	25
Lattice ...... Lock Device	26
Locking Mechanism ...... Pontoon Bridge	27
Retractile Draw Bridge ...... Overpass	28
Packing Ring ...... Pedestal Pier	29
Pile Pier or Bent ...... Pin Joint	30
Pin Packing ...... Priming Coat	31
Protection Fence ...... Reinforced Concrete Cantilever Wall	32
Rigid Frame Bridge ...... Rocker and Camshaft	33
Rolled Beams, Rolled Shapes ...... Sag Rod	34
Sash Brace ...... Shafts	35
Shear Lock ...... Skew Angle	36
Skewback ...... Span	37
Spandrel ...... Spreader	38
Springing Line ...... Stress	39
Stress (cont'd) ...... Sump	40
Superelevation ...... Sway Brace	41
Sway Frame ...... Toggle Joint	42
Tolerance ...... Truss	43
Truss Bridge ...... Warren Truss	44
Washer ...... Weep Hole	45
Weld ...... Wing Wall	46
Wing Wall (cont'd) ...... Working Stress	47

GLOSSARY OF BRIDGE ENGINEERING AND INSPECTION TERMS

A

Abutment. A substructure composed of stone, concrete, brick, or timber supporting the end of a single span or the extreme end of a multispan superstructure and, in general, retaining or supporting the approach embankment placed in contact therewith. (See also RETAINING WALLS, WING WALLS.)

The following types are now commonly used:

Cantilever Abutments. An abutment in which the stem or breast wall is fixed rigidly to the footing. The stem, acting as a cantilever beam transmits the horizontal earth pressure to the footing, which maintains stability by virtue of the dead weight of the abutment and of the soil mass resting on the rear portion, or heel, of the footing.

Cellular Abutment. An abutment in which the space between wings, breast wall, approach slab, and footings, instead of containing the approach fill, is hollow. This amounts to an R/C box or boxes comprising the abutment. On some bridges curtain walls are placed between the pier and abutment to simulate a cellular abutment.

Counterforted Abutment. An abutment which develops resistance to bending moment (or horizontal force) in the stem by use of counterforts. This permits the breast wall to be designed as a horizontal beam or slab spanning between counterforts, rather than as a vertical cantilever slab.

Gravity Abutment. A heavy abutment which resists the horizontal earth pressure by its own dead weight.

Integral Abutment. A small abutment cast monolithically with the end diaphragm of the deck. Although such abutments usually encase the ends of the deck beams and are pile supported, spread footings with a combination backwall and end diaphragm may also be used.

L-Abutment. A cantilever abutment with the stem flush with the toe of the footing, forming an L in cross section.

Spill-Thru Abutment. Consists essentially of two or more columns supporting a grade beam spanning the space between them. The approach embankment is retained only in part by the abutment since the embankment's sloped front and side portions extend with their normal slope to envelop the columns. Also called an arched abutment.

Shoulder Abutment. (*Full-Height Abutment.*) A cantilever abutment extending from the grade line of the road below to that of the road overhead. Usually set just off the shoulder.

Semi-Stub Abutment. Cantilever abutment founded part way up the slope, intermediate in size between a shoulder abutment and a stub abutment.

Straight Abutment. (*Trapezoidal or Block.*) An abutment whose stem and wings are in the same plane or whose stem is included within a length of retaining wall. In general, the stem wall is straight but will conform to the alignment of the retaining wall.

Stub Abutment. (*Perched Abutment, Dwarf Abutment.*) An abutment within the topmost portion of the end of an embankment or slope and, therefore, having a relatively small vertical height. While often engaging and supported upon piles driven through the underlying embankment or in-situ material, stubs may also be founded on gravel fill, the embankment, or natural ground itself.

Aggregate. The sand, gravel, broken stone, or combinations thereof with which the cementing material is mixed to form a mortar or concrete. The fine material used to produce mortar for stone and brick masonry and for the mortar component of concrete is commonly termed "fine aggregate" while the coarse material used in concrete only is termed "coarse aggregate."

Allowable Unit Stress. See STRESS.

Anchorage. The complete assemblage of members and parts whether composed of metal, masonry, wood or other material designed to hold in correct position the anchor span of a cantilever bridge, the end of a suspension span cable or a suspension span backstay; the end of a restrained beam, girder or truss span; a retaining wall, bulkhead, or other portion or part of a structure.

Anchor Span. The span which in conjunction with the uplift resisting anchorage device (if any) located at its outermost end, counterbalances and holds in equilibrium the fully cantilevered portion or arm extending in the opposite direction from the major point of support. See CANTILEVER BEAM, GIRDER, OR TRUSS.

Anchor Bolt. A bolt-like piece of metal commonly threaded and fitted with a nut, or a nut and washer at one end only, used to secure in a fixed position upon the substructure the end of a truss or girder, the base of a column, a pedestal, shoe, or other member of a structure. The end intended to engage the masonry may be formed in various ways depending somewhat upon the conditions attending its setting in final position. Among these are the following:

Hooked. Bent either cold or in a heated condition to form a hook-like anchorage. The hooked bolt is commonly built into the masonry preliminary to the placing of the member to be anchored and it may, therefore, be utilized to engage an anchor bar or other device imbedded in the masonry.

Ragged, Barbed or Fanged. Cut with a chisel to produce fin-like projections upon the surface.

Threaded. Shaped with a machine-cut thread. The thread anchorage is commonly supplemented by a nut, or a nut and anchor plate, when the bolt is to be built into the masonry instead of being set in a drilled hole.

Swedged. (*Notched, Hacked.*) Indented and bulged by swedging or nicked transversely and diagonally, or both, by cutting with a chisel.

Angle of Repose. (*Angle of Internal Friction.*) As applied to approach embankments or other earthwork construction: the batter or slope angle with the horizontal at which a given earth material will slide upon itself from a higher to a lower elevation. At all angles less than the angle of repose, the particles of earth are held in equilibrium by the forces of gravity and friction. Relatively slight variations in the quantity of contained moisture produce marked differences in the angle of repose. The inclined surface of a cut or of an embankment either naturally or artificially produced at the angle of repose is commonly described as being at "natural slope."

Anisotropy. The property of some engineering materials, such as wood, exhibiting different strengths in different directions.

Approach Slab. A heavy R/C slab placed on the approach roadway adjacent to and usually resting upon the abutment back wall. The function of the approach slab is to carry wheel loads on the approaches directly to the abutment, preventing the transfer of a horizontal dynamic force through the approach fill to the abutment stem.

Apron. A waterway bed protection consisting of timber, concrete, riprap, paving or other construction placed adjacent to substructure abutments and piers to prevent undermining by scour.

Arch. In general, any structure producing at its supports reactions having both vertical and horizontal components. However, this definition is not intended to include structures of the rigid frame type, although applicable thereto, but instead to apply only to those having throughout their length a curved shape, either actual or approximated.

Specific types of arches adapted to bridge construction derive their names either from the form of curve (or combination of curves assumed for the development of their intradosal surfaces), the support conditions, or their type of construction. The following constitute a portion of the types in use:

Elliptic Arch. One in which the intrados surface is a full half of the surface of an elliptical cylinder. This terminology is sometimes incorrectly applied to a multicentered arch. (An elliptic arch is fitted to stone masonry arches.)

Circular Arch. One in which the intrados surface is a portion of the surface of a right circular cylinder.

Multi-Centered Arch. One in which the intrados surface is outlined by two or more arcs having different radii by intersection tangentially and disposed symmetrically.

Open Spandrel Arch. An arch having spandrel walls with its spandrel unfilled. The arch ring receives its superimposed loads through these walls and, if necessary, through interior spandrel walls, tie or transverse walls, and/or interior columns.

A structure having the spandrel walls replaced by bays or panels with arches, lintel spans, or other constructions supporting the deck construction and these in turn supported by cross walls or columns resting upon the arch ring. See OPEN SPANDREL RIBBED ARCH.

Open Spandrel Ribbed Arch. A structure in which two or more comparatively narrow arch rings function in the place of an arch barrel. The ribs are rigidly secured in position by arch rib struts located at intervals along the length of the ring. The arch rings support a column type open spandrel construction sustaining the floor system and its loads.

Parabolic Arch. One in which the intrados surface is a segment of a symmetrical parabolic surface (suited to concrete arches).

Spandrel Arch. A stone or reinforced concrete arch span having spandrel walls to retain the spandrel fill or to support either entirely or in part the floor system of the structure when the spandrel is not filled.

Segmental Arch. An arch in which the intrados surface is less than half of the surface of a cylinder or cylindroid. Likewise it may take shape wherein any right section will show a parabolic curvature.

Two-Hinged Arch. An arch which is supported by a pinned connection at each support.

Three-Hinged Arch. An arch with end supports pinned and a third hinge (or pin) located somewhere near mid-span making the structure determinate.

Voussoir Arch. A hingeless arch with both supports fixed against rotation. Originally built of wedge-shaped stone blocks or voussoirs, the hingeless arch may also be built of concrete.

Arch Barrel. An arch ring that extends the width of the structure.

Arch Rib. An arch ring unit used in unfilled and open spandrel arch construction in reinforced concrete. Two or more relatively narrow arch ring units or sections support the columns of the bays or panels. The construction may involve a combination of arch ribs with spandrel walls providing an outward appearance akin to that of an unfilled spandrel arch.

One of the arched girders of a plate girder rib arch.

Arm. 1. The portion of a swing bridge or of a retractile draw bridge which forms the span or a portion of the span of the structure. 2. The rear or counterweight leaf of a bascule span. 3. The overhanging (or cantilever) portion of a cantilever bridge which supports the suspended span. 4. In statics, the perpendicular distance between the two parallel equal and opposite forces of a moment.

Armor. A secondary steel member installed to protect a vulnerable part of another member, e.g., steel angles placed over the edges of a joint.

Axle Load. The load borne by one axle of a traffic vehicle, a movable bridge, or other motive equipment or device and transmitted through a wheel or wheels to a supporting structure.

B

Back. See EXTRADOS.

Backfill. Material placed adjacent to an abutment, pier, retaining wall or other structure or part of a structure to fill the unoccupied portion of the foundation excavation.

Soil, usually granular, placed behind and within the abutment and wingwalls.

Backstay. The portion of the main suspension member of a suspension bridge extending between the tower and the anchorage. When this member continues over the towers from anchorage to anchorage, it does not support any portion of the bridge floor system which may be located between the tower and anchorage members of the structure.

A cable or chain attached at the top of a tower and extending to and secured upon the anchorage to resist overturning stresses exerted upon the tower by the suspension span attached to and located between towers.

Backwall. The topmost portion of an abutment above the elevation of the bridge seat, functioning primarily as a retaining wall with a live load surcharge. It may serve also as a support for the extreme end of the bridge deck and the approach slab.

Backwater. The water of a stream retained at an elevation above its normal level through the controlling effect of a condition existing at a downstream location such as a flood, an ice jam or other obstruction.

The increase in the elevation of the water surface above normal produced primarily by the stream width contraction beneath a bridge. The wave-like effect is most pronounced at and immediately upstream from an abutment or pier but extends downstream to a location beyond the body of the substructure part.

Balance Blocks. Blocks of cast iron, stone, concrete or other heavy weight material used to adjust the counterbalance of swing and lift spans.

Balance Wheel. (*Trailing Wheel.*) One of the wheels attached to the superstructure, normally having only a trailing contact upon a circular track surrounding the pivot of a center bearing swing bridge. These wheels maintain the proper balance and lateral stability of the superstructure by preventing excessive rocking or other motion due to wind pressures, shock from operating irregularities, or other causes. When correctly adjusted, a balance wheel will transmit only its own weight to the track and will revolve without load upon its axle.

Balancing Chain. See COUNTERBALANCING CHAIN.

Ballast. Filler material, usually broken stone or masonry, used either to stabilize a structure (as in filling a crib) or to transmit a vertical load to a lower level (as with a railroad track ballast).

Baluster. One of the column-like pieces composing the intermediate portion of a balustrade. Balusters may be varied in cross-sectional shape from round to square. See BALUSTRADE.

Balustrade. A railing composed of brick, stone or reinforced concrete located upon the retaining wall portion of an approach cut, embankment or causeway or at the outermost edge of the roadway or the sidewalk portion of a bridge to serve as a protection to vehicular and/or pedestrian traffic. Its major elements are: (1) plinth, (2) balusters, and (3) capping. However, the web portion may be built without openings instead of balustered or other open construction. See PARAPET.

Base Metal, Structure Metal, Parent Metal. The metal at and closely adjacent to the surface to be incorporated in a welded joint which will be fused, and by coalescence and interdiffusion with the weld will produce a welded joint.

Base Plate. A plate-shaped piece of steel, whether cast, rolled or forged, riveted upon or by other means made an integral part of the base portion of a column, pedestal or other member to transmit and distribute its load either directly or otherwise to the substructure or to another member.

Batten Plate. 1. A plate used to cover the joint formed by two abutting metal plates or shapes but ordinarily not considered as serving to transmit stress from one to the other. 2. A plate used in lieu of lacing to tie together the shapes comprising a built-up member. 3. A term sometimes used as synonymous with Stay Plates to indicate a plate in which the bar latticing or lacing of a bolted, riveted, or welded member terminates.

Batter. The inclination of a surface in relation to a horizontal or a vertical plane or occasionally in relation to an inclined plane. Batter is commonly designated upon bridge detail plans as so many inches to one foot. See RAKE.

Batter Pile. A pile driven in an inclined position to resist forces which act in other than a vertical direction. It may be computed to withstand these forces or, instead, may be used as a subsidiary part or portion of a structure to improve its general rigidity.

When driven and made fast upon the end of a pile bent or a piled pier located in a stream, river, or other waterway, it functions as a cutwater in dividing and deflecting floating ice and debris.

Bay. As applied to a stringer of multibeam structure, the area between adjacent stringers.

Bead. (*Run.*) A narrow continuous deposit of weld metal laid down in a single pass of fused filler metal.

Beam. 1. A simple or compound piece receiving and transmitting transverse or oblique stresses produced by externally applied loads, when supported at its end or at intermediate points and ends. The beam derives its strength from the development of internal bending or flexural stresses. 2. A rolled metal I-shaped or H-shaped piece. 3. An I-shaped piece or member composed of plates and angles or other structural shapes united by bolting, riveting or welding. In general, such pieces or members are described as built-up beams. These terms are applied to and define, in general terms only, variations in shape, size and arrangement of beam type members of reinforced concrete structures.

Reinforced Concrete Beam. Reinforced concrete beam is a construction wherein the tensile stresses, whether resulting from bending, shear, or combinations thereof produced by transverse loading, are by design carried by the metal reinforcement. The concrete takes compression (and some shear) only. It is commonly rectangular or Tee-shaped with its depth dimension greater than its stem width.

Reinforced Concrete T-Beam. Reinforced concrete T-beam derives its name from a similarity of shape to the letter "T," the head or topmost element of the letter consisting of a portion of the deck slab which is constructed integrally with the R/C beam stem.

Bearing Failure. Concerning the usual materials of construction, a crushing under extreme compressive load on an inadequate support; concerning soil, a shear failure in the supporting soil caused by excessively high pressures applied by a footing or pile.

Bearing. (*Fixed.*) A bearing which does not allow longitudinal movement.

Bearing Pad. A thin sheet of material placed between a masonry plate and the masonry bearing surface used to fill any voids due to imperfection of the masonry plate and bearing surface, to seal the interface, and to aid in even distribution of loads at the interface. The bearing pads may be made of alternating layers of red lead and canvas, of sheet lead, or of preformed fabric pads.

Bearing Seat. Top of masonry supporting bridge bearing.

Bearings. (*Live Load, Front Load, Outer.*) Live load bearings are a class of special bearings or supports installed on movable swing and bascule spans. These are engaged when the bridge is in the closed position taking the load off the trunnions and center pivot and preventing the outer end of the lift span from hammering on the rest pier under live load. Front load bearings are live load bearings placed on the support pier of a bascule bridge, and outer bearings are those on swing span and bascule rest piers.

Bed Rock. (*Ledge Rock.*) A natural mass formation of igneous, sedimentary, or metamorphic rock material either outcropping upon the surface, uncovered in a foundation excavation, or underlying an accumulation of unconsolidated earth material.

Bench Mark. A point of known elevation.

Bent. A supporting unit of a trestle or a viaduct type structure made up of two or more column or column-like members connected at their topmost ends by a cap, strut, or other member holding them in their correct positions. This connecting member is commonly designed to distribute the superimposed loads upon the bent, and when combined with a system of diagonal and horizontal bracing attached to the columns, the entire construction functions somewhat like a truss distributing its loads into the foundation.

When piles are used as the column elements, the entire construction is designated a "pile bent" or "piled bent" and, correspondingly, when those elements are framed, the assemblage is termed a "frame bent."

Berm. (*Berme.*) The line, whether straight or curved, which defines the location where the top surface of an approach embankment or causeway is intersected by the surface of the side slope. This term is synonymous with "Roadway Berm."

A horizontal bench located at the toe of slope of an approach cut, embankment or causeway to strengthen and secure its underlaying material against sliding or other displacement into an adjacent ditch, borrow pit, or other artificial or natural lower lying area.

Blanket. A protection against stream scour placed adjacent to abutments and piers and covering the stream bed for a distance from these structures considered adequate for the stream flow and stream bed conditions. The stream bed covering commonly consists of a deposit of stones of varying sizes which, in combination, will resist the scour forces. A second type consists of a timber framework so constructed that it can be ballasted and protected from displacement by being loaded with stones or with pieces of wrecked concrete structures or other adaptable ballasting material.

Boster. A block-like member composed of wood, metal, or concrete used to support a bearing on top of a pier cap or abutment bridge seat. It may adjust bearing heights and avoid constructing the bridge seat to the crown of the roadway, provide an area that may be ground to a precise elevation, or raise a bearing above moisture and debris that may collect on the bridge seat. See also BRIDGE PAD and BRIDGE SEAT PEDESTAL.

Bolted Joint. See RIVETED JOINT.

Bond. 1. In reinforced concrete, the grip of the concrete on the reinforcing bars, thereby preventing slippage of the bars. 2. The mechanical bond resulting from irregularities of surface produced in the manufacturing operations is an important factor in the strength of a reinforced concrete member. For plain round bar reinforcement, it is the difference between the force required to produce initial slip and the ultimate, producing failure. "Deformed" bars utilize this mechanical bond in conjunction with the surface bond. 3. The mechanical force developed between two concrete masses when one is cast against the already hardened surface of the other.

Bond Stress. A term commonly applied in reinforced concrete construction to the stress developed by the force tending to produce movement or slippage at the interface between the concrete and the metal reinforcement bars or other shapes.

Bowstring Truss. A general term applied to a truss of any type having a polygonal arrangement of its top chord members conforming to or nearly conforming to the arrangement required for a parabolic truss.

A truss having a top chord conforming to the arc of a circle or an ellipse. See PARABOLIC TRUSS.

Box Beam. A rectangular-shaped precast, and usually prestressed, concrete beam. These beams may be placed side by side, connected laterally, and used to form a bridge deck, with or without a cast-in-place slab or topping. In such cases, the beam units act together similar to a slab. Where a C-I-P slab is used and the units are spread, they act as beams.

Box Girder (concrete). A large concrete box-shaped beam, either reinforced or prestressed, usually multi-celled with several interior webs. The bottom slab of the girder serves as a flange only, while the top slab is both a flange and a transverse deck slab.

Box Girder (steel). A steel beam or girder, with a rectangular or trapezoidal cross section, composed of plates and angles or other structural shapes united by bolting, riveting, or welding, and having no interior construction except stiffeners, diaphragms, or other secondary bracing parts.

Recently, large steel multi-cell boxes with interior webs have been used as have composite steel box girders in which the concrete slab forms the top side of the box.

Bracing. A system of tension or of compression members, or a combination of these, forming with the part or parts to be supported or strengthened a truss or frame. It transfers wind, dynamic, impact, and vibratory stresses to the substructure and gives rigidity throughout the complete assemblage. In general, the bracing of a girder or of a truss span employs:

(1) A system of horizontal bracing in the planes of the top and bottom flanges or chords, designated according to its location, the top flange, top chord, top or overhead lateral brac-

ing, and the bottom flange, bottom chord or lower lateral bracing.

(2) Cross or X-bracing when placed transversely in vertical planes between beams and stringers and having diagonal members crossed, sometimes termed "Cross Frame." It functions as a diaphragm.

(3) Sway or buck bracing when placed transversely in vertical or nearly vertical planes between trusses. The term "overhead bracing," when applied here, is more appropriate than when applied to the top chord lateral bracing.

(4) Portal bracing consisting of a system of struts, ties and braces placed in the plane of the end posts of the trusses. Portal bracing may be in the plane of one flange of the end posts and described as a "single plane" portal or it may engage both flanges and be described as a "box portal." Without regard to its shape or details the entire portal bracing member is frequently designated as a "portal."

In general, the bracing of trestle and viaduct bents and towers employs:

(1) Transverse bracing engaging the columns of bents and towers in planes located either perpendicular or slightly inclined and transversely to the bridge alignment.

(2) Longitudinal bracing engaging the columns of bents and towers in planes located either perpendicular or slightly inclined and lengthwise with the bridge alignment.

(3) Horizontal bracing engaging the strut members of the transverse and longitudinal bracing of towers. Commonly this bracing is located in a horizontal position and is supported against sagging by vertical hangers or ties.

Bracket. A projecting support or brace-like construction fixed upon two intersecting members to function: (1) as a means of transferring reactions or shear stress from one to the other, or (2) to strengthen and render more rigid a joint connection of the members, or (3) to simply hold one member in a fixed position with relation to the other.

Breast Wall. (*Face Wall, Stem.*) The portion of an abutment between the wings and beneath the bridge seat. The breast wall supports the superstructure loads, and retains the approach fill.

Brick Veneer. See STONE FACING.

Bridge. A structure providing a means of transit for pedestrians and/or vehicles above the land and/or water surface of a valley, arroyo, gorge, river, stream, lake, canal, tidal inlet, gut or strait; above a road, highway, railway or other obstruction, whether natural or artificial.

In general, the essential parts of a bridge are: (1) the substructure consisting of its abutments and pier or piers supporting the superstructure, (2) the superstructure slab, girder, truss, arch or other span or spans supporting the roadway loads and transferring them to the substructure, and (3) the roadway and its incidental parts functioning to receive and transmit traffic loads.

Bridge (composite). A bridge whose concrete deck acts structurally with longitudinal main carrying members.

Bridge (indeterminate). A structure in which forces in the members cannot be determined by static equations alone.

Bridge (prestressed). A bridge whose main carrying members are made of prestressed concrete.

Bridge Pad. The raised, levelled area upon which the pedestal, shoe, sole, plate or other corresponding element of the superstructure takes bearing by contact. Also called Bridge Seat Bearing Area.

Bridge Seat. The top surface of an abutment or pier upon which the superstructure span is placed and supported. For an abutment it is the surface forming the support for the superstructure and from which the backwall rises. For a pier it is the entire top surface.

Bridge Site. The selected position or location of a bridge.

Bridging. A carpentry term applied to the cross-bracing, nailed or otherwise, fastened between wooden floor stringers, usually at the one-third span points, to increase the rigidity of the floor construction and to distribute more uniformly the live load and minimize the effects of impact and vibration.

Brush Curb. A narrow curb, 9 inches or less in width, which prevents a vehicle from brushing against the railing or parapet.

Buckle. To fail by an inelastic change in alignment (usually as a result of compression).

Buffer. (*Bumper.*) A mechanism designed to absorb the concussion or impact of a moving superstructure or other moving part when it swings, rises or falls to its limiting position of motion.

Built-Up Column. (*Built-Up Girder.*) A column, beam or girder, as the case may be, composed of plates and angles or other structural shapes united by bolting, riveting or welding to render the entire assemblage a unit. A built-up girder is commonly described as a plate girder.

Bulkhead. 1. A retaining wall-like structure commonly composed of driven piles supporting a wall or a barrier of wooden timbers or reinforced concrete members functioning as a constraining structure resisting the thrust of earth or of other material bearing against the assemblage. 2. A retaining wall-like structure composed of timber, steel, or reinforced concrete members commonly assembled to form a barrier held in a vertical or an inclined position by members interlocking therewith and extending into the restrained material to obtain the anchorage necessary to prevent both sliding and overturning of the entire assemblage.

Bumper. See BUFFER.

Buttress. A bracket-like wall, of full or partial height, projecting from another wall. The buttress strengthens and stiffens the wall against overturning forces applied to the opposite face by virtue of its depth in the direction of the loads. A buttress may be either integral with or independent of, but must be in contact with, the wall it is designed to reinforce. All parts of a buttress act in compression.

Buttressed Wall. See RETAINING WALL.

Butt Weld. A weld joining two abutting surfaces by depositing weld metal within an intervening space. This weld serves to unit the abutting surfaces of the elements of a member or to join members or their elements abutting upon or against each other.

C

Cable. One of the main suspension members of a suspension type bridge. Its function is to receive the bridge floor loads and transmit them to the towers and anchorages. See SUSPENSION BRIDGE.

Cable Band. The attachment device serving to fix a floor suspender upon the cable of a suspension bridge. In general this device consists of a steel casting provided with bolts or other appliances to securely seize it upon the cable and prevent the bank from slipping from its correct location.

Camber. The slightly arched form or convex curvature, provided in a single span or in a multiple span structure, to compensate for dead load deflection and to secure a more substantial and aesthetic appearance than is obtained when uniformly straight lines are produced. In general, a structure built with perfectly straight lines appears slightly sagged. This optical illusion is unsatisfactory and is most manifest in relatively long structures over rivers or other water areas.

The superelevation given to the extreme ends of a swing span during erection to diminish the deflection or "droop" of the arms when in open position-cantilevered from the center bearing. The decreased deformation below the normal position reduces the energy required to raise the ends in the closed position to permit the arms to function as simple spans.

Cantilever. A projecting beam, truss, or slab supported at one end only.

Cantilever Abutment. See ABUTMENT.

Cantilever Bridge. A general term applying to a bridge having a superstructure of the cantilever type.

Cantilever Beam, Girder, or Truss. A girder or truss having its members or parts so arranged that one or both of its end portions extend beyond the point or points of support. In general, it may have the following forms: (1) two projecting ends counterbalanced over a center support; (2) a projecting end counterbalanced in part by a portion extending beyond the point of support in the opposite direction, and having at its end an uplift resisting anchorage to complete the condition of equilibrium or, instead, the counterbalancing portion or anchor arm may in itself be adequate to counteract the projecting portion; (3) two projecting ends with an intermediate suspended portion, whose weight is completely counterbalanced by the anchor spans and/or anchorages. The end portions may or may not be alike in design.

Cantilever Span. A superstructure span of a cantilever bridge composed of two cantilever arms or of a suspended span connected with one or two cantilever arms.

Cap. (*Cap Beam, Cap Piece.*) The topmost piece or member of a viaduct, trestle, or frame bent serving to distribute the loads upon the columns and to hold them in their proper relative positions.

The topmost piece or member of a pile bent in a viaduct or trestle serving to distribute the loads upon the piles and to hold them in their proper relative positions. See PIER CAP and PILE CAP.

Capillary Action. The process by which water is drawn from a wet area to a dry area through the pores of a material.

Capstone. 1. The topmost stone of a masonry pillar, column or other structure requiring the use of a single capping element. 2. One of the stones used in the construction of a stone parapet to make up its topmost or "weather" course. Commonly this course projects on both the inside and outside beyond the general surface of the courses below it.

Carnegie Beam. See WIDE FLANGE.

Catch Basin. A receptacle, commonly box-shaped and fitted with a grilled inlet and a pipe outlet drain designed to collect the rain water and floating debris from the roadway surface and retain the solid material so that it may be removed at intervals. Catch basins are usually installed beneath the bridge floor or within the approach roadway with the grilled inlet adjacent to the roadway curb.

Catchment Area. See DRAINAGE AREA.

Catwalk. A narrow walkway for access to some part of a structure.

Cement Paste. The plastic combination of cement and water that supplies the cementing action in concrete.

Cement Matrix. The binding medium in a mortar or concrete produced by the hardening of the cement content of the mortar, concrete mixture of inert aggregates, or hydraulic cement and water.

Center Bearing. The complete assemblage of pedestal castings, pivot, discs, etc., functioning to support the entire dead load of a swing span when the end lifts are released or the span is revolving to "open" or to "closed position."

Center Discs. The assemblage of bronze, steel or other metal discs enclosed in the pivot of a center bearing swing span to reduce the frictional resistance in the operation of the span.

Center Lock. A locking device that transmits shear at the centerline of a double leaf bascule or double swing span bridge. This eliminates deflection and vibration at the center of the span.

Center Wedges. On a swing bridge, the assembly of pedestals and wedges located upon the pivot pier beneath the loading girder and operated mechanically to receive the pivot pier live loads and transmit them direct to the substructure, thus relieving the pivot casting from all, or nearly all, live load stress.

Centering. The supporting structure upon which the arch ring is constructed. This commonly consists of timber or metal framework having its topmost portion shaped to conform with the arch intrados and finished by covering with lagging or with bolsters, the latter being spaced to permit treatment of the mortared joints of stone masonry.

Support for formwork for any slab, beam, or other generally horizontal concrete structure.

Centering Device. The mechanical arrangement or device which guides the span of a bascule or a vertical lift span to its correct location upon its supports when being moved from open to closed position.

Channel Profile. Longitudinal section of a channel.

Chase. A channel, groove or elongated recess built into a structure surface for 1) the reception of a part forming a joint or (2) the installation of a member or part of the structure.

Check Analysis. See LADLE ANALYSIS.

Chord. In a truss, the upper and the lower longitudinal members, extending the full length and carrying the tensile and compressive forces which form the internal resisting moment, are termed chords. The upper portion is designated the upper, or top, chord and correspondingly the lower portion is designated the lower, or bottom, chord. The chords may be paralleled, or the upper one may be polygonal or curved (arched) and the lower one horizontal, or both may be polygonal. In general, the panel points of polygonal top chords are designed to follow the arc of a parabola and are, therefore, truly parabolic chords. Polygonal shaped chords are commonly described as "broken chords."

Chord Members. Trusses are commonly divided lengthwise into panels, the length of each being termed a panel length. The corresponding members of the chords are described as upper, or top, chord members and lower, or bottom, chord members.

Clearance. The unobstructed space provided: (1) in a through or half-through truss or a through plate girder type bridge, and (2) upon a deck truss or girder type bridge for the free passage of vehicular and pedestrian traffic. Clearance is measured in vertical and horizontal (lateral) dimensions and may or may not be determined or regulated by standard (clearance diagram) requirements. Vertical clearance for vehicles is measured above the elevation of the floor surface at its crown dimension while horizontal clearance is commonly measured from or with reference to the edge of travelway.

The unobstructed space provided below a bridge superstructure for (1) the passage of a river or stream with its surface burden of floating debris; (2) the passage of navigation craft commonly designated "clear headway" and (3) the passage of vehicular and pedestrian traffic. This form of clearance is frequently designated "under-clearance" to differentiate it from the provision for the requirements of the transportation service supported by the structure.

The space allowed for (1) the tolerance permitted in the dimensions of structural shapes; (2) the free assembling and adjustment of the elements of members or the members of a structure; and (3) the variations in dimensions incident to workmanship, temperature changes and minor irregularities. Among shop and field workers this condition is sometimes described as "the go and come" or "the play" allowance.

Clear Headway. (*Headway.*) The vertical clearance beneath a bridge structure available for the use of navigation. See CLEARANCE. In tidal waters headway is measured above mean high tide elevation.

Clear Span. The unobstructed space or distance between the substructure elements measured, by common practice, between faces of abutments and/or piers. However, when a structure is located upon a stream, river, tidal inlet or other waterway used by navigation, the clear span dimension is measured at mean low water elevation and may be the distance between guard or fender piers, dolphins or other constructions for the protection of navigation.

Clevis. A forked device used to connect the end of a rod upon a gusset plate or other structural part by means of a pin. It commonly consists of a forging having a forked end arranged to form two eyes or eyelets for engaging a pin and a nut-like portion, constructed integrally therewith, for engaging the correspondingly threaded end of a rod. However, the forked end (clevis) may form an integral portion of a rod without provision for adjustment of its length. An adjustable member having a fixed clevis at one end may be fitted with a thread and nut at its opposite end while one having fixed clevises at its ends may be fitted with either a sleeve nut or a turnbuckle in its midlength portion. Lateral bracing and tie-rod diagonals on old steel trusses often use clevises.

Clevis Bar. A member consisting of a rod having upset threaded ends fitted with clevises for engaging end connection pins. To render a clevis bar adjustable after assembling in a structure its ends are right and left threaded, or it may be constructed with a sleeve nut or a turnbuckle within its length, the end threads upon each of its sections being right and left hand and its clevises forged integrally with the body sections of the bar.

Clip Angle. See CONNECTION ANGLE.

Coefficient of Thermal Expansion. The unit strain produced in a material by a change of one degree in temperature.

Cofferdam. In general, an open box-like structure constructed to surround the area to be occupied by an abutment, pier, retaining wall or other structure and permit unwatering of the enclosure so that the excavation for the preparation of a foundation and the abutment, pier, or other construction may be effected in the open air. In its simplest form, the dam consists of interlocking steel sheet piles. See SHEET PILE COFFERDAM.

Collision Strut. A redundant member intended to reinforce the inclined end post of a through truss against damage from vehicular traffic. It joins the end post at a height above the roadway conceived to be the location of collision contact and, commonly, connects it with the first interior bottom chord panel point. The use of collision struts in highway bridges is limited.

Cold Work. The forming, such as rolling or bending, of a material at ordinary room temperature. Also applied to such deformation of steel elements in service under concentrated forces.

Column. A general term applying to a member resisting compressive stresses and having, in general, a considerable length in comparison with its transverse dimensions. This term is sometimes used synonymously for "post."

A member loaded primarily in compression. See also STRUT, POST, PILLAR.

Composite Joint. A joint in which the strength, rigidity or other requisites of its function are developed by combined mechanical devices, or by a fusion weld in conjunction with one or more mechanical means or appliances. The uncertain functioning of joints of this type makes their use undesirable.

Compound Roller. A roller consisting of a large solid cylinder at the center surrounded by a nest of smaller solid rollers having circular spacing bars engaging their ends and enveloped in a large hollow cylinder which forms the exterior surface of the assemblage. The large roller is commonly bored throughout its length at its center to permit observation of its interior material.

Compression (inelastic). Compression beyond the yield point.

Concrete. A composite material consisting essentially of a binding medium within which are embedded particles or fragments of a relatively inert mineral filler. In portland cement concrete, the binder or matrix, either in the plastic or the hardened state, is a combination of portland cement and water. The filler material, called aggregate, is generally graded in size from fine sand to pebbles or stones which may, in some concrete, be several inches in diameter.

Concrete is used in conjunction with stone fragments or boulders, of "one man" size or larger, imbedded therein to produce "cyclopean" or "rubble" concrete.

Connection Angle. (*Clip Angle.*) A piece or pieces of angle serving to connect two elements of a member or two members of a structure.

Consolidation. The time-dependent change in volume of a soil mass under compressive load caused by pore-water slowly escaping from the pores or voids of the soil. The soil skeleton is unable to support the load by itself and changes structure, reducing its volume and usually producing vertical settlements.

Continuous Girder. A general term applied to a beam or girder constructed continuously over one or more intermediate supports.

Continuous Spans. A beam, girder, or truss type superstructure designed to extend continuously over one or more intermediate supports.

Continuous Truss. A truss having its chord and web members arranged to continue uninterruptedly over one or more intermediate points of support, i.e., having three or more points of support.

Continuous Weld. A weld extending throughout the entire length of a joint.

Coping. A course of stone laid with a projection beyond the general surface of the masonry below it and forming the topmost portion of a retaining wall, pier, abutment, wingwall, etc. In general, the top surface is battered (washed) to prevent accumulation of rain or other moisture thereon.

A course of stone capping the curved or V-shaped extremity of a pier, providing a transition to the pier head proper. When so used it is commonly termed the "starling coping," "nose coping," the "cut-water coping" or the "pier extension coping."

In concrete construction the above terms are used without change.

Corbel. A piece or part constructed to project from the surface of a wall, column or other portion of a structure to serve as a support for a brace, short, beam or other member.

A projecting course or portion of masonry serving: (1) as a support for a superimposed member or members of a structure, or (2) as a part of the architectural treatment of a structure. In stone and brick masonry construction, this form of corbel is termed a "corbel course" implying greater length than that of a simple corbel.

Corrosion. The general disintegration and wasting of surface metal or other material through oxidation, decomposition, temperature, and other natural agencies.

Corrosion (electrolytic). Corrosion resulting from galvanic action.

Cotter Bolt. A bolt having a head at one end and near the opposite end a round hole or a hexagonal slot fitted with a cotter pin in the former or a tapered wedge in the latter. A cotter pin is usually formed by bending a piece of half-round rod to form a loop eye and a split body permitting its end to be splayed, thus holding it in position while a cotter wedge may be split for the same purpose, but either of these locking devices may be undivided and only bent sharply to prevent withdrawal. Cotter bolts are commonly fitted with one or two washers.

A cotter bolt fitted with a key is sometimes termed a "key bolt."

Counter. A truss web member which functions only when the span is partially loaded and shear stresses are opposite in sign to the normal conditions. The dead load of the truss does not stress the counter. See WEB MEMBERS.

Counterbalancing Chain. (*Balancing Chain.*) The chains made a part of the operating equipment of a vertical lift bridge to function as a weight counteracting the varying weight of the supporting cables incidental to the movements of the span.

Counterfort. A bracket-like wall projecting from another wall to which it adds stability by being integrally built with or otherwise securely attached to the side to which external forces are applied tending to overturn it. A counterfort, as opposed to a buttress, acts entirely to resist tensile and bending stresses. It may extend from the base either part or all the way to the top of the wall it is designed to reinforce.

Counterforted Wall. See RETAINING WALL.

Counterweight. A weight placed in position so as to counter balance the weight of a movable part (such as bascule leaf or vertical lift span).

Counterweight Well. (*Tail Pit.*) The enclosed space located beneath the bridge floor at the approach end to accommodate the counterweight and its supporting frame during the opening-closing cycle of the movable span of certain types of bascule bridge structures.

Course. In stone masonry, a layer of stone composed of either cut or uncut pieces laid with horizontal or slightly longitudinally inclined joints.

In brick masonry, a layer of bricks bedded in mortar.

Cover. In reinforced concrete, the clear thickness of concrete between a reinforcing bar and the surface of the concrete.

Cover Plate. A plate used in conjunction with flange angles or other structural shapes to provide additional flange section upon a girder, column, strut or similar member.

Covered Bridge. An indefinite term applied to a wooden bridge having in its construction a truss of any type adaptable to its location requirements. To prevent or delay deterioration of the timbers through infiltration of moisture into the framed or other joints, the entire structure, or instead, only its trusses are covered by a housing consisting of boards and shingles or other covering materials, fastened upon the side girts, rafters, purlins, or other parts intended to receive them. A covered bridge may be either a through or a deck structure. The former may be constructed with pony trusses.

Cracking (reflection). Visible cracks in an overlay indicating cracks in the concrete underneath.

Creep. An inelastic deformation that increases with time while the stress is constant.

Crib. A structure consisting of a foundation grillage combined with a superimposed framework providing compartments or coffers which are filled with gravel, stones, concrete or other material satisfactory for supporting the masonry or other structure to be placed thereon. The exterior portion may be planked or sheetpiled to protect the crib against damage by erosion or floating debris.

A structure consisting of a series of box-like compartments built of round or squared timbers having the crosstimbers (compartment division and end wall timbers) drift bolted and dove-tail framed or half framed to interlock with the side timbers, thus producing a rigid framework of the height desired. A portion of the compartment is constructed with floors to serve as ballast boxes for loading and sinking the crib in its final position after which the remaining compartments are filled or partially filled with gravel, stones or other material to render the entire structure stable against the forces to which it may be subjected.

This latter type of crib is used as a protection against wave action and stream currents producing scour and erosion adjacent to bridge structures to prevent undermining of abutments and piers or other substructure elements and also to serve as a training wall averting changes in shore and bank locations.

Cribbing. A construction consisting of wooden, metal or reinforced concrete units so assembled as to form an open cellular-like structure for supporting a superimposed load or for resisting horizontal or overturning forces acting against it.

Cross Frames. Transverse bracings between two main longitudinal members. See DIAPHRAGM and BRACING.

Cross Girder, Transverse Girder. A term applied to large timber members and to metal and reinforced concrete girder-like members placed generally perpendicular to and connected upon the main girders or trusses of a bridge span, including intermediate and end floor beams.

Cross Wall. See DIAPHRAGM WALL.

Crown of Roadway. 1. The crest line of the convexed surface. 2. The vertical dimension describing the total amount the surface is convexed or raised from gutter to crest. This is sometimes termed the cross fall of roadway.

Culvert. A small bridge constructed entirely below the elevation of the roadway surface and having no part or portion integral therewith. Structures over 20 feet in span parallel to the roadway are usually called bridges, rather than culverts; and structures less than 20 feet in span are called culverts even though they support traffic loads directly.

Curb. A stone, concrete or wooden barrier paralleling the side limit of the roadway to guide the movement of vehicle wheels and safeguard bridge trusses, railings or other constructions existing outside the roadway limit and also pedestrian traffic upon sidewalks from collision with vehicles and their loads.

Curb Inlet. See SCUPPER.

Curtain Wall. A term commonly applied to a thin masonry wall not designed to support superimposed loads either vertically or transversely.

A thin vertically placed and integrally built portion of the paving slab of a culvert intended to protect the culvert against undermining by stream scour. A similar construction placed in an inclined position is termed an "apron wall" or "apron."

A wall uniting the pillar or shaft portions of a dumbbell pier. However, its service function is that of a frame composed of struts and braces rendering the entire structure integral in its action. As here applied the term is synonymous with "diaphragm wall."

Curve Banking. See SUPERELEVATION.

Curves in Plan and Profile. A roadway may be curved in its lateral alignment, its vertical contour, or in both alignment and contour combined. The primary curves are described as:

1. Horizontal Curve. A curve in the plan location defining the alignment.

2. Vertical Curve. A curve in the profile location defining the elevation.

Cut. (*Cutting.*) That portion of a highway, railway, canal, ditch or other artificial construction of similar character produced by the removal of the natural formation of earth or rock whether sloped or level. The general terms "side hill cut" and "through cut" are used to describe the resulting cross sections of the excavations commonly encountered.

Cut Slope. A term applied to the inclined surface of an approach cut terminating in the ditch or gutter at its base, which in turn serves to remove accumulations of water from all areas drained into it.

Cylinder Pier. See PIER.

D

Dead Load. A static load due to the weight of the structure itself.

Dead Man. A general term applied to an anchorage member engaging the end of a stay rod, cable or other tie-like piece or part. The anchorage member is made secure through the resistance to movement produced by the earth, stone, brickbats, or other material used to embed and cover the anchor piece which may consist of a wooden log or timber, a metal beam or other structural shape, a quarried stone boulder or any other adaptable object. This type of anchor member is used to restrain and hold in position piles, bulkheads, cribs, and other constructions against horizontal movement as well as to resist the stresses of tie members acting in inclined and vertical directions.

Debris Rack. A grill type barrier used to intercept debris above a sewer or culvert inlet.

Deck. That portion of a bridge which provides direct support for vehicular and pedestrian traffic. The deck may be either a reinforced concrete slab, timber flooring, a steel plate or grating, or the top surface of abutting concrete members or units. While normally distributing load to a system of beams and stringers, a deck may also be the main supporting element of a bridge, as with a reinforced concrete slab structure or a laminated timber bridge.

Deck Bridge. A bridge having its floor elevation at, nearly at, or above the elevation of the uppermost portion of the superstructure.

Decking. A term specifically applied to bridges having wooden floors and used to designate the flooring only. It does not include the floor stringers, floor beams, or other members serving to support the flooring.

Deformation (elastic). Deformation occurring when stress in a material is less than the yield point. If the stress is removed, the material will return to its original shape.

Depth of Truss. As applied to trusses having parallel chords and to polygonal trusses having a midspan length with parallel chords; the vertical distance between the centerlines of action of the top and bottom chords.

Design Load. The loading comprising magnitudes and distributions of wheel, axle or other concentrations used in the determination of the stresses, stress distributions and ultimately the cross-sectional areas and compositions of the various portions of a bridge structure.

The design loading or loadings fixed by a specification are very commonly composite rather than actual, but are predicated upon a study of various types of vehicles. In lieu of a loading so determined for use as "standard," an equivalent uniform load designed to produce resulting structures practically identical with those evolved by the use of such loadings may be used. One or more concentrated loads may be used in conjunction with the uniform load to secure the effect corresponding to the incorporation of especially heavy vehicles within the normally maximum traffic considered as likely to pass upon a given bridge or a series of bridges. Such equivalent loadings are merely a convenience facilitating design operations.

In rating bridges for the Bridge Inspection Manual, either the H or HS trucks with their alternate lane loadings may be used. Or, if desired, the special legal limit trucks: Type 3, Type 3S 2, and Type 3–3, may be used.

Diagonal. See WEB MEMBERS.

Diagonal Stay. A cable support in a suspension bridge extending diagonally from the tower to the roadway system to add stiffness to the structure and diminish the deformations and undulations resulting from traffic service.

Diaphragm. A reinforcing plate or member placed within a member or deck system, respectively, to distribute stresses and improve strength and rigidity. See BRACING.

Diaphragm Wall (cross wall). A wall built transversely to the longitudinal centerline of a spandrel arch serving to tie together and reinforce the spandrel walls together with providing a support for the floor system in conjunction with the spandrel walls. To provide means for the making of inspections the diaphragms of an arch span may be provided with manholes.

The division walls of a reinforced concrete caisson dividing its interior space into compartments and reinforcing its walls. A wall serving to subdivide a box-like structure or portion of a structure into two or more compartments, or sections.

Dike. (*Dyke*). An earthen embankment constructed to provide a barrier to the inundation of an adjacent area which it encloses entirely or in part.

When used in conjunction with a bridge, its functions are commonly those of preventing stream erosion and localized scour and/or to so direct the stream current that debris will not accumulate upon bottom land adjacent to approach embankments, abutments, piers, towers, or other portions of the structure.

This term is occasionally misapplied to crib construction used to accomplish a like result. See CRIB.

Spur Dike. A projecting jetty-like construction placed adjacent to an abutment of the "U," "T," block or arched type upon the upstream and downstream sides, but sometimes only on the upstream side, to secure a gradual contraction of the stream width and induce a free even flow of water adjacent to and beneath a bridge. They may be constructed in extension of the wing wall or a winged abutment.

The common types of construction used for water wings are: (1) Wooden cribs filled with stones; (2) embankments riprapped on the waterway side; and (3) wooden and metal sheet piling.

Spur dikes serve to prevent stream scour and undermining of the abutment foundation and to relieve the condition which otherwise would tend to gather and hold accumulations of stream debris against and adjacent to the upstream side of the abutment.

Dimension Stone. A stone of relatively large dimensions, the face surface of which is either chisel or margin drafted but otherwise rough and irregular, commonly called either "rock face" or "quarry face."

Stones quarried with the dimensions large enough to provide cut stones with given finished dimensions.

Distribution Girder. A beam or girder-like member forming a part of the frame by which the dead and live loads are transmitted to the drum girder of a rim-bearing swing span.

Ditch. See DRAIN.

Diversion Drain. (*Diversion Flume.*) An open top paved drain constructed for the purpose of diverting and conveying water from a roadway gutter down the inclined surface of a bridge approach embankment or causeway.

Dolphin. A group or cluster of piles driven in one to two circles about a center pile and drawn together at their top ends around the center pile to form a buffer or guard for the protection of channel span piers or other portions of a bridge exposed to possible injury by collision with waterbound traffic. The tops of the piles are served with a wrapping consisting of several plies of wire, rope, coil, twist link, or stud link anchor chain, which, by being fastened at its ends only, renders itself taut by the adjustments of the piles resulting from service contact with ships, barges, or other craft. The center pile may project above the others to serve as a bollard for restraining and guiding the movements of water-borne traffic units.

Single steel and concrete piles of large size may also be used as dolphins.

Double Movable Bridge. A bridge in which the clear span for navigation is produced by joining the arms of two adjacent swing spans or the leaves of two adjacent bascule spans at or near the center of the navigable channel. The arms or leaves may act as cantilevers with a shear lock at their junction to provide for the passage of traffic over the joint. The leaves of bascules may be equipped to act as a hinged arch. Spans comprised of two bascule leaves are called double leaf bascule bridges. See MOVABLE BRIDGE.

Dowel. A short length of metal bar, either round or square, used to attach and prevent movement and displacement of wooden, stone, concrete, or metal pieces when placed in a bored, drilled, or cored hole located in their contact surfaces. A dowel may or may not be sized to provide a driving fit in the hole. In stone and premolded concrete structures the dowels are commonly set in lead, mortar, or other material filling the portions of the holes not occupied by the dowels. In concrete construction the plastic concrete is usually either placed around a dowel or the dowel is thrust into it.

In general, dowels function to resist shear forces, although footing dowels in reinforced concrete walls and columns resist bending forces.

Drain. (*Ditch, Gutter.*) A trench or trough-like excavation made to collect water. In general a drain is considered as functioning to collect and convey water whereas a ditch may only serve to collect it.

A gutter is a paved drain commonly constructed in conjunction with the curbs of the roadway or instead built closely adjacent to the paved portion of the roadway.

Drain Hole. (*Drip Hole.*) An aperture extending through a wall to provide an egress for water which might otherwise accumulate upon one of its sides. In this connection the term "weep hole" and "drain hole" are commonly used. See WEEP HOLE.

A cored, punched or bored hole in a box or trough shaped member or part to provide means for the egress of accumulated water or other liquid matter. In areas exposed to freezing temperatures, these holes are used to prevent damage by the expansive force incident to the freezing of water accumulations.

Drainage. The interception and removal of water from the roadway and/or sidewalk surfaces of a bridge or its approaches; from beneath the paved or otherwise prepared roadway and/or sidewalk surfaces of the approaches and from the sloped surfaces of hillsides, cuts, embankments, and causeways; from the backfill or other material in contact with abutments, retaining walls, counterweight wells or parts of a bridge or incidental structure.

A ditch, drain, gutter, gully, flume, catch basin, downspout, scupper, weep hole, or other construction or appliance facilitating the interception and removal of water.

Drainage Area, Catchment Area. The area from which the run-off water passing beneath a bridge or passing a specific location in a river or stream is produced.

Drawbridge. A general term applied to a bridge over a navigable stream, river, lake, canal, tidal inlet, gut or strait having a movable superstructure span of any type permitting the channel to be freed of its obstruction to navigation. A popular but imprecise term.

Probably the earliest use of a drawbridge was for military purposes, utilizing a single leaf hinged frame lifted up or let down by a comparatively simple manually operated mechanism.

Draw Rest. A support constructed upon a fender or guard pier and equipped with a latch block for holding a swing span in open position. This support may consist of a block of masonry, a rigid metal frame or other construction adapted to the service requirements.

Draw Span. A general term applied to either a swing or a retractile type movable superstructure span of a bridge over a navigable stream, river, lake, canal, tidal inlet, gut or strait. See MOVABLE BRIDGE.

Drift Bolt. A short length of metal bar, either round or square, used to connect and hold in position wooden members placed in contact. It may or may not be made with a head and a tapered point. Drift bolts are commonly driven in holes having a diameter slightly less than the bolts. This condition appears to be the recognized practical difference between a drift bolt and a dowel. The difference is more a matter of usage of terms rather than of functions to be performed.

Drip Bead. A channel or groove in the under side of a belt course, coping, or other protruding exposed portion of a masonry structure intended to arrest the downward flow of rain water and cause it to drip off free from contact with surfaces below the projection.

Drip Hole. See DRAIN HOLE.

Drop Inlet. A box-like construction commonly built integrally with the upstream end of a culvert with provision for the water to flow in at its top and to enter the culvert proper at its bottom or within its bottom portion. Vegetable or other material likely to become lodged in the culvert may be retained in the base portion of this receiving device by constructing its base to form a sump below the inlet elevation of the culvert. The culvert inlet may or may not be provided with a grating.

Drum Girder. (*Rim Girder.*) The circular plate girder forming a part of a swing bridge turntable transferring its loadings to the rollers and to the circular track upon which they travel. When the swing span is in "closed" position the drum girder track receives the superstructure dead and live loads and transmits these to the substructure bearing area beneath the track.

Ductility. The ability to withstand non-elastic deformation without rupture.

Dyke. See DIKE.

E

Efflorescence. A white deposit on concrete or brick caused by crystallization of soluble salts brought to the surface by moisture in the masonry.

Elastic Deformation. See DEFORMATION.

Elastomer. A natural or synthetic rubber-like material.

Electrolytic Corrosion. See CORROSION (ELECTROLYTIC).

Element. Metal Structures. An angle, beam, plate or other rolled, forged or cast piece of metal forming a part of a built piece. For Wooden Structures. A board, plank, joist, scantling or other fabricated piece forming a part of a built piece.

End Block. On a prestressed concrete beam, the thickening of the web or increase in beam width at the end to provide adequate anchorage bearing for the post-tensioning wires, rods, or strands.

End Hammer. The hammering action of an end lift device upon its pedestal or bearing plate resulting from the deflections and vibrations set up by the movements of traffic upon a swing span when the lifting device is improperly adjusted.

End Lift. The mechanism consisting of wedges, toggles, link-and-roller, rocker-and-eccentric or other devices combined with shafts, gears, or other operating parts requisite to remove the camber or "droop" of a swing span.

End Post. The end compression member of a truss, either vertical or inclined in position and extending from chord to chord, functioning to transmit the truss end shear to its end bearing.

Epoxy. A synthetic resin which cures or hardens by chemical reaction between components which are mixed together shortly before use.

Equalizer. A balance lever engaging the counterweight and the suspending cables of a vertical lift span as a means of adjustment and equalization of the stresses in the latter.

Equilibrium. In statics, the condition in which the forces acting upon a body are such that no external effect (or movement) is produced.

Equivalent Uniform Load. A load having a constant intensity per unit of its length producing an effect equal or practically equal to that of a live load consisting of vehicle axle or wheel concentrations spaced at varying distances apart, when used as a substitute for the latter in determining the stresses in a structure.

Expansion Bearing. A general term applied to a device or assemblage designed to transmit a reaction from one member or part of a structure to another and to permit the longitudinal movements resulting from temperature changes and superimposed loads without transmitting a horizontal force to the substructure.

The expansion bearing is designed to permit movement by overcoming sliding, rolling or other friction conditions. In general, provision is made for a movement equal to $1\frac{1}{4}''$ in $100'$, thus providing for ordinary irregularities in field erection and adjustment.

Expansion Dam. The part of an expansion joint serving as an end form for the placing of concrete at a joint. Also applied to the expansion joint device itself.

Expansion Joint. A joint designed to provide means for expansion and contraction movements produced by temperature changes, loadings or other agencies.

Expansion Rocker. An articulated assemblage forming a part of the movable end of a girder or truss and facilitating the longitudinal movements resulting from temperature changes and superimposed loads. Apart from its hinge connection the rocker proper is a cast or built-up member consisting essentially of a circular segment integrally joined by a web-like portion to a hub fitted for hinge action either with a pin hole or by having its ends formed into trunnions. In its service operation the rocker is commonly supported upon a shoe plate or pedestal. Strictly speaking, this is a segment of a roller. A short cast or built-up member hinged at both ends, or instead hinged at one end and provided with a circular segment or spherical type bearing at the other to facilitate expansion and contraction on other longitudinal rotational movements.

Expansion Roller. A cylinder so mounted that by revolution it facilitates expansion, contraction or other movements resulting from temperature changes, loadings or other agencies.

Expansion Shoe. (*Expansion Pedestal.*) An expansion bearing member or assemblage designed to provide means for expansion and contraction or other longitudinal movements. In general, the term "shoe" is applied to an assemblage of structural plates or plate-like castings permitting movement by sliding while the term "pedestal" is used to describe assemblages of castings or built-up members securing a somewhat greater total depth and providing for movement either by sliding or by rolling.

The masonry plate or casting is commonly held in a fixed position by anchor bolts and the superimposed shoe plate or pedestal is free to move longitudinally upon it or upon intervening rollers but is restrained from transverse movement either by a rib and slot, by pintles, by anchorage or by anchorage in combination with one of the first two mentioned. The term "bed plate" is sometimes used to designate the bottom portion of the assemblage.

Extrados. (*Back.*) 1. The curved surface of an arch farthest from its longitudinal construction axis or axes. 2. The curve defining the exterior surface of an arch.

Eyebar. A member consisting of a rectangular bar body with enlarged forged ends or heads having holes through them for engaging connecting pins.

An adjustable eyebar is composed of two sections fitted with upset threaded ends engaging a sleevenut or a turnbuckle.

Eyebolt. (*Ringbolt.*) A bolt having a forged eye at one end used, when installed in a structure, to provide means for making fast the end of a cable, a hooked rod or other part or portion of the bridge, or instead to provide a means of anchorage for unrelated equipment or structures.

A ringbolt is essentially an eyebolt fitted with a ring to serve the same purpose as described above for an eyebolt with added articulation.

F

Face Stones. The stones exposed to view in the face surfaces of abutments, piers, arches, retaining walls or other stone structures.

Face Wall.
   Abutment. See BREAST WALL.
   Spandrel Arch Structure. The outermost spandrel walls providing the face surfaces of the completed structure. See SPANDREL ARCH.

Factor of Safety. A factor or allowance predicated by common engineering practice upon the failure stress or stresses assumed to exist in a structure or a member or part thereof. Its purpose is to provide a margin in the strength, rigidity, deformation and endurance of a structure or its component parts compensating for irregularities existing in structural materials and workmanship, uncertainties involved in mathematical analysis and stress distribution, service deterioration and other unevaluated conditions.

Falsework. A temporary wooden or metal framework built to support without appreciable settlement and deformation the weight of a structure during the period of its construction and until it becomes self-supporting. In general, the arrangement of its details are devised to facilitate the construction operations and provide for economical removal and the salvaging of material suitable for reuse.

Fascia. An outside, covering member designed on the basis of architectural effect rather than strength and rigidity although its function may involve both.

A light, stringer-like member spanning longitudinally between cantilever brackets which support large overhangs on girder or beam bridges.

Fascia Girder. As exposed outermost girder of a span sometimes treated architecturally or otherwise to provide an attractive appearance.

Fatigue. The tendency of a member to fail at a lower stress when subjected to cyclical loading than when subjected to static loading.

Felloe Guard. See WHEEL GUARD.

Fender. 1. A structure placed at an upstream location adjacent to a pier to protect it from the striking force, impact and shock of floating stream debris, ice floes, etc. This structure is sometimes termed an "ice guard" in latitudes productive of lake and river ice to form ice flows. 2. A structure commonly consisting of dolphins, capped and braced rows of piles or of wooden cribs either entirely or partially filled with rock ballast, constructed upstream and downstream from the center and end piers (or abutments) of a fixed or movable superstructure span to fend off water-borne traffic from collision with these substructure parts, and in the case of a swing span, with the span while in its open position.

Fender Pier. A pier-like structure which performs the same service as a fender but is generally more substantially built. These structures may be constructed entirely or in part of stone or concrete masonry. See GUARD PIER.

Field Coat. A coat of paint applied upon the priming or base coat or upon a coat subsequently applied and, generally, after the structure is assembled and its joints completely connected by bolts, rivets or welds. This application is quite commonly a part of the field erection procedure and is, therefore, termed field painting.

Fill. (*Filling.*) Material, usually earth, used for the purpose of raising or changing the surface contour of an area, or for constructing an embankment.

Filler (Filler Plate). In wooden and structural steel construction. A piece used primarily to fill a space beneath a batten, splice plate, gusset, connection angle, stiffener or other element.

Filler Metal. Metal prepared in wire, rod, electrode or other adaptable form to be fused with the structure metal in the formation of a weld.

Filler Plate. See FILLER.

Fillet. 1. A curved portion forming a junction of two surfaces which would otherwise intersect at an angle. 2. In metal castings and rolled structural shapes a fillet is used to disseminate and relieve the shrinkage or other stresses tending to overstress and, perhaps, rupture the junction material. In castings it may also provide means for movement to take place at locations where the rigidity of the mold would otherwise resist and obstruct this action. 3. In concrete construction the use of mitered fillets in internal corners of forms not only serves the purposes applying to castings but also facilitates both the placing of concrete and the subsequent removal of forms.

Fillet Weld. A weld joining intersecting members by depositing weld metal to form a near-triangular or fillet shaped junction of the surfaces of the members so joined. This weld serves to unite the intersecting surfaces of two elements of a member.

Filling. See FILL.

Finger Dam. Expansion joint in which the opening is spanned by meshing steel fingers or teeth.

Fish Belly. A term applied to a girder or a truss having its bottom flange or its bottom chord, as the case may be, constructed either haunched or bow-shaped with the convexity downward. See LENTICULAR TRUSS.

Fixed-Ended Arch. See VOUSSOIR ARCH.

Fixed Bearing. The plates, pedestals, or other devices designed to receive and transmit to the substructure or to another supporting member or structure the reaction stresses of a beam, slab, girder, truss, arch or other type of superstructure span.

The fixed bearing is considered as holding the so-termed "fixed end" of the structure rigidly in position, but in practice the clearance space commonly provided in the anchorage may permit a relatively small amount of movement.

Fixed Bridge. A bridge having its superstructure spans fixed in position except that provision may be made in their construction for expansion and contraction movements resulting from temperature changes, loadings, or other agencies.

Fixed Span. A superstructure span having its position practically immovable, as compared to a movable span.

Flange. The part of a rolled I-shaped beam or of a built-up girder extending transversely across the top and bottom edges of the web. The flanges are considered to carry the compressive and tensile forces that comprise the internal resisting moment of the beam, and may consist of angles, plates, or both.

Flange Angle. An angle used to form a flange element of a built-up girder, column, strut or similar member.

Floating Bridge. In general this term means the same as "Pontoon Bridge." However, its parts providing buoyancy and supporting power may consist of logs or squared timbers, held in position by lashing pieces, chains or ropes, and floored over with planks, or the bridge itself may be of hollow cellular construction.

Floating Foundation. A term sometimes applied to a "foundation raft" or "foundation grillage." Used to describe a soil-supported raft or mat foundation with low bearing pressures.

Flood Gate. (*Tide Gate.*) An automatically operated gate installed in a culvert or bridge waterway to prevent the ingress of flood or tide water to the area drained by the structure.

Floor. See DECK.

Floor Beam. A beam or girder located transversely to the general alignment of the bridge and having its ends framed upon the columns of bents and towers or upon the trusses or girders of superstructure spans. A floor beam at the extreme end of a girder or truss span is commonly termed an end floor beam.

Floor System. The complete framework of floor beams and stringers or other members supporting the bridge floor proper and the traffic loading including impact thereon.

Flow Line. The surface of a water course.

Flux. A material which prevents, dissolves, and removes oxides from metal during the welding process. It may be in the coating on a metal stick electrode or a granular mass covering the arc in submerged arc welding and protects the weld from oxidation during the fusion process.

Footbridge. (*Pedestrian Bridge.*) A bridge designed and constructed to provide means of traverse for pedestrian traffic only.

Footing. (*Footing Course, Plinth.*) The enlarged, or spread-out, lower portion of a substructure, which distributes the structure load either to the earth or to supporting piles. The most common footing is the concrete slab, although stone piers also utilize footings. Plinth refers to stone work as a rule. "Footer" is a local term for footing.

Foot Wall. See TOE WALL.

Forms. (*Form Work, Lagging, Shuttering.*) The constructions, either wooden or metal, providing means for receiving, molding and sustaining in position the plastic mass of concrete placed therein to the dimensions, outlines and details of surfaces planned for its integral parts throughout its period of induration or hardening.

The terms "forms" and "form work" are synonymous. The term "lagging" is commonly applied to the surface shaping areas of forms producing the intradoses of arches or other curved surfaces, especially when strips are used.

Forms. (SIP, Stay-in-Place.) A prefabricated metal concrete deck form that will remain in place after the concrete has set.

Form Work. See FORMS.

Foundation. The supporting material upon which the substructure portion of a bridge is placed. A foundation is "natural" when consisting of natural earth, rock or near-rock material having stability adequate to support the superimposed loads without lateral displacement or compaction entailing appreciable settlement or deformation. Also, applied in an imprecise fashion to a substructure unit.

Consolidated Soil Foundation. A foundation of soft soil rendered more resistant to its loads by (1) consolidating the natural material, (2) by the incorporation of other soil material (sand, gravel, etc.) into the soft material, and (3) by the injection of cementing materials into the soil mass which will produce consolidation by lapidification.

Pile or Piled Foundation. A foundation reinforced by driving piles in sufficient number and to a depth adequate to develop the bearing power required to support the foundation load.

Foundation Excavation. (*Foundation Pit.*) The excavation made to accommodate a foundation for a retaining wall, abutment, pier or other structure or element thereof.

Foundation Grillage. A construction consisting of steel, timber, or concrete members placed in layers. Each layer is normal to those above and below it and the members within a layer are generally parallel, producing a crib or grid-like effect. Grillages are usually placed under very heavy concentrated loads.

Foundation Load. The load resulting from traffic, superstructure, substructure, approach embankment, approach causeway, or other incidental load increment imposed upon a given foundation area.

Foundation Pile. A pile, whether of wood, reinforced concrete, or metal used to reinforce a foundation and render it satisfactory for the supporting of superimposed loads.

Foundation Pit. See FOUNDATION EXCAVATION.

Foundation Seal. A mass of concrete placed underwater within a cofferdam for the base portion of an abutment, pier, retaining wall or other structure to close or seal the cofferdam against incoming water from foundation springs, fissures, joints or other water carrying channels. See TREMIE.

Foundation Stone. The stone or one of the stones of a course having contact with the foundation of a structure.

Frame. A structure having its parts or members so arranged and secured that the entire assemblage may not be distorted when supporting the loads, forces, and physical pressures considered in its design. The framing of a truss relates to the design and fabrication of the joint assemblages.

Framing. The arrangement and manner of joining the component members of a bent, tower, truss, floor system or other portion of a bridge structure to insure a condition wherein each element and member may function in accord with the conditions attending its design. Framing must be interpreted as including both design and fabrication for the complete structure.

Friction Roller. A roller placed between parts or members intended to facilitate change in their relative positions by reducing the frictional resistance to translation movement.

Frost Heave. The upward movement of and force exerted by soil due to alternate freezing and thawing of retained moisture.

Frost Line. The depth to which soil may be frozen.

G

Galvanic Action. Electrical current between two unlike metals.

Gauge. The distance between parallel lines of rails, rivet holes, etc. A measure of thickness of sheet metal or wire.

Girder. A flexural member which is the main or primary support for the structure, and which usually receives loads from floor beams and stringers.

Any large beam, especially if built up.

Girder Bridge. A bridge whose superstructure consists of two or more girders supporting a separate floor system of slab and floor beams, or slab, stringer, and floor beam, as differentiated from a multi-beam bridge or a slab bridge.

Any bridge utilizing large, built-up steel beams, prestressed concrete beams, or concrete box girders.

With reference to the vertical location of the floor system, plate girder spans are divided into two types, viz.:

1. Through bridges having the floor system near the elevation of the bottom flanges, whereby traffic passes between the top flanges.

2. Deck bridges having the floor system at or above the elevation of the top flanges whereby traffic passes above the girders.

Girder Span. A span in which the major longitudinal supporting members are girders. It may be simple, cantilever or continuous in type.

Gothic Arch. (*Pointed Arch.*) An arch in which the intrados surface is composed of two equal cylinder segments intersecting obtusely at the crown.

The Tudor Arch is a modification of the Gothic, produced by the introduction of shorter radius cylinder segments at the haunches thus rendering it a four-centered form or type.

Grade Crossing. A term applicable to an intersection of two or more highways, two railroads or one railroad and one highway at a common grade or elevation; now commonly accepted as meaning the last of these combinations.

Grade Intersection. The location where a horizontal and an inclined length of roadway or, instead, two inclined lengths meet in profile. To provide an easy transition from one to the other they are connected by a vertical curve and the resulting profile is a sag or a summit depending upon whether concaved or convexed upward.

Grade Separation. A term applied to the use of a bridge structure and its approaches to divide or separate the crossing movement of vehicular, pedestrian or other traffic, by confining portions thereof to different elevations. See OVERPASS.

Gradient. The rate of inclination of the roadway and/or sidewalk surface(s) from horizontal applying to a bridge and its approaches. It is commonly expressed as a percentage relation of horizontal to vertical dimensions.

Gravity Wall. See RETAINING WALL.

Grillage. A platform-like construction or assemblage used to insure distribution of loads upon unconsolidated soil material. See FOUNDATION GRILLAGE.

A frame composed of I-beams or other structural shapes rigidly connected and built into a masonry bridge seat, skewback or other substructure support to insure a satisfactory distribution of the loads transmitted by the superstructure shoes, pedestals, or other bearing members.

Grout. A mortar having a sufficient water content to render it a free-flowing mass, used for filling (grouting) the interstitial spaces between the stones or the stone fragments (spalls) used in the "backing" portion of stone masonry; for fixing anchor bolts and for filling cored spaces in castings, masonry, or other spaces where water may accumulate.

Guard Pier. (*Fender Pier.*) A pier-like structure built at right angles with the alignment of a bridge or at an angle therewith conforming to the flow of the stream current and having adequate length, width, and other provisions to protect the swing span in its open position from collision with passing vessels or other water-borne equipment and materials. It also serves to protect the supporting center pier of the swing span from injury and may or may not be equipped with a rest pier upon which the swing span in its open position may be latched. The type of construction varies with navigation and stream conditions from a simple pile and timber structure or a wooden crib-stone ballasted structure to a solid masonry one, or to a combination construction. In locations where ice floes or other water-borne materials may accumulate upon the upstream pier end, a cutwater or a starling is an essential detail. See FENDER PIER.

Guard Railing. (*Guard Rail, Guard Fence, Protection Railing.*) A fencelike barrier or protection built within the roadway shoulder area and intended to function as a combined guide or guard for the movement of vehicular and/or pedestrian traffic and to prevent or hinder the accidental passage of such traffic beyond the berm line of the roadway.

Guide. A member or element of a member functioning to hold in position and direct the movement of a moving part.

Guide Roller. A roller fixed in its location or position and serving both as a friction roller and as a pilot or guide for a part or member in contact with it.

Gusset. A plate serving to connect or unite the elements of a member or the members of a structure and to hold them in correct alignment and/or position at a joint. A plate may function both as a gusset and splice plate while under other conditions it may function as a gusset and stay plate. See SPLICE PLATE and STAY PLATE.

Gutter. See DRAIN.

Gutter Grating. A perforated or barred cover placed upon an inlet to a drain to prevent the entrance of debris gathered and brought to the inlet by the water stream.

Guy. A cable, chain, rod or rope member serving to check and control undulating, swaying or other movements, or to hold a fixed alignment or position a structure or part thereof by having one of its ends bolted, clamped, tied or otherwise fastened upon it, the other end being secured upon a part or member of the structure or upon a disconnected anchorage.

H

H-Beam. (*H-Pile.*) A rolled steel bearing pile having an H-shaped cross section.

Hand Hole. Holes provided in cover plates of built-up box sections to permit access to the interior for maintenance and construction purposes.

Hand Operated Span. A manpower-operated movable span to which the force for operating is applied upon a capstan, winch, windlass or wheel.

The terms "Hand Draw Bridge," "Hand Swing Bridge" and "Lever Swing Bridge" are applied to swing spans of hand-operated type.

Hand Rail. See RAILING.

Hanger. A tension element or member serving to suspend or support a member attached thereto. A tension member, whether a rod, eyebar, or built-up member supporting a portion of the floor system of a truss, arch or suspension span. In suspension bridge construction wire cable is used and the complete member is commonly termed a "suspender."

Haunch. A deepening of a beam or column, the depth usually being greatest at the support and vanishing towards or at the center. The curve of the lower flange or surface may be circular, elliptic, parabolic, straight or stepped.

Head. A measure of water pressure expressed in terms of an equivalent weight or pressure exerted by a column of water. The height of the equivalent column of water is the head.

Headwater. The depth of water at the inlet end of a pipe, culvert, or bridge waterway.

Headway. See CLEAR HEADWAY.

Heat Treatment. Any of a number of various operations involving heating and cooling that are used to impart specific properties to metals. Examples are tempering, quenching, annealing, etc.

Heel of Span. The rotation end of a bascule span.

Heel Stay. See SHEAR LOCK.

Hemispherical Bearing. A bearing which utilizes the ball and socket principle by having male and female spherical segments forming the bearing areas or surfaces of the interlocking elements, thus providing for movements by revolution in any direction.

In order to insure accurate adjustment of the mating elements it is essential that a pintle or other self-centering device be provided as a part of the construction details.

Hinged Joint. A joint constructed with a pin, cylinder segment, spherical segment or other device permitting movement by rotation.

Hip Joint. (*The Hip of Truss.*) The juncture of the inclined end post with the end top chord member of a truss. In the truss of a swing span, the juncture of the inclined end post located adjacent to the center of span, with the combined top chord and the connecting tie member between the swing span arms, is designated an "interior hip joint" or an "interior hip of truss."

Hip Vertical. The vertically placed tension member engaging the hip joint of a truss and supporting the first panel floor beam in a through truss span, or instead, only the bottom chord in a deck truss span.

Hook Bolt. 1. A bolt having a forged hook at one end used for essentially the same purposes as described for an eyebolt. See EYEBOLT. 2. A bolt having its head end bent at or nearly at a right angle with its body portion and, when in use, acting as a clamp.

Howe Truss. A truss of the parallel chord type originally adapted to wooden bridge construction but with the later development of metal bridge trusses it was adopted only to a limited extent due to the uneconomical use of metal in its compression members. The web system is composed of vertical(tension) rods at the panel points with an X pattern of diagonals.

Hydrolysis. A chemical process of decomposition in the presence of elements of water.

Hydroplaning. Loss of contact between a tire and the deck surface when the tire planes or glides on a film of water covering the deck.

I

Ice Guard. See FENDER.

Impact. As applied to bridge design—a dynamic increment of stress equivalent in magnitude to the difference between the stresses produced by a static load when quiescent and by a load moving in a straight line.

Impact Load. (*Impact Allowance.*) A load allowance or increment intended to provide for the dynamic effect of a load applied in a manner other than statically.

Indeterminate Stress. A stress induced by the incorporation of a redundant member in a truss or of an additional reaction in a beam rendering stress distributions indeterminate by the principles of statics.

In redundant beams or trusses the distribution of the stresses depends upon the relative stiffnesses or areas of the members.

Inelastic Compression. See COMPRESSION (INELASTIC).

Inspection Ladders. (*Inspection Platforms and Walks.*) Special devices or appliances designed to afford a safe and efficient means for making inspections and tests to determine the physical condition of a structure and to facilitate repair operations incident to its maintenance which must include these service conveniences. To prevent displacement they will be, in general, rigidly fixed upon the structure. However, certain types of structures are adapted to the use of movable platform devices for suspension from the railings or other parts which are or may be adapted thereto.

The term "catwalk" is applied to narrow permanent walks supported, usually, by brackets or by hangers and located below and/or above the bridge floor. This term is also applied to temporary walks used in the construction of suspension and other types of bridges as utilities facilitating the movements of labor and materials, and the supervision and inspection operations.

Intercepting Ditch. A ditch constructed to prevent surface water from flowing in contact with the toe of an embankment or causeway or down the slope of a cut.

Intergranular Pressure. Pressure between soil grains.

Intermittent Weld. A noncontinuous weld commonly composed of a series of short welds with intervening spaces arranged with fixed spacing and length.

Intrados. (*Soffit.*) The curved surface of an arch nearest its longitudinal (constructional) axis or axes. Properly speaking the intrados is the curve defining the interior surface of the arch.

J

Jack Stringer. The outermost stringer supporting the bridge floor in a panel or bay. It is commonly of less strength than a main stringer.

Joint. In Stone Masonry. The space between individual stones.

In Concrete Construction. The divisions or terminations of continuity produced at predetermined locations or by the completion of a period of construction operations. These may or may not be open.

In a Truss or Frame Structure. (1) A point at which members of a truss or frame are joined, (2) the composite assemblage of pieces or members around or about the point of intersection of their lines of action in a truss or frame.

K

Keystone. A stone of the crown string course of an arch. However, this term is most commonly applied to the symmetrically shaped wedge-like stone located in a head ring course at the crown of the arch, which thus exposed to view produces desired architectural effects. This head ring stone commonly extends short distances above and below the extradosal and intradosal limits of the voussoirs of adjoining string courses. The final stone placed, thereby closing the arch.

King-Post. (*King Rod.*) The post member in a "King-post" type truss or in a "King-post" portion of any other type of truss.

King-Post Truss. A truss adapted to either wooden or metal bridge construction. It is composed of two triangular panels with a common vertical. A beam or chord extends the full truss length.

In the through form of this truss the inclined members are struts and the vertical or King-post is a hanger. In the deck truss, the two inclined members become tie (tension) members and the vertical becomes a post (compression) member.

The King-post truss is the simplest of trusses belonging to the triangular system. However, it is described with equal accuracy as a trussed girder.

K-Truss. A truss having a web system wherein the diagonal members intersect the vertical members at or near the mid-height. When thus arranged the assembly in each panel forms a letter "K"; hence the name "K-Truss."

Knee Brace. A member usually short in length, engaging at its ends two other members which are joined to form a right angle or a near-right angle. It thus serves to strengthen and render more rigid the connecting joint.

Knee Wall. A return of the abutment backwall at its ends to enclose the bridge seat on three of its sides. The returned ends may or may not serve to retain a portion of the bridge approach material, but do hide the bridge seat, beam ends, and bearings.

Knuckle. An appliance forming a part of the anchorage of a suspension bridge main suspension member permitting free longitudinal movement of the anchorage chain at locations where it changes its direction and providing for elastic deformations induced by temperature changes and the pull exerted by the suspension member.

L

Lacing. See LATTICE.

Ladle Analysis. (*Ladle Test, Check Analysis.*) As applied to the chemical determination of the constituents of steel or other ferrous metals, the terms "ladle analysis" and "ladle test" are synonymous and are used to designate the analysis of drillings or chips taken from the small ingot or ingots cast from a spoon sample taken from each melt during the pouring (teeming) operation.

The term "check analysis" is applied to the analysis of drillings taken from the finished material after being rolled, forged or otherwise worked. It is primarily intended as a check determination of the results secured from the ingots made at the furnace. Specifications may provide a tolerance or margin of variation between the ingot and the finished material analyses.

Lagging. See FORMS.

Laminated Timber. Timber planks glued together to form a larger member. Laminated timber is used for frames, arches, beams, and columns.

Lap Joint. A joint in which a splice is secured by fixing two elements or members in a position wherein they project upon or overlap each other.

Latch. (*Latch Block.*) The device or mechanism commonly provided at one or both ends of a swing span to hold the span in its correct alignment when in its closed position, and in readiness for the application of the end wedges or lifts.

Latch Lever. A hand-operated lever attached by a rod, cable or chain to the latching device of a movable span and used to engage and to release the latch.

Lateral Bracing. (*Lateral System.*) The bracing assemblage engaging the chords and inclined end posts of truss and the flanges of plate girder spans in the horizontal or inclined planes of these members to function in resisting the transverse forces resulting from wind, lateral vibration, and traffic movements tending to produce lateral movement and deformation. See BRACING.

Lattice. (*Latticing, Lacing.*) An assemblage of bars, channels, or angles singly or in combination bolted, riveted or welded in inclined position upon two or more elements of a member to secure them in correct position and assure their combined action. When the bars form a double system by being inclined in opposite directions the assemblage is termed "double lattice." When so arranged the bars are commonly connected at their intermediate length intersections.

Lattice Truss. In general, a truss having its web members inclined but more commonly the term is applied to a truss having two or more web systems composed entirely of diagonal members at any interval and crossing each other without reference to vertical members. Vertical members when used perform the functions of web stiffeners. They may be utilized for connecting vertically placed brace frames to the girders.

Leaf. The portion of a bascule bridge which forms the span or a portion of the span of the structure.

Ledge Course. In masonry or concrete construction, a course forming a projection beyond the plane of a superimposed course or courses. The projecting portion may be wash dressed to permit an unobstructed flow of rain water down the wall surface. A ledge course differs from a belt or string course in having a projection only upon its topmost bed. This construction is also known as a "Ledger Course."

Ledge Rock. See BED ROCK.

Lenticular Truss. (*Fish Belly Truss.*) A truss having polygonal top and bottom chords curved in opposite directions with their ends meeting at a common joint. The chords nearly coincide with parabolic arcs. In through spans the floor system is suspended from the joints of the bottom chord and the end posts are vertical.

Lifting Girder. A girder or girder-like member engaging the trusses or girders of a vertical lift span and to which the suspending cables are attached.

Lift Span. A superstructure span moved by revolution in a vertical plane or by lifting in a vertical direction to free a navigable waterway of the obstruction it presents to navigation. See MOVABLE BRIDGE.

Link and Roller. An adjustable device or assemblage consisting of a hinged strut-like link fitted with a roller at its bottom end, supported upon a shoe plate or pedestal and operated by a thrust strut serving to force it into a vertical position and to withdraw it therefrom. When installed at each outermost end of the girders or the trusses of a swing span their major function is to lift them to an extent that their camber or droop will be removed and the arms rendered free to act as simple spans. When the links are withdrawn to an inclined position fixed by the operating mechanism the span is free to be moved to an open position.

Lintel Bridge. A bridge having a single span or a series of spans composed of slabs of stone or reinforced concrete spanning the interval or intervals between its substructure elements.

Lintel Stone. A stone used to support a wall over an opening.

Live Load. A dynamic load such as traffic load that is supplied to a structure suddenly or that is accompanied by vibration, oscillation or other physical condition affecting its intensity.

Loading Girder. A term applied to the girder or girders of a center bearing type swing span, located above the pivot pier and functioning to concentrate the superimposed load upon the pivot.

Location. The longitudinal line assumed for construction purposes, which may or may not coincide with the center line of bridge; together with the gradients upon the bridge and its approaches established upon the construction plans and/or on the bridge site preparatory to construction operations.

Lock Device. A mechanism which locks the movable span of a bridge in its "closed" position and prevents movement to "open" position until released. The device on a swing span may also be used to lock the span in its "open" position at times when wind or other conditions render this prevention of movement desirable.

Locking Mechanism. A general term applied to the various devices used for holding in their closed or traffic service position a bascule, vertical lift or swing span of any type. This term applies not only to the locking or latching appliance but includes also the levers, shafts, gears or other parts incidental to their service operation.

Longitudinal Bracing. (*Longitudinal System.*) The bracing assemblage engaging the columns of trestle and viaduct bents and towers in perpendicular or slightly inclined planes located lengthwise with the bridge structure and functioning to resist the longitudinal forces resulting from traffic traction and momentum, wind or other forces tending to produce longitudinal movement and deformation. See BRACING.

M

Margin. See TOLERANCE.

Masonry. A general term applying to abutments, piers, retaining walls, arches and allied structures built of stone, brick or concrete and known correspondingly as stone, brick or concrete masonry.

Masonry Plate. A steel plate or a plate-shaped member whether cast, rolled or forged, built into or otherwise attached upon an abutment, pier, column, or other substructure part to support the rocker, shoe, or pedestal of a beam, girder or truss span and to distribute the load to the masonry beneath.

Mattress. A mat-like protective covering composed of brush and poles, commonly willow, compacted by wire or other lashings and ties and placed upon river and stream beds and banks; lake, tidal or other shores to prevent erosion and scour by water movement action.

Meander. The tortuous channel that characterizes the serpentine curvature of a slow flowing stream in a flood plain.

Member. An individual angle, beam, plate forging, casting or built piece, with or without connected parts for joints, intended utlimately to become an integral part of an assembled frame or structure.

Milled. In steel fabrication, a careful grinding of an edge or surface to assure good bearing or fit.

Mortar. An intimate mixture, in a plastic condition, of cement, or other cementitious material with fine aggregate and water, used to bed and bind together the quarried stones, bricks, or other solid materials composing the major portion of a masonry construction or to produce a plastic coating upon such constructions.

The indurated jointing material filling the interstices between and holding in place the quarried stones or other solid materials of masonry construction. Correspondingly, this term is applied to the cement coating used to produce a desired surface condition upon masonry constructions and is described as the "mortar finish," "mortar coat," "floated face or surface," "parapet," etc.

The component of concrete composed of cement, or other indurating material with sand and water when the concrete is a mobile mass and correspondingly this same component after it has attained a rigid condition through hardening of its cementing constituents.

Movable Bridge. A bridge of any type having one or more spans capable of being raised, turned, lifted, or slid from its normal vehicular and/or pedestrian service location to provide for the passage of navigation. The movements of the superstructure may be produced either manually or by engine power.

Bascule Bridge. A bridge having a superstructure designed to swing vertically about a fixed or a moving horizontal axis. The axis may be the center of a hinge pin or trunnion, or it may be only a line fixing the center of a circular rotation combined with translation, (rolling lift bridge).

Vertical Lift Bridge. A bridge having a superstructure designed to be lifted vertically by cables or chains attached to the ends of the movable span and operating over sheaves placed upon the tops of masts or towers or by other mechanical devices functioning to lift the span to "open" position and to lower it into its "closed" position with its ends seated upon bridge seat pedestals.

Pontoon Bridge. A bridge ordinarily composed of boats, scows or pontoons so connected to the deck or floor construction that they are retained in position and serve to support vehicular and pedestrian traffic. A pontoon bridge may be so constructed that a portion is removable and thus serve to facilitate navigation. Modern floating bridges may have pontoons built integrally with the deck.

Retractile Draw Bridge. (*Traverse Draw Bridge.*) A bridge having a superstructure designed to move horizontally either longitudinally or diagonally from "closed" to "open" position, the portion acting in cantilever being counterweighted by that supported upon rollers.

Rolling Lift Bridge. A bridge of the bascule type devised to roll backward and forward upon supporting girders when operated throughout an "open and closed" cycle.

Swing Bridge. A bridge having a superstructure designed to revolve in a horizontal plane upon a pivot from its "closed" position to an "open" one wherein its alignment is normal or nearly normal to the original alignment. For a structure having its substructure skewed the design commonly provides for revolution in one direction only and through an arc less than 90°. The superstructure is balanced upon a center and its ends acting as cantilevers when the end bearings are released may be either equal in length or unequal with the shorter one counterweighted to permit free revolution movement. A swing bridge with its end bearings released may be supported: (1) upon a single center bearing; (2) upon a circular rim or drum supported upon rollers and (3) upon a center bearing and rim in combination.

Movable Span. A general term applied to a superstructure span designed to be withdrawn, swung, lifted or otherwise moved longitudinally, horizontally or vertically to free a navigable waterway of the obstruction it presents to navigation.

Mud Sill. A single piece of timber or a unit composed of two or more timbers placed upon a soil foundation as a support for a single column, a framed trestle bent, or other similar member of a structure.

A load distribution piece aligned with and placed directly beneath the sill piece of a framed bent is termed a "Sub-sill" although it may serve also as a mud sill.

N

N-Truss. See PRATT TRUSS.

Natural Slope. See ANGLE OF REPOSE.

Neat Line. (*Neat Surface.*) The general alignment position or the general surface position of a face or other surface exlusive or regardless of the projections of individual stones, belts, belt courses, copings or other incidental or ancillary projections in a masonry structure.

Neutral Axis. The axis of a member in bending along which the strain is zero. On one side of the neutral axis the fibers are in tension, on the other side in compression.

Normal Roadway Cross Section. The roadway cross section with its crown in countradistinction to the superelevated cross sections used upon horizontal curves of different degrees of curvature and the transition lengths required for their development.

Nose. A projection acting as a cut water on the upstream end of a pier. See STARLING.

Notch Effect. Stress concentration caused by an abrupt discontinuity or change in section. Such concentrations may have a marked effect on fatigue strength of a member.

O

Operator's House. (*Operator's Cabin.*) The building containing the power plant and operating machinery and devices required for the operator's (bridge tender's) work in executing the complete cycle of opening and closing a movable bridge span.

Overpass. (*Underpass.*) The applications of these terms are definitely indicated by their constructions. For any given combination of highways, railways, and canals, the basic element is a separation of grades. The use of these terms is fixed by the relative elevations of the traffic ways involved; for the lower roadway, the structure is an underpass; for the upper roadway, an overpass.

P

Packing Ring. See SEPARATOR.

Paddleboard. Striped, paddle-shaped signs or boards placed on the roadside in front of a narrow bridge as a warning.

Panel. (*Sub-Panel.*) The portion of a truss span between adjacent points of intersection of web and chord members and, by common practice, applied to intersections upon the bottom chord. A truss panel divided into two equal or unequal parts by an intermediate web member, generally by a subdiagonal or a hanger, forms the panel division commonly termed "subpanels."

Panel Point. The point of intersection of primary web and chord members of a truss.

Parabolic Truss. (*Parabolic Arched Truss.*) A polygonal truss having its top chord and end post vertices coincident with the arc of a parabola; its bottom chord straight and its web system either triangular or quadrangular.

Parapet. A wall-like member composed of brick, stone or reinforced concrete construction upon the retaining wall portion of an approach cut, embankment or causeway or along the outermost edge of the roadway or the sidewalk portion of a bridge to serve as a protection to vehicular and/or pedestrian traffic. While the terms balustrade and parapet are used, in a measure, synonymously, the latter is commonly regarded as applying to barriers of the block type without openings within the body portion. See BALUSTRADE.

Parker Truss. See PRATT TRUSS.

Pedestal. A cast or built-up metal member or assemblage functioning primarily to transmit load from one member or part of a structure to another member or part. A secondary function may be to provide means for longitudinal, transverse or revolution movements.

A block-like construction of stone, concrete or brick masonry placed upon the bridge seat of an abutment or pier to provide a support for the ends of the beams.

Pedestrian Bridge. See FOOT BRIDGE.

Penetration. When Applied to Creosoted Lumber. The depth to which the surface wood is permeated by the creosote oil.

When Applied to Welding. The depth to which the surface metal of the structure part (Structure metal) is fused and coalesced with the fused weld metal to produce a weld joint. See WELD PENETRATION.

When Applied to Pile Driving. The depth a pile tip is driven into the ground.

Pier. A structure composed of stone, concrete, brick, steel or wood and built in shaft or block-like form to support the ends of the spans of a multi-span superstructure at an intermediate location between its abutments.

The following types of piers are adapted to bridge construction. The first three are functional distinctions, while the remaining types are based upon form or shape characteristics.

Anchor Pier. A pier functioning to resist an uplifting force, as for example: The end reaction of the anchor arm of a cantilever bridge. This pier functions as a normal pier structure when subjected to certain conditions of superstructure loading.

Pivot Pier. Center Pier. A term applied to the center bearing pier supporting a swing span while operating throughout an opening-closing cycle. This pier is commonly circular in shape but may be hexagonal, octagonal or even square in plan.

Rest Pier. A pier supporting the end of a movable bridge span when in its closed position.

Cylinder Pier. A type of pier produced by sinking a cylindrical steel shell to a desired depth and filling it with concrete. The foundation excavation may be made by open dredging within the shell and the sinking of the shell may proceed simultaneously with the dredging.

Dumbbell Pier. A pier consisting essentially of two cylindrical or rectangular shaped piers joined by a web constructed integrally with them.

Hammerhead Pier. (*Tee Pier.*) A pier with a cylindrical or rectangular shaft, and a relatively long, transverse cap.

Pedestal Pier. A structure composed of stone, concrete or brick built in block-like form—supporting a column of a bent or tower of a viaduct. Foundation conditions or other practical considerations may require that two or more column supports be placed upon a single base or footing section. To prevent accumulation of stream debris at periods of high water or under other conditions the upstream piers may be constructed with cut-waters and in addition the piers may be connected by an integrally built web between them. When composed only of a wide blocklike form, it is called a wall or solid pier.

Pile Pier or Bent. A pier composed of driven piles capped or decked with a timber grillage or with a reinforced concrete slab forming the bridge seat.

Rigid Frame Pier. Pier with two or more columns and a horizontal beam on top constructed to act like a frame.

Pier Cap. (*Pier Top.*) The topmost portion of a pier. On rigid frame piers, the term applies to the beam across the column tops. On hammerhead and tee piers, the cap is a continuous beam.

Pilaster. A column-like projection upon a face surface rarely intended to serve as a structural member but instead functioning as an architectural treatment to relieve the blankness of a plane surface.

Pile. A rod or shaft-like linear member of timber, steel, concrete, or composite materials driven into the earth to carry structure loads thru weak strata of soil to those strata capable of supporting such loads. Piles are also used where loss of earth support due to scour is expected.

Bearing Pile. One which receives its support in bearing through the tip (or lower end) of the pile.

Friction Pile. One which receives its support through friction resistance along the lateral surface of the pile.

Sheet Piles. Commonly used in the construction of bulkheads, cofferdams, and cribs to retain earth and prevent the inflow of water, liquid mud, and fine grained sand with water, are of three general types, viz.: (1) Timber composed of a single piece or of two or more pieces spiked or bolted together to produce a compound piece either with a lap or a tongued and grooved effect. (2) Reinforced concrete slabs constructed with or without lap or tongued and grooved effect. (3) Rolled steel shapes with full provision for rigid interlocking of the edges.

Pile Cap. Concrete footings for a pier or abutment supported on piles. Also applied to the concrete below the pile tops when footing reinforcing steel is placed completely above the piles.

Pile Cut-Off. The portion of a pile removed or to be removed from its driven butt end to secure the elevation specified or indicated.

Pile Shoe. A metal piece fixed upon the point or penetration end of a pile to protect it from injury in driving and to facilitate penetration in every dense earth material.

Pile Splice. One of the means of joining one pile upon the end of another to provide greater penetration length.

Piling. (*Sheet Piling.*) General terms applied to assemblages of piles in a construction. See PILE.

Pin. A cylindrical bar used as a means of connecting, holding in position, and transmitting the stresses of, the members forming a truss or a framed joint. To restrain the pin against longitudinal movement its ends are fitted with pin nuts, cotter bolts, or both. The nuts are commonly of the recessed type taking bearing at their edges upon the assemblage of members. To prevent the loosening of the nuts and the displacement of the pins by vibration, joint movements, and other service conditions, the pin ends may be burred or they may be fitted with cotters.

Pin-Connected Truss. A general term applied to a truss of any type having its chord and web members connected at the truss joints by pins.

Pinion. The small driving gear on the powertrain of a movable bridge.

Pinion Bracket. The frame supporting the turning pinion with its shaft and bearings upon the drum girder or the loading girder of a swing span.

Pin Joint. A joint in a truss or other frame in which the members are assembled upon a cylindrical pin.

Pin Packing. An arrangement of truss members on a pin at a pinned joint.

Pin Plate. A plate or shape riveted or otherwise rigidly attached upon the end of a member to secure a desired bearing upon a pin or pin-like bearing; to develop and distribute the stress of the joint and/or secure additional strength and rigidity in the member.

Pintle. A small steel pin or stud, engaging the rocker in an exansion bearing, thereby permitting rotation, transferring shear, and preventing translation.

Pitch. The longitudinal spacing between rivets, studs, bolts, holes, etc., which are arranged in a straight line.

Plate Girder. An I-shaped beam composed of a solid plate web with either flange plates or flange angles bolted, riveted or welded upon its edges. Additional cover plates may be attached to the flanges to provide greater flange area.

Plinth. See FOOTING.

Plinth Course. The course or courses of stone forming the base portion of an abutment, pier, parapet or retaining wall and having a projection or extension beyond the general surface of the main body of the structure. See also BASE and FOOTING.

Plug Weld. (*Slot Weld.*) A weld joining two elements of a member or two members so assembled that an area of contact will be secured and the weld produced by depositing weld metal within circular, square, slotted or other shaped holes cut through one or more of the elements or members. This weld serves to unite the elements of a member or to join the members intersecting at truss at other joints of a structure.

Pointed Arch. See GOTHIC ARCH.

Pointing. The operations incident to the compacting of the mortar in the outermost portion of a joint and the troweling or other treatment of its exposed surface to secure water tightness or desired architectural effect or both.

Polygonal Truss. A general term applied to a truss of any type having an irregular or "broken" alignment of straight top chord members which forms with the end posts and the bottom chord the perimeter of a polygon.

Pony Truss. A general term applied to a truss having insufficient height to permit the use of an effective top chord system of lateral bracing above the bridge floor.

Pop-Out. Conical fragment broken out of concrete surface. Normally about one inch in diameter. Shattered aggregate particles usually found at bottom of hole.

Portable Bridge. A bridge so designed and constructed that it may be readily erected for a temporary communication-transport service; disassembled and its members again reassembled and the entire structure rendered ready for further service.

Portal. The clear unobstructed space of a through bridge forming the entrance to the structure.

The entire portal member of the top chord bracing which fixes the uppermost limit of the vertical clearance. See BRACING. The portal of a skew bridge is described as a "skew portal."

Post. A term commonly applied to a relatively short member resisting compressive stresses, located vertical or nearly vertical to the bottom chord of a truss and common to two truss panels. Sometimes used synonymously for column. See COLUMN.

Posted. A limiting dimension, speed, or loading, e.g., posted load, posted clearance, posted speed, indicating larger dimensions and higher speeds and loads can not be safely taken by the bridge.

Pot Holes. Small worn or distintegrated areas of bridge floor or approach surface concaved by the wearing action of vehicle wheels.

Pratt Truss. (*N-Truss*.) A truss with parallel chords and a web system composed of vertical posts with diagonal ties inclined outward and upward from the bottom chord panel points toward the ends of the truss except the counters required in midlength panels. The Parker Truss is an adaptation of the Pratt Truss by making the top chord polygonal in shape.

Priming Coat. (*Base Coat.*) The first coat of paint applied to the metal or other material of a bridge. For metal structures this is quite commonly a fabricating shop application and is, therefore, termed the "shop coat."

Protection Fence. See GUARD RAILING.

Protection Railing. See GUARD RAILING.

Q

Queen-Post Truss. A parallel chord type of truss adapted to either timber or metal bridge construction, having three panels with one of the chords occupying only the length of the center panel. Unless center panel diagonals are provided, it is a trussed beam.

R

Rack. A bar with teeth on one of its sides, designed to mesh with the gears of a pinion or worm. The rack is usually attached to the moving portion of a movable bridge and receives the motive power from the pinion.

Radial Rod. (*Spider Rod.*) A radially located tie rod connecting the roller circle of a rim-bearing swing span with the center pivot or center bearing casting.

Radial Strut. A radially located brace member of the drum construction of a rim-bearing swing span.

Railing. (*Handrail.*) A wooden, brick, stone, concrete or metal fence-like construction built at the side of the roadway, or the sidewalk, upon the retaining wall portion of an approach cut, embankment, or causeway or at the outermost edge of the roadway or the sidewalk portion of a bridge to guard or guide the movement of both pedestrian and vehicular traffic and to prevent the accidental passage of traffic over the side of the structure.

The term "handrail" is commonly applied only to railing presenting a latticed, barred, balustered or other open web construction.

Rake. The slope, batter or inclination from a horizontal, vertical or other assumed plane, of the sides of an embankment or other inclined earth construction; the batter of a face or other surface of masonry; of the plane of a truss side of a tower or other portion of a bridge superstructure or of any member thereof.

Ramp. An inclined traffic-way leading from one elevation to another. The general term used to designate an inclined roadway and/or sidewalk approach to a bridge and commonly applied to a rather steep incline.

Random Stone. A general term applied to quarried stone block of any dimensions whether intended for ashlar or for random masonry construction.

Range of Stress. The algebraic difference between the minimum and maximum stresses in a member or in an element or part thereof either computed to be produced by a given condition of loading or produced by its actual service loading.

Rebar. A steel reinforcing bar.

Redundant Member. A member in a truss or frame which renders it a statistically indeterminate structure. The structure would be stable without the redundant member whose primary purpose is to reduce the stresses carried by the determinate structure.

Re-Entrant Corner. A corner with more than 180° of material and less than 180° of open space.

Reinforcing Bar. A steel bar, plain or with a deformed surface, which bonds to the concrete and supplies tensile strength to the concrete.

Retaining Wall. A structure designed to restrain and hold back a mass of earth.

Buttressed Wall. A retaining wall designed with projecting buttresses to provide strength and stability.

Counterforted Wall. A retaining wall designed with projecting counterforts to provide strength and stability.

Gravity Wall. A wall composed of brick, stone or concrete masonry designed to be stable against sliding and rotation (overturning) upon its foundation or upon any horizontal plane within its body by virtue of its shape and weight.

Reinforced Concrete Cantilever Wall. A wall consisting of a base section integral with stem constructed approximately at a right angle thereto giving its cross section a letter "L" or an inverted "T" shape. The stem portion resists the horizontal or other forces tending to produce overturning by acting as a cantilever beam.

Rigid Frame Bridge. A bridge with rigid or moment resistant connections between deck slabs or beams and the substructure walls or columns, producing an integral, elastic structure. The structure may be steel or concrete.

In general this type of bridge may be regarded as a form of arch or curved beam having its intermediate intradosal section or portion either straight or slightly curved and its end sections located normal to the straight portion or to the tangent of the curved one at its center length position.

Rim Girder. See DRUM GIRDER.

Rim Plate. Toothed or plain segmental rim on a rolling lift bridge.

Ringbolt. See EYEBOLT.

Ring Stone. See VOUSSOIR.

Riprap. Brickbats, stones, blocks of concrete or other protective covering material of like nature deposited upon river and stream beds and banks, lake, tidal or other shores to prevent erosion and scour by water flow, wave or other movement.

Rise of an Arch. For a symmetrical arch; the vertical distance from the chord through its springing lines to the intrados at its crown.

For an unsymmetrical arch, assumed to be in a normal vertical position, the vertical distances from its springing lines to the intrados at its crown.

Riveted Joint. (Bolted Joint.) A joint in which the assembled elements and members are united by rivets. The design of a riveted joint contemplates a proper distribution of its rivets to develop its various parts with relation to the stresses and the purposes which each must serve.

A bolted joint differs from a riveted one only in the use of bolts as the uniting medium instead of rivets. The conditions of design are generally the same, but different allowable unit stresses are employed.

Roadway. (*Travel Way.*) 1. The portion of the deck surface of a bridge intended for the use of vehicular or vehicular and pedestrian traffic. 2. The top surface portion of an approach embankment, causeway or cut intended for the general use of vehicular or vehicular and pedestrian traffic. In general, its width corresponds (1) to the distance curb to curb; (2) to the distance between the outside limits of sidewalks; or (3) to the width of the roadway pavement or traveled way when no curbs exist.

Roadway Shoulder Area. (*Shoulder Area.*) The portion or area of the top surface of an approach embankment, causeway, or cut immediately adjoining the roadway, used to accommodate stopped vehicles in emergencies and to laterally support base and surface courses.

Rocker Bearing. A cylindrical, sector-shaped member attached by a pin or trunnion at its axis location to the expansion end of a girder or truss and having line bearing contact upon its perimetral surface with the masonry plate or pedestal, thus providing for the longitudinal movements resulting from temperature changes and superimposed loads by a wheel-like translation.

The design condition that the entire reaction stress is concentrated upon a line contact renders it especially essential that the masonry plate or pedestal be accurately leveled and that the rocker be carefully adjusted to secure a uniform even bearing thereon. A relatively large percentage of this type of bearings lack correct adjustment.

Rocker Bent. A bent composed of metal, reinforced concrete or timber, hinged or otherwise articulated at one or both ends to provide the longitudinal movements resulting from temperature changes and the superimposed loads of the span or spans supported thereon.

Rocker and Camshaft. An adjustable bearing device or assemblage consisting of a rocker bearing combined with a camshaft, properly mounted and geared to produce by its rotation a vertical lifting action, reacting upon a shoe plate or pedestal fixed upon the bridge seat. When installed at each outermost end of the girders, or the trusses of a swing span, the lifting action raises them to an extent that their camber or droop will be removed and the areas rendered free to act as simple spans. When the camshafts are revolved through an angle of 180° from their total or full lift position the rocker bearings are released and lifted and the span is free to be moved to "open" position.

Rolled Beams, Rolled Shapes. See STRUCTURAL SHAPES, WIDE FLANGE BEAMS.

Roller. 1. A steel cylinder forming an element of a roller nest or any other device or part intended to provide movements by rolling contact. The so-termed "segmental roller" consisting essentially of two circular segments integrally joined by a web-like portion is used in the construction of roller nests requiring relatively large bearing length with the least practicable shoe plate area and a correspondingly decreased weight of metal in the entire assemblage. 2. One of the wheel-like elements forming the roller circle of a rim-bearing swing span.

Roller Bearing. A single roller or a group of rollers so housed as to permit movement of a part or parts of a structure thereon.

Roller Nest. A group of steel cylinders forming a part of the movable end of a girder or truss and located between the masonry plate and shoe or pedestal to facilitate the longitudinal movements resulting from temperature changes and superimposed loads. Commonly the rollers are assembled in a frame or a box. Roller nests may be used for other services than those herein described. The term "Expansion Rollers" is sometimes used synonymously for roller nest.

Roller Track. The circular track upon which the drum rollers of a rim-bearing swing span travel. This is sometimes described as the lower track.

Roller Tread. See TREAD PLATES.

Rolling Lift Bridge. See MOVABLE BRIDGE.

Rubble. Irregularly shaped pieces of stone in the undressed condition obtained from the quarry and commonly ranging in size from relatively small usable pieces to one-man or two-man stones. This term is also applied to large boulders and fragments requiring mechanical equipment for handling. When shaped ready for use in rubble masonry, this stone is commonly described as "worked" or "dressed" rubble.

Run-Off. As applied to bridge design, the portion of the precipitation upon a drainage (catchment) area which is discharged quickly by its drainage stream or streams and which, therefore, becomes a factor in the design of the effective water discharge area of a bridge. Run-off is dependent upon soil porosity (varied by saturated or frozen condition), slope or soil surfaces, intensity of rainfall or of melting snow conditions, and other pertinent factors.

S

Saddle. A member located upon the topmost portion of the tower of a suspension bridge, designed to support the suspension cable or chain and to provide for its horizontal movements resulting from elastic deformations induced by temperature changes and the stresses incident to the service loadings.

Safe Load. The maximum loading determined by a consideration of its magnitudes and distributions of wheel, axle or other concentrations as productive of unit stresses in the various members and incidental details of a structure, permissible for service use, due consideration being given to the physical condition of the structure resulting from its previous service use.

Safety Curb. A narrow curb between 9 inches and 24 inches wide serving as a refuge or walkway for pedestrians crossing a bridge.

Sag. A deformation of an entire span; of any part of a span, or of one or more of its members from the horizontal, vertical, or inclined position intended as a condition of its original design and construction. This variation may result from elastic deformation of structural material; from irregularities produced by inadequate temporary supports during the progress of construction operations; or from incorrect adjustments and unworkmanlike procedures made a part of the work.

In existing structures sag may be attributable to (1) original construction irregularities; (2) to excessive stresses resulting from overloading; (3) to corrosion, decay or other deterioration of the structure materials, and (4) plastic flow of material.

The total deflection of the cable members of a suspension bridge. The so-termed "sag ratio" is the relation existing between the sag and the length of span.

Sag Rod. A rod usually fitted with threads and nuts at its ends; used to restrain a structure member from sagging due to its own weight or to external force or forces.

Sash Brace. (*Sash Stay, Sash Strut.*) A horizontal or nearly horizontal piece bolted or otherwise secured upon the side of a pile or framed bent between the cap and ground surface or the cap and sill, as the case may be, thus adding rigidity to the assemblage.

The horizontal member in a tier of bracing attached to a timber, reinforced concrete, or metal trestle bent or tower.

Scab. (*Scab Piece.*) A plank spiked or bolted over the joint between two members to hold them in correct adjustment and strengthen the joint.

A short piece of I-beam or other structural shape bolted, riveted or welded upon the flange and/or web of a metal pile to increase its resistance to penetration. Similarly, for the same purpose, a piece of dense hardwood fitted upon the flange and/or web and having bearing upon a lug angle at one or both its ends.

Scour. An erosion of a river, stream, tidal inlet, lake or other water bed area by a current, wash or other water in motion, producing a deepening of the overlying water, or a widening of the lateral dimension of the flow area.

Screw Jack and Pedestal. An adjustable device or assemblage consisting of a screw operated within a fixed nut and having upon its bottom end a pedestal-like bearing conjoined with it by a ball and socket or other equally adaptable articulation permitting its adjustment upon a shoe plate or pedestal fixed upon the bridge seat. When installed at each outermost end of the girders or the trusses of a swing span their major function is to lift them to an extent that their camber or droop will be removed and the arms rendered free to act as simple spans.

Scupper. (*Curb Inlet.*) An opening in the floor portion of a bridge, commonly located adjacent to the curb or wheel guard, to provide means for rain or other water accumulated upon the roadway surface to drain through it into the space beneath the structure. Bridges having reinforced concrete floors with concrete curbs may be effectively drained through scuppers located within the curb face surfaces.

Scupper Block. One of the short wooden pieces fixed between the wooden planks of a bridge floor and the bottom side of the wheel guard to provide open spaces beneath the latter for draining rain or other water accumulation from the floor surface.

Seam Weld. A weld joining the edges of two elements of a member or of two members placed in contact. This weld serves to form a continuous surface whether plane or curved, and to prevent infiltration of moisture between the parts. In general, it is not a stress carrying weld.

Seat Angle. (*Shelf Angle.*) A piece of angle attached upon the side of a column girder or other member to provide support for a connecting member either temporarily during its erection or permanently. The outstanding leg of the angle may be strengthened by a stiffener placed vertically beneath it.

Segmental Girder and Track Girder. These terms apply to the rolling lift type of bascule bridge combining circular rotation and translation movements in the "opening-closing" cycle.

The term "segmental girder" is used to designate one of the movable operating girders of a span or leaf to which a span girder or truss is rigidly attached. It commonly consists of a plate girder having its bottom flange curved to form a segment of a circle. This curved flange is fitted with tread castings which take line bearing contact upon the tread castings fitted upon the top flange of the supporting track girder with which they interlock to insure positive translation movement.

The term "track girder" is used to designate one of the plate girders or trusses intended to provide support for the movable span throughout an "opening-closing" cycle. Its tread castings fitted upon its top flange or chord form the track upon which the segmental girder moves by a rack and pinion-like action.

Segmental Rim. The curved rim or circular segment of a rolling lift bridge.

Seizing. The ligature of wire or other material applied upon a suspension bridge cable to hold the individual wires in satisfactory contact condition.

Separator. See SPREADER.

Shafts. Pieces conveying torsion stress only, which are, in general, used only in movable structures.

Shear Lock. (*Heel Stay, Tail-Lock.*) The device or mechanism provided at the heel of a bascule span to engage and hold the leaf in its closed position and prevent rotation.

Sheave. A wheel having a groove or grooves in its face surface. This term may be applied collectively to include both the sheave and its housing block.

Sheave Girder. A girder or girder-like member supporting the operating cable sheaves at the top of a tower of a vertical lift bridge.

Sheave Hood. A protecting covering placed above a sheave engaging the suspending cables of a vertical lift bridge to prevent accumulations of moisture, sleet and ice upon the sheave face.

Sheet Pile Cofferdam. In general a wall-like, watertight or nearly watertight barrier composed of driven timber or metal sheet piling constructed to surround the area to be occupied by an abutment, pier, retaining wall or other structure and permit unwatering of the enclosure so that the excavation for the preparation of a foundation and the abutment, pier or other construction may be produced in the open air. The alignment of the piles may be facilitated by the use of walers, struts and ties.

This type of dam is adapted to construction located in still or slow flowing shallow water. Its watertightness is sometimes rendered more complete by depositing earth material against the exterior side of the dam.

Sheet Piling. (*Sheeting.*) A general or collective term used to describe a number of sheet piles taken together to form a crib, cofferdam, bulkhead, etc.

Shelf Angle. See SEAT ANGLE.

Shim. A comparatively thin piece of wood, stone, or metal inserted between two elements, pieces or members to fix their relative position and/or to transmit bearing stress.

Shoe. In general, a pedestal-shaped member at the end of a plate girder or truss functioning to transmit and distribute its loads to a masonry bearing area or to any other supporting area or member. A shoe may be a cast or a built-up member; the base plate or plate-like part of which is commonly termed the "shoe plate," which may take bearing directly upon a masonry plate or upon an intervening expansion device.

Shore. A strut or prop placed in a horizontal, inclined or vertical position against or beneath a structure or a portion thereof to restrain movement.

Shoulder Area. See ROADWAY SHOULDER AREA.

Sidewalk. The portion of the bridge floor area serving pedestrian traffic only and, for safety and convenience to its users, commonly elevated above the portion occupied by vehicles.

Sidewalk Bracket. As applied to metal structures: A trianguar shaped frame attached to and projecting from the outside of a girder, truss or bent to serve as a support for the sidewalk stringers, floor and railing or parapet. In general, these brackets are in effect a cantilevered extension of the floor beams and are commonly connected to them by bars or other tension pieces designed to sustain the bending moment at the junction plane.

As applied to reinforced concrete structures: A cantilever beam commonly triangular in shape, attached to and projecting from the outside of a girder, truss, or bent to serve as a support for the sidewalk floor slab and the railing or parapet.

Sill. (*Sill Piece.*) The base piece or member of a viaduct or trestle bent serving to distribute the column loads directly upon the foundation or upon mud sills embedded in the foundation soil transversely to the alignment of the bent.

Silt. Very finely divided siliceous or other hard and durable rock material derived from its mother rock through attritive or other mechanical action rather than chemical decomposition. In general, its grain size shall be that which will pass a Standard No. 200 sieve.

Simple Span. A superstructure span having, at each end, a single unrestraining bearing or support and designed to be unaffected by stress transmission to or from an adjacent span or structure.

S-I-P Forms. See FORMS.

Skew Angle. As applied to oblique bridges; the skew angle, angle of skew or simply "skew" is the acute angle subtended by a line normal to the longitudinal axis of the structure and a line parallel to or coinciding with the alignment of its end.

Skewback. The course of stones, in an abutment or pier, located at the extremity of an arch and having its beds inclined (battered) as required to transmit the stresses of the arch. The bed adjoining the voussoirs forming the first string course of the arch ring will be normal to the axis of the arch. The individual stones of the skewback course are designated "skewback stones."

A casting or a combination of castings; or a built-up member designed to function as a skewback.

Skewback Shoe. (*Skewback Pedestal.*) The shoe or pedestal member, transmitting the thrust of a trussed arch or a plate girder arch to the skewback course or cushion course of an abutment or pier. Skewback shoes and pedestals are commonly hinged.

Slab. A thick plate, usually of reinforced concrete, which supports load by flexure. It is usually treated as a widened beam.

Slab Bridge. A bridge having a superstructure composed of a reinforced concrete slab constructed either as a single unit or as a series of narrow slabs placed parallel with the roadway alignment and spanning the space between the supporting abutments or other substructure parts. The former is commonly constructed in place but the latter may be precast.

Slag Inclusion. Small particles of slag trapped inside a weld during the fusion process.

Sleeve Nut. A device used to connect the elements of an adjustable rod or bar member. It consists of a forging having an elongated nut-shaped body with right- and left-hand threads within its end portions, thus permitting its adjustment with a wrench to provide a desired tension in the member.

Slenderness Ratio. Measure of stiffness of a member, expressed as the length of the member divided by its radius of gyration.

Slope. A term commonly applied to the inclined surface of an excavated cut or an embankment.

Slope Pavement. (*Slope Protection.*) A thin surfacing of stone, concrete or other material deposited upon the sloped surface of an approach cut, embankment or causeway to prevent its disintegration by rain, wind or other erosive action.

Slot Weld. See PLUG WELD.

Soffit. See INTRADOS.

Sole Plate. A plate bolted, riveted, or welded upon the bottom flange of a rolled beam, plate girder, or truss to take direct bearing upon a roller nest, bearing pedestal, or masonry plate. It distributes the reaction of the bearing to the beam, girder, or truss member. The sole plate may also function as a combined sole and masonry plate at the fixed end of a beam, girder, or truss.

Soldier Beam. A steel pile driven into the earth with its butt end projecting, used as a cantilever beam to support horizontal lagging retaining an excavated surface.

Spalls. Circular or oval depression in concrete caused by a separation of a portion of the surface concrete, revealing a fracture parallel with or slightly inclined to the surface. Usually part of the rim is perpendicular to the surface.

The pieces of spalled concrete themselves.

Span. This term has various applications depending upon its use whether in design, in field construction, or in its common nontechnical application, viz.:

When applied to design of a beam, girder, truss or arch structure. The distance center to center of the end bearings or the distance between the lines of action of the reactions whether induced by substructure or other supporting members.

When applied to the field construction of substructure abutments and piers. The unobstructed space or distance between the faces of the substructure elements. For arch structures this length is measured at the elevation of the springing lines. These lengths or dimensions are commonly referred to as "clear span length." See CLEAR SPAN.

The complete superstructure of a single span bridge or a corresponding integral part or unit of a multiple span structure. This application of "span" is rendered more specific when subdivided into: (a) Fixed Span: A superstructure anchored in its location upon the substructure and (b) Movable Span: A superstructure intended to be swung or lifted to provide an unobstructed waterway space for the passage of waterborne traffic.

Spandrel. The space bounded by the arch extrados, the substructure abutments and/or pier(s), and the roadway surface or other elevation limit fixed by the construction details.

Spandrel Column. A column superimposed upon the ring or a rib of an arch span and serving as a support for the deck construction of an open spandrel arch. See OPEN SPANDREL ARCH.

Spandrel Fill. The filling material placed within the spandrel space of a spandrel arch.

Spandrel Tie. A wall or a beam-like member connecting the spandrel walls of an arch and securing them against bulging and other deformation. In stone masonry arches the spandrel tie walls served to some extent as counterforts. In reinforced concrete spandrel arch spans spandrel tie walls may likewise serve as counterforts. See TIE WALLS.

Spandrel Wall. A wall built upon an arch to function as a retaining wall for the spandrel fill and the roadway in a spandrel filled structure; but, when the spandrel is not filled, to support the floor system and its loads. In wide structures having unfilled spandrels one or more interior walls may be used, thus providing a cellular construction when combined with tie walls. See TIE WALLS.

Specifications. A detailed enumeration of the chemical and physical properties determining the quality of construction materials together with requirements for handling, shipping and storage thereof; the conditions governing the loads, load applications and unit stress considerations of bridge foundation, substructure and superstructure design; the development of construction details and their applications incident to fabrication; erecton or other constructon procedures pertinent to the production of serviceable bridge structures.

When general or so called "standard" specifications are used, it occasionally becomes necessary to supplement the requirements by items having specific application to a given bridge structure or group of structures. The special items may either designate and authorize departures from the "standard" or apply entirely to requirements and conditions not dealt with therein. The status of these supplemental or special specifications is commonly fixed by the "standard" specifications. Likewise the "standard" specification commonly recognizes the possibility of discrepancies between the specifications and the general plans and working (detail) drawings by fixing a coordination status for such occurrences.

Spider. The collar-like plate connecting the spider frame of a rim bearing or a combined rim and center bearing swing span to the pivot.

Spider Frame. The frame assemblage of struts, radial rods, spacer rings and roller adjusting devices holding the conical roller ring of a rim bearing or a combined rim and center bearing swing span in correct position with relation to the pivot.

Spider Rod. See RADIAL ROD.

Splay Saddle. A member at the anchorage ends of suspension bridge cables which permits the wires or strands to spread so that they may be connected to the anchorage.

Splice. This term has two applications depending upon its use whether in design or in shop and field construction, viz.:

When applied to design and the development of construction details: The joining or uniting of elements of a member, parts of a member or members of a structure to provide desired conditions for the transmittal of stress and the development of rigidity and general strength fulfilling the service requirements of the member or of the structure of which it is a part.

When applied to shop and field construction: the complete assemblage of parts used in producing the union of elements of a member or members of a structure.

Splice Joint. A joint in which the elements of a member or the members of a structure are joined by a splice plate or by a part or piece functioning to secure a required amount of strength and stability.

Spreader. 1. A cast or fabricated piece used to hold angles, beams, channels or fabricated pieces or parts in the locations or positions in which they function as parts of a member or structure. 2. A ring-like or sleeve-like piece placed upon a pin to hold the eyebars or other members assembled upon it in their correct member positions. This piece is sometimes described as a "pin-filler," or "packing ring."

Springing Line. The line within the face surface of an abutment or pier at which the intrados of an arch takes its beginning or origin.

Starling. An extension at the upstream end only, or at both the upstream and downstream ends of a pier built with surfaces battered thus forming a cutwater to divide and deflect the stream waters and floating debris and, correspondingly, when on the downstream end, functioning to reduce crosscurrents, swirl and eddy action which are productive of depositions of sand, silt and detritus downstream from the pier.

Statics. The branch of physical science which is concerned with bodies acted on by balanced forces. Therefore, these bodies are either at rest or static.

Stay-In-Place Forms. See FORMS.

Stay Plate. (*Tie Plate.*) A plate placed at or near the end of a latticed side or web of a compression or other member and also at intermediate locations where connections for members interrupt the continuity of the latticing. This plate serves to distribute the lattice bar stress to the elements of the member and adds stiffness and rigidity to joint assemblages.

Stem. The vertical wall portion of an abutment retaining wall, or solid pier. See also BREASTWALL.

Stiffener. An angle, tee, plate or other rolled section riveted, bolted or welded upon the web of a plate girder or other "built-up" member to transfer stress and to prevent buckling or other deformation.

A stiffener forged at its ends to fit upon the web and the web-legs of the flange angles of a plate girder is termed "crimped."

Stiffening Girder, Stiffening Truss. A girder or truss incorporated in a suspension bridge to function in conjunction with a suspension cable or chain by restraining the deformations of the latter and by distributing the concentrated or other irregularly distributed loads thus resisting and controlling the vertical oscillations of the floor system imparted to it by the cable or chain deformations.

Stirrup. In timber and metal bridges: A U-shaped rod, bar or angle piece providing a stirrup-like support for an element of a member or a member.

In reinforced concrete bridges: A U-shaped bar placed in beams, slabs or similar constructions to resist diagonal tension stresses.

Stirrup Bolt. A U-shaped rod or bar fitted at its ends with threads, nuts and washers and used to support streamer or other timber pieces of wooden truss structures suspended from the bottom chord.

Stone Facing. (*Stone Veneer, Brick Veneer.*) A stone or brick surface covering or sheath laid in imitation of stone or brick masonry but having a depth thickness equal to the width dimension of one stone or brick for stretchers and the length dimension for headers. The backing portion of a wall or the interior portion of a pier may be constructed of rough stones imbedded in mortar or concrete, cyclopean concrete, plain or reinforced concrete, brick bats imbedded in mortar, or even of mortar alone. The backing and interior material may be deposited as the laying of the facing material progresses to secure interlocking and bonding with it, or the covering material may be laid upon its preformed surface.

Strain. The distortion of a body produced by the application of one or more external forces and measured in units of length. In common usage, this is the proportional relation of the amount of distortion divided by the original length.

Stress. The resistance of a body tp distortion when in a solid or plastic state and when acting in an unconfined condition. Stress is produced by the strain (distortion) and holds in equilibrium the external forces causing the distortion. It is measured in pounds or tons. Within the elastic limit the strain in a member of a structure is proportional to the stress in that member.

Allowable Unit Stress. As applied to the investigation of an existing structure in determining its adequacy for existing or prospective service; it is the stress per unit of area of the material of the entire structure or any portion or member thereof which is determined to be a safe unit for service use, due consideration being given to the quality of the material, physical condition, the adequacy of the construction details or other physical factors incident or pertinent to the service conditions to which they are or will be subjected and, if necessary, to the conditions contemplated to exist in the event of repair, replacement or strengthening operations.

Unit Stress. The stress per square inch (or other unit of surface or crosssectional area). The Allowable Unit Stress is: (a) Assumed in determining the composition and construction details of a memer or the members of a proposed structure, or (b) assumed for judging the safe load-capacity of an existing structure; while working stress is (c) produced in the members and parts of an existing structure when subjected to loads, impacts and other stress-producing elements and factors to which the structure is proposed to be or may have been subjected.

Working Stress. The unit stress in a member under service or design load.

Stress Sheet. A drawing showing a structure in skeletal form sufficient only to impart or suggest in conjunction with notations thereon its general makeup, major dimensions and the arrangement and composition of its integral parts. Special construction details may be shown by section views and sketches with or without dimensional data. Upon the skeletal outline of the structure or in tabulated form the drawing should show the computed stresses resulting from the application of a system of loads together with the design composition of the individual members resulting from the application of assumed unit stresses for the material or materials to be used in the structures. The assumed design load or loads should appear either in diagrammatic form with dimensions and magnitudes, or reference be made to readily available information relating thereto by a special note conspicuously displayed upon the drawing. A future investigation of a given structure to determine its reliability for a given load or combination of loads may be greatly facilitated and expedited by an adequate stress sheet record of its original design conditions.

Stringer. A longitudinal beam supporting the bridge deck, and in large bridges or truss bridges, framed into or upon the floor beams.

Structural Members. Basically these are of three types, viz.: (1) Ties: Pieces subject to axial tension only; (2) Columns or Struts: Pieces subject to axial compression only; (3) Beams: Pieces transversely loaded and subject to both shear and bending moment.

However, the arrangement of the members of a structure and the application of its design loads may embody combinations of these basic stress types.

Structural Shapes. As applied to bridge structures: The various types and forms of rolled iron and steel having flat, round, angle, channel, "I", "H", "Z" and other cross-sectional shapes adapted to the construction of the metal members incorporated in reinforced foundations, substructures and superstructures.

Structural Tee. A tee-shaped rolled member formed by cutting a wide flange longitudinally along the centerline of web.

Strut. A general term applying to a piece or member acting to resist compressive stress.

Sub-Panel. See PANEL.

Subpunched and Reamed Work. A term applied to structural steel shapes having rivet holes punched a specified dimension less in diameter than the nominal size of the rivets to be driven therein and subsequently reamed to a specified diameter greater than the rivet size.

This term is also applied to completely assembled and riveted members and structures in which the rivet holes have been produced by subpunching and reaming procedure.

Substructure. The abutments, piers, grillage or other constructions built to support the span or spans of a bridge superstructure whether consisting of beam, girder, truss, trestle or other type or types of construction.

Sump. A pit or tank-like depression or receptacle into which water is drained. The removal of the water so accumulated may be effected by pumping or by siphoning.

Superelevation. (*Curve Banking.*) The transverse inclination of the roadway surface within a horizontal curve and the relatively short tangent lengths adjacent thereto required for its full development. The purpose of superelevation is to provide a means of resisting or overcoming the centrifugal forces of vehicles in transit.

Superstructure. The entire portion of a bridge structure which primarily receives and supports highway, railway, canal, or other traffic loads and in its turn transfers the reactions resulting therefrom to the bridge substructure. The superstructure may consist of beam, girder, truss, trestle or other type or types of construction.

A superstructure may consist of a single span upon two supports or of a combination of two or more spans having the number and distribution of supports required by their types of construction, whether consisting of simple, continuous, cantilever, suspension, arch or trestle span-tower-bent construction.

Surcharge. An additional load placed atop existing earth or dead loads. In the case of abutments and retaining walls, the surcharge load is assumed to be replaced by an earth load of equivalent total weight.

Suspended Span. A superstructure span having one or both of its ends supported upon or from adjoining cantilever arms, brackets or towers, and designed to be unaffected by other stress transmission to or from an adjacent structure. The ordinary use of a suspended span is in connection with cantilever span construction.

Suspender. A wire cable, a metal rod or bar designed to engage a cable band or other device connecting it to the main suspension member of a suspension bridge at one end and a member of the bridge floor system at the other thus permitting it to assist in supporting the bridge floor system and its superimposed loads by transferring loads to the main suspension members of the structure.

A member serving to support another member in a horizontal or an inclined position against sagging, twisting or other deformation due to its own weight.

Suspension Bridge. A bridge in which the floor system and its incidental parts and appliances are supported in practically a horizontal position by being suspended upon cables which are supported at two or more locations upon towers and are anchored at their extreme ends. The cables constitute the main suspension members and commonly their anchorage may be one of three forms, viz.: (1) By extension of these members beyond the towers to the anchorages; (2) By fixing their ends upon the towers and backstaying the towers against overturning by the suspension members pulling upon them; (3) By an integral inclusion of the anchorages within the structure whereby the entire horizontal and vertical components of the main suspension member stresses are resisted by a rigid floor system construction functioning as a column, upon the extreme ends of which the main suspension members are securely connected. This form is commonly described as "self anchored."

Suspension Cable. (*Suspension Chain.*) One of the main members upon which the floor system of a suspension bridge is supported. Its ends may be fixed at the tops of towers which are backstayed to resist the horizontal components of the cable or chain stresses or instead it may rest upon saddles at the tops of two or more towers and be extended and fixed upon anchorage members. When the extension portions from the tops of towers to the anchorages do not directly support any part of the bridge floor, they function essentially as backstays; but when they engage floor suspenders located between the towers and anchorages they function as suspension cables for the end spans of the structure.

Sway Anchorage. (*Sway Cable.*) A guy, stay cable or chain attached at an intermediate length location upon the floor system of a suspension bridge and anchored upon the end portion of an abutment or pier or in the adjacent land surface to increase the resistance of the suspension span to lateral movement.

Sway Brace. 1. A piece bolted, or otherwise secured in an inclined position upon the side of a pile or frame bent between the cap and ground surface or the cap and sills, as the case may be, to add rigidity to the assemblage. See BRAC-

ING. 2. An inclined member in a tier of bracing forming a part of a timber, metal, or R/C bent or tower. 3. One of the inclined members of the sway bracing system of a metal girder or truss span. In plate girder construction the term X-brace is sometimes used.

Sway Frame. A complete panel or frame of sway bracing. See BRACING.

Swedge Bolt. See ANCHOR BOLT.

Swing Span. A superstructure span designed to be entirely supported upon a pier at its center, when its end supports have been withdrawn or released, and equipped to be revolved in a horizontal plane to free a navigable waterway of the obstruction it presents to navigation when in its normal traffic service position. See MOVABLE BRIDGE.

Swing Span Pivot. The center casting upon or about which the movable portion of a swing span revolves in making an opening-closing cycle.

In the center bearing type span, this casting functions not only as a pivotal member but also as the support for the movable span when the end lifting device is released.

In the rim-bearing type span this casting functions as a pivotal anchor member regulating the location of the movable parts throughout an opening-closing cycle but does not support the movable span.

In the combined center and rim-bearing type this casting functions as a support for a portion of the weight of the movable span when the end lifting device is released.

T

Tack Weld. A weld of the butt, fillet or seam type intended only to fix an element of a member or a member of a structure in correct adjustment and position preparatory to fully welding. Tack welds may be used to restrain welded parts against deformation and distortion resulting from expansion of the metal by atmospheric and welding temperatures.

Tail Lock. See SHEAR LOCK.

Tail Pit. See COUNTERWEIGHT WELL.

Tail Water. Water ponded below the outlet of a culvert, pipe, or bridge waterway, thereby reducing the amount of flow through the waterway. Tailwater is expressed in terms of its depth. See also HEADWATER.

Temporary Bridge. A structure built for emergency or interim use to replace a previously existing bridge demolished or rendered unserviceable by flood, fire, wind or other untoward occurrence, or instead, to supply bridge service required for a relatively short period.

Tendon. A prestressing cable or strand.

Tension. An axial force or stress caused by equal and opposite forces pulling at the ends of the members.

Throat. Of a fillet weld. The dimension normal to the sloping face of a fillet weld between the heel of the weld and the sloping faces.

Through Bridge. A bridge having its floor elevation more nearly at the elevation of the bottom than at the top portion of the superstructure, thus providing for the passage of traffic between the supporting parts.

Tide Gate. See FLOOD GATE.

Tie Plate. See STAY PLATE.

Tie Rod. (*Tie Bar.*) A rod-like or bar-like member in a truss or other frame functioning to transmit tensile stress.

Tie Walls. (*Spandrel Tie Wall.*) One of the walls built at intervals above the arch ring to tie together and reinforce the spandrel walls. See DIAPHRAGM WALL.

Any wall designed to serve as a restraining member to prevent bulging and distortion of two other walls connected thereby.

Toe of Slope. The location defined by the intersection of the sloped surface of an approach cut, embankment or causeway or other sloped area with the natural or an artifical ground surface existing at a lower elevation.

Toe Wall. (*Footwall.*) A relatively low retaining wall placed near the "toe-of-slope" location of an approach embankment or causeway to produce a fixed termination or to serve as a protection against erosion and scour or, perhaps, to prevent the accumulation of stream debris.

Toggle Joint. A mechanical arrangement wherein two members are hinged together, in fact or in effect, at a central location and hinged separately at their opposite ends; their alignment forming an obtuse angle so that a force applied at the common hinge location will produce a thrust acting at the end hinges, laterally to the alignment or direction of the original force.

Tolerance. (*Margin.*) A range or variation in physical or chemical properties specified or otherwise determined as permissible for the acceptance and use of construction materials.

Tower. 1. A three dimension substructure framework in a viaduct type structure having the vertical bents at its ends joined longitudinally by struts and braces thus rendering the assemblage so formed effective in resisting forces acting longitudinally upon the structure. 2. A four-sided frame supporting the ends of two spans or instead one complete span (tower span) and the ends of two adjacent spans of a viaduct; having its column members strutted and braced in tiers and the planes of either two or four sides battered. 3. A pier or a frame serving to support the cables or chains of a suspension type bridge at the end of a span. 4. A frame functioning as an end support, guide frame and counterweight support for a vertical lift span during an operating cycle.

Track Girder. See SEGMENTAL GIRDER.

Track Plate. The plate, toothed or plain, upon which the segmental girder of a rolling lift span rolls.

Track Segment. One of the assemblage pieces of the circular track supporting the balance wheels of a center bearing swing span or the drum bearing wheels of a drum or combined center and drum bearing span.

Transition Length. The tangent length within which the change from a normal to a superelevated roadway cross section is developed.

Transverse Bracing. (*Transverse System.*) The bracing assemblage engaging the columns of trestle and viaduct bents and towers in perpendicular or slightly inclined planes and in the horizontal or nearly horizontal planes of their sash braces to function in resisting the transverse forces resulting from wind, lateral vibration and traffic movements tending to produce lateral movement and deformation of the columns united thereby. See BRACING.

Transverse Girder. See CROSS GIRDER.

Travel Way. See ROADWAY.

Tread Plates. (*Roller Tread.*) The plates attached upon the bottom flange of the drum girder; shaped to form a circular surface taking a uniform even bearing upon the drum rollers and thereby transferring to them the live and dead loads of the superimposed structure. The assemblage of tread plates is sometimes described as the "Upper Track."

Tremie. A long trunk or pipe used to place concrete under water. A tremie usually has a hopper at its upper end.

The concrete placed under water by use of a tremie is often called tremie concrete. In placing tremie concrete, it is important that the mouth of the tremie be kept immersed within the mass of concrete already deposited to prevent the water from mixing with the concrete, thereby weakening or destroying it.

Trestle. A bridge structure consisting of beam, girder or truss spans supported upon bents. The bents may be of the piled or of the frame type, composed of timber, reinforced concrete or metal. When of framed timbers, metal or reinforced concrete they may involve two or more tiers in their construction. Trestle structures are designated as "wooden," "frame," or "framed," "metal," "concrete," "wooden pile," "concrete pile," etc., depending upon or corresponding to the material and characteristics of their principal members.

Trailing Wheel. See BALANCE WHEEL.

Triangular Truss. See WARREN TRUSS.

Trunnion. As applied to a bascule bridge. The assemblage consisting essentially of a pin fitted into a supporting bearing and forming a hinge or axle upon which the movable span swings during an opening-closing cycle.

Trunnion Girder. The girder supporting the trunnions on a bascule bridge.

Truss. A jointed structure having an open built web construction so arranged that the frame is divided into a series of triangular figures with its component straight members primarily stressed axially only. The triangle is the truss element and each type of truss used in bridge construction is an assemblage of triangles. The connecting pins are assumed to be frictionless.

Truss Bridge. A bridge having a truss for a superstructure: The ordinary single span rests upon two supports, one at each end, which may be abutments, piers, bents or towers, or combinations thereof. The superstructure span may be divided into three parts, viz.: (1) the trusses, (2) the floor system and (3) the bracing.

Truss Panel. See PANEL.

Trussed Beam. A beam reinforced by one or more rods upon its tension side attached at or near its ends and passing beneath a support at the midlength of the span producing in effect an inverted King post truss. The support, if a wooden block, is commonly termed a "saddle block" but, if a cast iron or structural steel member it is termed a "stanchion."

Tubular Truss. A truss whose chords and struts are composed of pipes or cylindrical tubes.

Tudor Arch. See GOTHIC ARCH.

Turnbuckle. A device used to connect the elements of adjustable rod and bar members. It consists of a forging having nut-like end portions right and left hand threaded and integrally connected by two bars upon its opposite sides thus providing an intervening open space through which a lever may be inserted to adjust the tension in the member.

Turning Pinion and Rack. The pinion to which the power to operate a swing span is applied and the circular rack fixed upon the pivot pier upon which the pinion travels to produce its rotation movement. When a swing span requires a very considerable amount of power to operate it, two operating pinions located at opposite sides of the circular rack or nearly so are commonly used to distribute the operating force upon the rack and its anchorage.

U

U–Bolt. A bar, either round or square, bent in the shape of the letter "U" and fitted with threads and nuts at its ends.

Underpass. See OVERPASS.

Uplift. A negative reaction or a force tending to lift a beam, truss, pile, or any other bridge element upwards.

V

Vertical-Lift Bridge. See MOVABLE BRIDGE.

Viaduct. A bridge structure consisting of beam, girder, truss, or arch span supported upon abutments with towers or alternate towers and bents or with a series of piers (cylindrical, dumbbell, rectangular or other types), or with any combination of these types of supporting parts.

In general, a viaduct is regarded as having greater height than a trestle. However, this notion is inconsistent with bridge engineering practice. A viaduct may be in all respects like a multiple span bridge.

Vierendeel Truss. A rigid frame consisting essentially of an assemblage of rectangles and trapezoids with no diagonal members. Its service in a bridge is the same as that assigned to a plate girder or a truss.

Voided Unit. A precast concrete deck unit containing cylindrical voids to reduce dead load.

Voussoir. (*Ring Stone.*) One of the truncated wedge shaped stones composing a ring course in a stone arch. The facing or head voussoirs are those placed at the terminations of a ring course.

W

Wale. (*Wale-Piece, Waler.*) A wooden or metal piece or an assemblage of pieces placed either inside or outside, or both inside and outside, the wall portion of a crib, cofferdam or similar structure, usually in a horizontal position to maintain its shape and increase its rigidity, stability, and strength. An assemblage of wale pieces is termed a "waling," or "strake o' wail."

Warren Truss. (*Triangular Truss.*) A parallel chord truss developed for use in metal bridge structures, wherein the web system is usually formed by a single triangulation of members at an angle to each other. There are no counters but web members near the center of a span may be subject to stress reversals and are to be designed accordingly. Verticals may or may not be used.

Washer. A small metal disc having a hole in its center to engage a bolt or a rivet. It may be used beneath the nut or the head of a bolt or as a separator between elements of a member or the members of a structure.

Water Table. The upper limit or elevation of ground water saturating a portion of a soil mass.

Waterway. The available width for the passage of stream, tidal or other water beneath a bridge, if unobstructed by natural formations or by artificial constructions beneath or closely adjacent to the structure. For a multiple span bridge the available width is the total of the unobstructed waterway lengths of the spans. See CLEAR SPAN.

Wearing Surface. (*Wearing Course.*) The surface portion of a roadway area which is in direct contact with the means of transport and is, therefore, primarily subject to the abrading, crushing or other disintegrating effect produced by hammering, rolling, sliding or other physical action tending to induce attrition thereof.

A topmost layer or course of material applied upon a roadway to receive the traffic service loads and to resist the abrading, crushing or other distintegrating action resulting therefrom.

Web. The portion of a beam, girder or truss, located between and connected to the flanges or the chords. It serves mainly to resist shear stresses. The stem of a dumbbell or solid wall type pier.

Web Members. The intermediate members of a truss extending, in general, from chord to chord but not including the end posts. Inclined web members are termed diagonals. A "tie" is a diagonal in tension while a brace or strut is a diagonal in compression. A vertical web member in compression is commonly designated a post, while one in tension due entirely to the external forces applied at its lower end, is designated a hanger. The joint formed by the intersection of an inclined end post with the top chord is commonly designated the hip joint or "the hip" end and the vertical tension member engaging the hip joint is commonly known as the hip vertical or the first panel hanger.

Web Plate. The plate forming the web element of a plate girder, built-up beam or column.

Wedge and Pedestals. An adjustable bearing device or assemblage consisting of a wedge operating between an upper and a lower bearing block or pedestal, and when installed at each outermost end of the girders or the trusses of a swing span, functioning to lift them to an extent that their camber or "droop" will be removed and the arms rendered free to act as simple spans. Furthermore, when installed beneath the loading girder of a center bearing swing span they serve to relieve the pivot bearing from all or nearly all live load and to stabilize the center portion of the span. When the wedges are withdrawn and the end latching device released, the span is free to be moved to an "open" position.

Lifting devices of the wedge and pedestal type may be used under the loading girder of a center bearing swing span in conjunction with rocker and eccentric, link and roller, or other end lifting devices at the ends of the span.

However, some swing spans of short length and placed in rather unimportant locations are designed to support both dead and live loads upon the center pivot and the ends of span are inadequately lifted with the result that they "end hammer" upon their pedestals.

Wedge Stroke. The theoretical travel distance a wedge must move upon its pedestal to lift the end of the arm of a swing span a distance equal to the vertical camber or "droop" of the arm due to elastic deformation minus the portion assumed to be provided in the field erection operation.

The actual elastic deformation of the arms of a given swing span may vary considerably from the theoretical due probably to temperature variations during the periods in which fabrication and erection are in progress, or to variation in the friction developed between the elements combined to form joints and to other incidental irregularities.

Weep Hole. (*Weep Pipe.*) An open hole or an embedded pipe in a masonry retaining wall, abutment, arch or other portion of a masonry structure to provide means of drainage for the embankment, causeway, spandrel backfill or retained soil wherein water may accumulate.

Weld. The process of uniting portions of one or more pieces, the elements of a member, or the members of a structure in an intimate and permanent position or status by (1) the application of pressure induced by the blow of a hammer or by a pressure machine, the portions to be united having been previously heated to a so-called welding temperature and the junction areas cleaned and purified by the application of fluxing material, or by (2) the use of a high temperature flame to preheat the metal adjacent to the weld location and when it has attained a molten temperature to add molten weld metal, in conjunction with fluxing material, in sufficient quantity to produce a fully filled joint when cooled or by (3) the use of the electric arc to obtain a molten temperature in the metal closely adjacent to the weld location and to supply in the arc stream molten filler metal and fluxing material requisite to produce by coalescence of the structure and electrode metals a fully filled joint.

The joint produced by the application of a welding process.

Weld Layer. A single thickness of weld metal composed of beads (runs) laid in contact to form a pad weld or a portion of a weld made up of superimposed beads.

Weld Metal. The fused filler metal which is added to the fused structure metal to produce by coalescence and interdiffusion a welded joint or a weld layer.

Weld Penetration. The depth beneath the original surface, to which the structure metal has been fused in the making of a fusion weld. See PENETRATION.

Weld Sequence. The order of succession required for making the welds of a built-up piece or the joints of a structure to avoid, so far as practicable, the residual stresses producing or tending to produce individual joint distortions and deformations of the structure or its members.

Welded Bridge. (*Welded Structure.*) A structure wherein the metal elements composing its members and the joints whereby these members are combined into the structure frame, are united by welds.

Welded Joint. A joint in which the assembled elements and members are united through fusion of metal. The design of a welded joint contemplates a proper distribution of the welds to develop its various parts with relation to the stresses and the purpose which each must serve, due consideration being given to factors productive of secondary stresses through weld shrinkage, warping and other conditions attending weld fabrication.

Wheel Base. A term applied to the axle spacing or lengths of vehicles. When applied to automobiles and trucks having wheel concentrations at the ends of the front and rear axles it is the length center to center of axles or the longitudinal dimension center to center of front and rear wheels.

Wheel Concentration. (*Wheel Load.*) The load carried by and transmitted to the supporting structure by one wheel. This concentration may involve the wheel of a traffic vehicle, a movable bridge, or other motive equipment or device. See AXLE LOAD.

Wheel Guard. (*Filloe Guard.*) A timber piece placed longitudinally along the side limit of the roadway to guide the movements of vehicle wheels and safeguard the bridge trusses, railings and other constructions existing outside the roadway limit from collision with vehicles and their loads.

Whiteway Lighting. The lighting provided for nighttime illumination along a road or bridge, as distinguished from sign lighting or colored regulatory and warning lights.

Wide Flange. (*Carnegie Beam.*) A rolled member having an H-shaped cross section, differentiated from an I-beam in that the flanges are wider and the web thinner.

Wind Bracing. The bracing systems in girder and truss spans and in towers and bents which function to resist the stresses induced by wind forces.

Wing Wall. The retaining wall extension of an abutment intended to restrain and hold in place the side slope material of an approach causeway or embankment. When flared at an angle with the breast wall it serves also to deflect stream water and floating debris into the waterway of the bridge and thus protects the approach embankment against erosion. The general forms of wing walls are:

(1) Straight—in continuation of the breast wall of the abutment.

(2) U-type—placed parallel to the alignment of the approach roadway.

(3) Flared—forming an angle with the alignment of the abutment breast wall by receding therefrom.

(4) Curved—forming either a convex or concave arc flaring from the alignment of the abutment breast wall.

The footing of a full abutment height wing wall is usually a continuation of the base portion of the breast wall but may be stepped to a higher or lower elevation to obtain acceptable foundation conditions.

A stub type of straight wing wall is sometimes used in connection with a pier-like or bent-like abutment placed within the end of an embankment. This type, commonly known as "elephant ear" or as "butterfly wing" serves to retain the top portion of the embankment from about the elevation of the bridge seat upward to the roadway elevation. The top surface is battered to conform with the embankment side slope.

Working Stress. See STRESS.

www.ingramcontent.com/pod-product-compliance
Lightning Source LLC
Chambersburg PA
CBHW081810300426
44116CB00014B/2299